W9-AFQ-945

Genderspeak

Other Books by Suzette Haden Elgin

NONFICTION

The Gentle Art of Verbal Self-Defense
More on the Gentle Art of Verbal Self-Defense
The Last Word on the Gentle Art of Verbal Self-Defense
Success with the Gentle Art of Verbal Self-Defense
Staying Well with the Gentle Art of Verbal Self-Defense
The Gentle Art of Written Self-Defense Letter Book

TEXTBOOKS

Guide to Transformational Grammar
Pouring Down Words
What Is Linguistics?

NOVELS

The Communipaths
Furthest
At the Seventh Level
Twelve Fair Kingdoms
The Grand Jubilee
And Then There'll Be Fireworks
Star-Anchored, Star-Angered
Native Tongue
Yonder Comes the Other End of Time
Native Tongue II: The Judas Rose
Native Tongue III

Audio Programs by Suzette Haden Elgin

Mastering the Gentle Art of Verbal Self-Defense
Success with the Gentle Art of Verbal Self-Defense
The Gentle Art of Verbal Self-Defense for Parents and Kids
(with Rebecca Haden, M.A.)
The Gentle Art of Verbal Self-Defense for Parents and Teenagers
(with Rebecca Haden, M.A.)

Genderspeak

Men, Women, and the
Gentle Art of Verbal Self-Defense

SUZETTE HADEN ELGIN, Ph.D.

John Wiley & Sons, Inc.
New York Chichester Brisbane Toronto Singapore

In recognition of the importance of preserving what has been written, it is a policy of John Wiley & Sons, Inc., to have books of enduring value published in the United States printed on acid-free paper, and we exert our best efforts to that end.

Copyright © 1993 by Suzette Haden Elgin
Published by John Wiley & Sons, Inc.
All rights reserved. Published simultaneously in Canada.

Reproduction or translation of any part of this work beyond that permitted by Section 107 or 108 of the 1976 United States Copyright Act without the permission of the copyright owner is unlawful. Requests for permission or further information should be addressed to the Permissions Department, John Wiley & Sons, Inc.

Library of Congress Cataloging-in-Publication Data
Elgin, Suzette Haden.
      Genderspeak : men, women, and the gentle art of verbal self-
   defense / by Suzette Haden Elgin.
         p.   cm.
      Includes index.
      ISBN 0-471-58016-3 (pbk.)
      ISBN 0-471-30506-5 (cloth)
      1. Verbal self-defense.   2. Sex differences (Psychology)
   I. Title.
   BF637.V47E42   1993
   153.6—dc20   92-37933

Printed in the United States of America
10 9 8 7 6 5 4 3 2 1

Contents

Preface

Does This Sound Familiar?

F: "Please . . . talk to me."

M: "All right. What do you want to talk about?"

F: "Anything! You never talk to me!"

M: "My mind's a blank. I'm sorry. Tell me what you want to talk about and I'll be happy to oblige."

F: "Oh, never mind! Just never mind!"

M: "Whatever you say."

F: "Good morning, darling. Did you sleep well?"

M: "I guess so. Sure."

F: [Long pause] "Well?"

M: "Well, what?"

M: "Are we going to your mother's for Easter?"

F: "Do we have a choice?"

M: "How would I know? She's your mother!"

F: "Well, you don't have to get nasty about it!"

F: "Why didn't you call me?"

M: "I meant to."

F: "Then why didn't you?"

M: "I don't know."

F: "That's not a reason!"

M: "Look—I told you . . . I meant to. I just didn't, that's all!"

M: "Did you do the laundry?"

F: "YOU KNOW I had to take the kids to the dentist!!"

M: "What did I say to deserve that?"

F: "We were really lucky, you know, getting all those little trees for a dollar fifty apiece."

M: "A dollar fifty-nine apiece!"

F: "Why do you always do that?"

M: "Do what?"

F: "You know what! WHY do you ALways CORRECT me like that?!"

M: "Why can't YOU ever get anything RIGHT?"

M: "I really like Pittsburgh—it's a fantastic town."

F: "What's the matter with Wichita?"

F: "That's a good-looking shirt, honey."

M: "You should have told me you wanted me to wear a jacket!"

It probably *does* sound familiar. Men might prefer to think that their communication with women never contains anything but pleasant words and judicious comments. Women might prefer to believe that when they argue with men, it's always about significant issues and matters of great importance. We would *all* like to think that we're the kind of wise and rational and courteous human beings who never find themselves involved in language interactions like those above.

Unfortunately, that's not the way it is. The way it is is more accurately represented by the dialogues. Look them over again. Most of them aren't about anything that matters. Those that have a point, of sorts—like the argument about making a phone call—aren't going to improve matters in any way. None of these exchanges can be called *productive* communication.

Because we *are* human, we are undoubtedly going to continue to get involved in misunderstandings and arguments when talking to members of the opposite sex. But we can get rid of the useless and foolish altercations that only waste our time and our energies without accomplishing anything useful. We can free our language environment of mystifying interactions in which both parties end up hurt and/or furious, and neither one knows why. We can learn to talk without fighting, even when we disagree. We can save our resources for those rare occasions when an argument has a point and a purpose and what is needed is negotiation. We can put the joy back into our talking, and make it a positive part of our lives and our relationships instead of a burden. When you picked up this book and began reading, you took the first step toward making that a reality for *you*.

Few topics lead to more controversy than the subject of today's communication problems between men and women. In the old order, men got up in the morning and went to work, surrounded by other men. The only women they interacted with in the workplace were subordinates who said little more than "Yes, sir," and "Thank you, sir." Cross-gender communication at work consisted for the most part of giving or taking orders. When men came home at night they expected tender, loving—and respectful—care, from women whose lives were devoted to cleaning, cooking, and children. Women both at home and at work had conversations almost exclusively with other women and with children. Men were expected to be providers; women were expected to be homemakers; communication between them, other than in formulas and rituals, was not part of anybody's expectations. That old order is gone now. Times have changed. Suddenly women and men find themselves obliged to talk to one another—*really* talk to one another—and they're not finding it easy.

Women complain that their husbands don't talk to them and won't listen, and that their male colleagues talk down to them or try to shut them out of all but trivial communication at work. Men complain that their wives talk endlessly without saying anything and make absurd demands for talk that wastes time and accomplishes nothing; they complain that the women they interact with now at work don't know how to play the game and have to be constantly tiptoed around and catered to. Both men and women insist that talking to members of the opposite sex is infuriating, baffling, and a major source of problems in every area of life. The misunderstandings and confusion are so serious that they have brought on the ultimate disclaimer, heard everywhere today: that men and women "don't even speak the same language."

Genderspeak was written to address this problem, by providing practical solutions to the male/female communication crisis. Solutions that any man or woman can understand quickly and put to immediate use in both personal and professional life. It's the seventh book in a series devoted to the communication system called *The Gentle Art of Verbal Self-Defense*. The information it contains is based on solid linguistic science and has been tested thoroughly over the course of more than two decades. (If you know the *Gentle Art* system well, this book will show you how to apply your knowledge specifically to language interactions between the sexes. If the system is new to you, you will find everything you need to know inside this volume, including a thorough overview of the *Gentle Art* for your reference.)

Male/female communication does not have to be either armed combat or endless mystifying tedium. It does not have to be the source of either rage or misery. It can and should be effective, efficient, and a source of mutual satisfaction. This book will show you how to make that true for you, in your own life, beginning right now.

Acknowledgments

My thanks go to Virginia Satir, to John Grinder, to Leonard Newmark, to Cheris Kramarae, to Sally McConnell-Ginet, to George Miller, to Thomas Gordon, to Peter J. Blanck, and to the many other scholars and researchers whose work has laid the foundations upon which mine is based. I am grateful to my colleagues, my students, my *Gentle Art* trainers, and my clients, and to the many readers who've taken time to write me with their comments and suggestions about the series; without their generous input, this book would not have been possible. I want to express my appreciation for the invaluable support and assistance I have received from editors Jeff McCartney and PJ Dempsey. Thanks are due as always to the members of my long-suffering household, and especially to my daughter and colleague, Rebecca Haden.

If you would like to comment on *Genderspeak*, or if you want more information about the *Gentle Art* system, please feel free to contact me directly.

Suzette Haden Elgin, Ph.D.
Ozark Center for Language Studies
P.O. Box 1137
Huntsville, AR 72740

How to Use This Book

Genderspeak provides you with a complete program to make your communication across the infamous gender gap successful and satisfying in every area of your personal and professional life. In each of its fourteen chapters, you will find the following:

- A scenario presenting a typical situation of communication breakdown between men and women, in narrative form.
- An analysis of the scenario, in which the personal viewpoint of each male and female major character is presented in detail, so that the reader of *either* gender will understand how that man or woman perceives the situation.
- One or more practical techniques for tackling the specific communication problem described in the scenario.
- A re-examination of the scenario, demonstrating how using the techniques would have changed the situation and prevented or repaired the communication breakdown.
- A set of varied dialogues illustrating many different communication difficulties between men and women, followed by detailed notes explaining the problems and offering suggestions for dealing with them.

In addition, this book contains:

- Concise, thorough, nontechnical explanations of the necessary basic terms and concepts in linguistic science and communications.
- A brief history of changing attitudes about male/female communication during the past two centuries.

- A brief discussion of the current theoretical positions on male/female communication, and of the research on which those positions are based.

- A detailed bibliography and readings list, to give you access to more information on the topics presented if you would like to explore them further.

- Special chapters on two critical topics: sexual harassment in the workplace, and achieving intimacy in the *couple* relationship.

- An overview of the *Gentle Art of Verbal Self-Defense* system.

- A complete and thorough index, to provide you with convenient access to the book's contents.

Notes on the Scenarios and Dialogues

The men and women in the scenarios include husbands and wives, employers and employees, friends and colleagues and associates and relatives, parents and children, and couples of every kind. They are involved in an ongoing narrative that shows the development of communication breakdowns in the lives of people you will recognize immediately, because their lives are like *your* life. (As my editor, PJ Dempsey, says: Every argument you ever had is in this book.) You might find it useful to begin by reading the scenarios through from beginning to end as you would read a novel or short story, to get a general feeling for the problems that will be discussed in the chapters.

The dialogues, by contrast, present a wide variety of different situations and characters; each of them stands alone. They are intended to give the broadest possible coverage to the crisis in cross-gender communication, from the largest possible number of viewpoints. You will recognize the people in these dialogues and understand what they are going through, and the lines they say will be lines you have said or heard yourself.

In both the scenarios and the dialogues (as well as in examples of speech elsewhere in the chapters), I've made an effort to overcome the serious dilemma usually described as "You just had to <u>be</u> there!" There's no way to "be there" with written language, and that means a loss of valuable information, especially about the way the speech *sounds*. I've tried to adapt English punctuation and usage conventions to help you hear the words you're reading. The examples below, each with the same *words* but sounding very different when spoken aloud, will help clarify that for you.

- "Why are you leaving?"

  This is a neutral question, from someone who simply wants the information.

- "<u>Why</u> are you leaving?"

  This question comes from a speaker who is in some way emotionally involved, rather than neutral.

- "<u>Why</u> are you <u>leaving</u>?"

  This question comes from a speaker who objects to the other person's leaving and is for some reason very anxious about it.

- "WHY are you leaving?" and "WHY are you LEAVing?"

  Both of these questions indicate *anger* on the part of the speaker; they are hostile questions.

If you have trouble visualizing (audiolizing?) the sound of the speech in the book, I recommend reading the sentences aloud, giving extra stress (emphasis) to words and parts of words that are either underlined or appear in all capital letters. Those in capital letters are intended to carry the most emotional information and should be given the strongest emphasis.

It goes without saying that real people don't talk as fluently and as tidily as the speakers in this book do. Real people use profanity and slang, stammer, make speech errors, throw in "uhs" and "y'knows" and "yeahs," forget what they were talking about, and flounder around in the ways typical of human beings using language. I've tried to avoid the extravagant use of time and trees that would be needed to represent speech *exactly*, as is sometimes attempted in linguistics literature; at the same time, I've tried to make it realistic enough so that readers can identify with the speakers.

It also goes without saying that many, if not most, of the lines spoken by characters in this book—each identified as a line from a man or a woman—could have been said by either sex. Try it . . . read the line yourself and then have someone of the opposite sex read it. You'll find that 99 percent of the time the line sounds equally natural either way. This is a significant indication that women and men speak the *same* language.

When you've finished this book you will feel more hopeful about the possibility for useful and satisfying male/female language interaction. You will be less likely to throw up your hands in despair because "nothing can be done about the problem." You will be less likely to accept the idea that cross-gender miscommunication is something we just have to accept as a fact of life, or to believe that the most we can hope for is an awareness of that "fact" on the part of both men and women. And you will find that this change in your perceptions of male/female communication, together with your new skills, will lead to dramatic improvements in your life that would not otherwise have been possible.

If it is true that "you just don't understand," you can stop worrying about that. It's a temporary condition, and you can fix it.

Enjoy the book.

A Note for Nontraditional Couples

Throughout this book, all the couples described have been two people of opposite sexual genders who are both speakers of American Mainstream English, with at least roughly similar backgrounds. A large proportion of the information provided applies only to such couples. The English VAPs, for example, are not the VAPs of other languages. The traffic rules of the AME-speaking culture are not identical to those of other ethnic groups in the United States. Body language rules are not the same for all Americans, nor do they all have the same grammar regarding space and time.

The further apart the native languages and dialects of the partners in a language interaction are, the more likely the two people are to have very different definitions of words and phrases as well as different rules for many areas of linguistic behavior—even when both are fluent in one shared language.

This doesn't mean that none of the information in the book is useful to the nontraditional couple. It does mean that adjustments and changes will have to be made. The only people who can do that are the individuals involved. They will need much patience, and I wish them the very best of luck in a difficult—but not impossible—task; I hope that they will share what they learn as they carry it out. America badly needs the books they would be able to write.

Genderspeak

CHAPTER 1

The Male/Female Communication Problem: An Overview

Scenario One

"And now," said Mary Clayton, "I'd like to hear your thoughts on the proposal." She sat down, glad to be at the end of a very complicated presentation, and waited for the reaction of the others sitting around the conference table.

Her boss spoke up immediately, as she'd expected; he always did. "I'd like to kick this off, Mary," he said, "by just saying thank you for all the hard work you've done over the past month getting ready for this meeting, and for a really terrific presentation. Very impressive. I'm sure everybody here agrees with me. Right, people?"

The nods around the table seemed genuine enough, and Mary began to relax. She knew there would be objections to details, later, but it looked as if there were no strong negative reactions at this point.

"Thank you, John," she said, "and my thanks to the rest of you. I appreciate the positive response."

"But that's not all!" John Gellis went on. "On behalf of every man in this room, I want you to know that looking at your pretty face this morning . . . and let me tell you, Mary, you look like a million dollars! . . . has brightened everybody's day. It made it a little harder for us to concentrate on the details, I'll admit, but it was a pleasure all the same."

Mary swallowed hard and looked straight ahead, avoiding his eyes. She felt her face and throat flush as the rest of the men grinned at her and nodded their agreement to the compliment; she was careful not to look at any of them, either. What, she wondered, could she <u>say</u>? It was obvious to her that John's secretary was wondering the same thing; the poor woman was frozen in her chair, afraid to move. But John solved the problem for them.

"That'll do it, then!" he said. "Let's get back to work, and I'll let you know when we're ready to move on this project. A couple of days, maybe . . . maybe a week."

Mary gathered her materials together and stood up, still avoiding their eyes. She knew the expression on her face as she hurried out of the room was a tight-lipped, phony smile. It was the best she could do.

Back at her desk, she sat down and took a deep breath. "I did an excellent job on that presentation," she told herself. "I am <u>not</u> going to let John's behavior spoil that for me!"

"Hey, Mary?"

Bill Cartwright—one of her colleagues, and a man she considered a good friend—was leaning in her door.

"Yes, Bill?"

"Great job you did in there!" he told her heartily. "Great stuff!"

"Thank you," she said. "I'm glad you feel that way." She meant it; it was kind of him to make it explicit.

He cocked his head then and grinned at her, his eyes dancing. "My compliments on the black sweater," he said. "It kept everybody's attention, even through the statistics. Smart move, Mary—good strategy!"

Mary stared at him, shocked, unable to say a word, but he didn't notice; he left with a cheerful "See you!" before she could come up with an answer. She sat still for a minute, biting her lip hard, and then she got up and closed her office door. She might not be able to keep from crying, but she could keep them from seeing her do it.

◆

What's Going On Here?

Mary's Point of View

Mary feels that she has put in a great deal of hard work and has given as competent, detailed, and technical a presentation as any man could have given. She knows that no one would have listened to the same presentation from a man and then complimented him on his appearance. Such compliments seem to her to be the men's way of guaranteeing that her work, no matter how good, will always carry the equivalent of a Big Pink Bow marking it as [+ FEMALE]. She knows no way to counter this tactic—which has been going on for many months now—without making herself look and sound like "a neurotic woman." It is tremendously hurtful and frustrating to her, both physically and emotionally, and has become a major source of stress in her life.

John's Point of View

As John perceives the situation, he has no choice but to put up with women in the workplace—the laws require him to do that—but he's under no obligation to make it easy for them. He considers Mary's inability to counter his strategies solid proof that she ought to be home in a traditional role instead of in his office. He knows how distressing it all is to Mary. But in his opinion, he's not being unkind—he's doing her a favor. The sooner he can maneuver her into giving up the idea of a business career, the sooner she'll be *out* of all this stress and tension.

He is of course careful at all times to maintain the surface position of a nonsexist male. That's part of doing business in America today, and he recognizes and responds to that fact in spite of his own more conservative views on the subject. He enjoys the strategic challenge this offers him, and he prides himself on his skill in dealing with it.

Bill's Point of View

As Bill sees it, Mary is an attractive and successful woman. She has his respect and his admiration. He's willing to help her and make concessions for her in a way he would never even consider doing for a male colleague. He goes out of his way to be sure she knows that she can count on his support. He would be amazed to learn that Mary did *not* wear the black sweater as a deliberate strategy. The effect a woman can create by careful attention to her physical appearance is something else that he respects: If he were a woman, he would make maximum use of that advantage. He takes it for granted that Mary sees things this way, because to him it is so obvious and right. And although he's glad his own wife doesn't have to work, he is all for women's involvement in business if they can do a creditable job. He knows John disagrees with him, but he finds that natural, too—John is a man from an older generation, and Bill understands his views. Under the circumstances, he feels John deserves a lot of credit for his efforts to adjust to a changing world that he doesn't entirely approve of.

Everybody's Speaking English Here—What's the Problem?

From the point of view of *logic*, none of these communication breakdowns should be happening. John and Mary and Bill are all native speakers of American Mainstream English (AME). They come from roughly the same background, are of the same ethnic group, and are trained to work in the same field. They share roughly the same values. Mary has strong objections to the men's behavior toward her, but she doesn't believe that either of them is being deliberately malicious or cruel. If John were Japanese and Mary were French; if Bill were the only American; the trouble these three people have understanding one another's motives and behavior might be expected. Nobody is surprised when interaction between differing languages and cultures leads to misunderstandings. But that's not the situation here.

Why, then, do they communicate with one another so badly? Why can't Mary defend herself? Why can't she convince John to stop using language tactics that are patronizing and demeaning? Why can't she demonstrate to him, in a way that earns his respect, that she won't tolerate that behavior? Why doesn't Bill realize that his well-meaning remarks and body language are actually hurting Mary rather than helping her?

The best way to begin finding answers to these questions is by taking a brief look at the way attitudes about male/female communication in American English have developed and changed over the past hundred years or so. This will give us a foundation from which to examine the situation we find ourselves in today.

A Brief History of the Male/Female Language Controversy

Before 1900 the generally accepted position on the difference between male and female language for most speakers of American English (and especially for male speakers) could be summed up as follows:

1. The language of women, whether spoken or written, was inferior to that of men.
2. A woman who was an exception to this rule was a sort of freak, an abnormal organism. Anyone who wanted to compliment her on her speech or writing did so by saying that she spoke or wrote "like a man."

Such statements rapidly lost their respectability after 1900, so that even individuals who still agreed with them were unlikely to express them *publicly*; it became politically incorrect to say such things openly. We can read the last hurrah for the position they represent in the words of linguist Otto Jespersen, telling his readers in 1905 that:

> There is one expression that continually comes to my mind whenever I think of the English language and compare it with others: it seems to me positively and expressly *masculine*, it is the language of a grown-up man and has very little *childish* or *feminine* about it . . . the language is more *manly* than any other language I know. (*Growth and Structure of the English Language*, 9th edition. Oxford: Basil Blackwell, 1962. p. 10)

The idea that men and women use language very differently continued to thrive as conventional wisdom over the decades. It was generally taken for *granted* that the difference existed, that it was as natural and inevitable as the difference between ovaries and testicles, and that it was one of the mysteries of the universe. Few believed that it should be investigated, or that anything could or should be done about it.

Then in the 1970s attitudes changed dramatically. A number of scholars wrote on the subject, but the publication that brought the matter into the public eye was Robin Lakoff's popular paperback book, *Language and Woman's Place*, which appeared in 1975 (Harper and Row). Lakoff proposed a list of characteristics that she suggested could be used to identify women's speech in AME-speaking America and distinguish it from that of AME-speaking men. Lakoff's list wasn't made up of subjective or judgmental labels; it was a list of *linguistic* characteristics that could be observed and tested. To say that women's language is "more emotional" or "less logical" than men's is not testable in any scientific manner. To say, as Lakoff did, that women use more tag questions (like "It's raining, isn't it?") than men do *is* testable. Researchers proceeded to carry out the necessary investigations; however, the results were contradictory and confusing.

The research on tag questions is typical. Six studies done between 1976 and 1980, involving eleven skilled researchers, produced the following results: Six found that women used more tag questions; one found that there was no difference between men and women in their use of tag questions; and five found that men used more tag questions than women do. One study done at a professional conference found that the men present used thirty-three such questions while the women used none at all. Similar studies on such questions as which gender talks more, which interrupts more often, and the like, have produced similarly ambiguous results. (See Thorne et al. 1983.) This is perhaps because the field is so new and because the many variables involved make research design difficult; whatever the cause, it complicates matters greatly.

Research has continued in spite of the confusion, and the field (sometimes called *gendrolinguistics*) has grown steadily since 1975. It might seem that this kind of inquiry would be of interest only to linguists and to scholars in related fields, but events have proved otherwise. The degree to which the subject matters to the public is made dramatically clear by the many months that Deborah Tannen's book, *You Just Don't Understand: Women and Men in Conversation* (Morrow 1990), spent on the bestseller lists, and by Tannen's celebrity status.

Models Proposed by Scholars

From the many varying positions in the current literature we can extract two basic theoretical models for male/female communication in American Mainstream English. (For a detailed discussion of these positions, see Henley and Kramarae 1991.)

The first model claims that women and men who are speakers of AME use different varieties of English, and that these two varieties can be described in scientifically testable terms. This is the model that has caused the media in the United States to trumpet that men and women "speak different languages."

The second model proposes that speakers who have the dominant role in a language interaction use one variety of AME, and speakers in the subordinate role use another. In a doctor's examining room, for example, the physician uses the dominant variety and the patient uses the subordinate. When a lawyer questions a witness in a courtroom, the lawyer uses the dominant variety and the subordinate one is used by the witness. According to this model, the statistical fact that women tend to appear more often in the subordinate *roles*—because there are so many more male doctors and lawyers, for example, and so many more men than women in positions of power in business and government—has created a false perception that the subordinate variety is "women's language."

In all versions of both models there is much controversy about the question of what is responsible for the proposed linguistic differences. When and where do they begin, for instance? Are they the result of inherent differences, or are they acquired through socialization and education? Both models have predictable consequences for men and women who must get along together in the real world.

The Problem of Perceptions

The exact facts about male/female language usage, as demonstrated by the tag question studies, are unclear. As a result, no scholar today would make open negative claims of the old-fashioned kind about the language of either men or women. However, human beings base their behavior not on "exact facts" but on *perceptions*. Let's look at a few examples of perceptions about male/female language in our society today.

• Psychologists asked subjects to evaluate an article, telling some that it had been written by a man, others that it had been written by a woman, others that it had an anonymous author. The results: ". . . people rated the articles as better written, more insightful, more persuasive and higher in overall quality when they were told they had been written by a man." (V. Bozzi, "Crosstalk: Byline Bias," *Psychology Today*, November 1985, p. 15)

• ". . . women's language is not the language that business people want applicants to speak. Even women don't want to hear it. They want a woman to talk like a man." (Leigh Knotts, "Job-hunting Advice for Women: Talk Like a Man," *Baltimore Evening Sun*, 28 May 1991)

• "Women use conversation to expand and understand relationships; men use talk to convey solutions, thereby ending conversation." (Anastasia Toufexis, "Coming from a Different Place," *Time*, Fall 1990, p. 65)

• "For most men, public discourse is a competitive sport. . . ." (Barbara Ehrenreich, *The Worst Years of Our Lives* [New York: Pantheon, 1990], p. 114)

• "Most men prefer exercise to communication." ("The Male Stress Syndrome," *Pest Control Technology*, June 1987, p. 44)

• Women "get cowed too easily and back down, even when they have a good point," "lack proper social presence when they're not making business conversation," tend to "be more emotional and to personalize professional matters," and "haven't developed the grace of leadership that comes naturally to most men." (Various men, all speaking anonymously, in "The Last Angry Men? What Men *Really* Feel About Working With Women," by Linda Heller; *Executive Female*, 10 September 1988, pp. 33–38)

Perceptions like these, even when false, have consequences that are real; in public life, at the moment, the consequences are worse for women. As Robin Lakoff says in *Talking Power* (Basic Books, 1990): "Women, to succeed, must become honorary men.'' Here are a few typical examples of real-world effects resulting from the stereotypes, to support her claim.

• When a woman in an architecture class got an A on an assigned project, her professor said ''Yesterday you were a girl, today you are a man.'' (Anthony Astrachan, *How Men Feel* [New York: Anchor/Double-day, 1986] p. 173)

• The dollhouse family sold by ''Rose's Doll House'' in 1991 is made up of ''Mr. Smith, the daddy,'' ''Billy Smith,'' the child, and ''Rose, the kind Mom.''

• The ad for Danbury Mint's ''Barbie'' collector's plate says Barbie is ''every little girl's dream of the woman she hopes to one day become—beautiful, glamorous, and always dressed reflecting the latest styles.'' The ad does not go on to say that she hopes to be intelligent, logical, eloquent, well-educated, or even competent.

• ''There's not a woman anywhere who made it in business who is not tough, self-centered and enormously aggressive.'' (Businesswoman Marion Howington, quoted in ''Why Can't a Woman Manage More Like . . . a Woman?'' by Barbara Rudolph, with William McWhirter, *Time*, Fall 1990, p. 53. Howington was given a jockstrap as her ''parting gift'' when she retired from her executive post recently.)

Even when the actual characteristics of the language *contradict* them, the stereotypes often win. Consider what happened in the debates between George Bush and Geraldine Ferraro when they were campaigning to become vice president of the United States in 1988. Anyone in the audience holding a checklist of ''male language'' and ''female language'' characteristics would have quickly noticed that it was Bush's language that fit the feminine stereotype and Ferraro's language that fit the accepted idea of masculine speech. Bush's voice repeatedly became high and shrill and agitated; Ferraro's stayed low and calm. Bush lost track of where he was in his sentences, wandered off his subject and into digressions, and—in tight corners—became intensely personal. Ferraro was the logical and coherent speaker, and she did not resort to personal attacks. But that's not what the media reported, and it wasn't the perception of the general public—Republican, Democrat, or other. George Bush, declared the winner, described his performance as having ''kicked a little ass.''

Given the cumulative effect of stereotypical perceptions, this response to the debates should not surprise anyone. Bush is a former head of the CIA, a war hero, a former oilman, a father and husband and grandfather;

he is a wealthy man of power and stature and aristocratic lineage. He had all this on his side, as well as the indisputable historical facts: No woman had ever been vice president, and no woman but Ferraro had ever been even a *candidate* for that office for either of the major political parties. In the face of all that, it wasn't possible for most people to perceive him as "talking like a woman" or as losing the debate to a woman.

This phenomenon—when women are perceived as "talking like women" and men as "talking like men," regardless of the linguistic facts—is not confined to public debates and weighty occasions. It is a persistent phenomenon that interferes with effective communication in everyday life. Look at these two brief dialogues.

M: "How long till dinner's ready?"
F: "Twenty minutes?"

F: "How long till we leave for the airport?"
M: "Twenty minutes?"

Both dialogues contain exactly the same reply to the question; in both, the reply means, "How about twenty minutes? Is that convenient for you?" But the woman's line is typically perceived as an example of "feminine" or "subordinate" speech—hesitant, uncertain, and submissive. The man, on the other hand, is perceived as "being considerate," with no suggestion that he appears unable to make up his own mind. It's easy to see why the research results are so often mystifying.

If the stereotypes applied only in public life—or if almost all women (or almost all men) stayed home almost all the time—the disputes over whether men and women "speak different languages" and what those languages are like could perhaps be relegated to the ivory tower and left for scholars to quibble over. But both men and women take their stereotypes with them everywhere they go, and today the majority of women work outside the home as well as within it. This makes the disputes matters of importance for everyone.

As you read the chapters that follow, please keep two things firmly in mind.

• That there are two basic theoretical models of male/female communication differences for AME, which we can call "Male versus Female Language" and "Subordinate versus Dominant Language."

• That what we're discussing is American Mainstream English, the kind of English most people use in businesses and colleges and public life in the United States, although they may switch to another variety of English in their private lives.

Another Look at Scenario One

Let's look again at Scenario One on page 1, taking into account this time the information we've just discussed. Here we see three ordinary people, all tangled in their culture's stereotypical ideas about the language of men and women and the equally stereotyped implications of those ideas.

When John Gellis compliments Mary Clayton on her physical attractiveness in the meeting, she's speechless. When Bill Cartwright compliments her on her shrewdness in wearing her black sweater during her presentation, she can't think of a word to say. In both cases, although she knows exactly what her objections are and is confident that she's in the right, she is unable to defend herself. She is a victim of the stereotypes not only with regard to the behavior of the two men but in her own behavior as well. She is *absolutely* certain that if she simply speaks up and explains her feelings the men will either perceive her as behaving irrationally and "like a neurotic woman" or will pretend that they do, and that they will then attack her verbally on those grounds. She may be right. But she doesn't give them, or herself, a chance to find out. Her perception of herself as a victim of the stereotypes is so firmly entrenched that it leaves her defenseless.

John feels safe using the stereotypes as part of his campaign to convince Mary she doesn't belong, because he knows their power so well and they have worked for him so often in the past. And despite the pain he causes Mary with his words, he's able to go on thinking of himself as a man who is basically fair and kind. He *believes* that success in business is impossible for most women because they just aren't capable of functioning on an equal basis with men in the workplace; from within the context of that stereotype, his behavior is unpleasant but not illogical.

Bill is equally trapped by the stereotypes, but he reacts to them somewhat differently. Unlike John, he has no hidden negative agenda, though he would object to his own wife working outside their home. He is so convinced that all women use their sexual attractiveness to distract men in the workplace, and that this is nothing but good common sense on their part, that he fails to realize the implications of the idea. The implications are:

• That women's work can't stand on its own if men are clear-headed and thinking only of the work itself.

- That competent male adults are easily distracted by such trivia as a black sweater.

The trite old science-fiction plots in which women weren't allowed on spaceship journeys because they might distract the male crew and cause disastrous accidents were as biased against men as against women; like their authors, Bill would probably fail to realize that. It's easy to laugh at the popular images; but the effects they have on real people are anything but funny.

Dialogues for Analysis

Let's go back now, briefly, to the dialogues you first saw on pages xiii–xiv, plus one more to round out the set.

DIALOGUE ONE

F: "Please . . . talk to me."

M: "All right. What do you want to talk about?"

F: "Anything! You never talk to me!"

M: "My mind's a blank. I'm sorry. Tell me what you want to talk about and I'll be happy to oblige."

F: "Oh, never mind. Just never mind!"

M: "Whatever you say."

This is the stereotype of the subservient woman and the condescending dominant male at its worst. Even if she responds to "What do you want to talk about?" by proposing a topic of conversation, she is taking the subordinate role. Suppose he really would like to talk to her, but picking a topic out of the blue is something he's just not good at. In that case her behavior embarrasses him and makes him feel guilty. Suppose he'd rather *not* talk to her, and he enjoys being able to string her along like this; then she's playing right into his hands. Either way, they both lose.

Suggestion for Her: Begin with a topic and stick to it, as in "The way Congress is behaving disgusts me," or "I think our maple tree is dying." If you don't know what you want to talk about, it's unreasonable to expect *him* to know.

Suggestion for Him: If there's something you've been *wanting* to talk about, this is your chance: Introduce your topic and carry on a conversation with her on that subject. If not, respond to "Please . . . talk to me" by giving her a choice. Say, "Sure! Would you rather talk about Congress or that maple tree we're both worried about?"

DIALOGUE TWO

F: "Good morning, darling. Did you sleep well?"

M: "I guess so. Sure."

F: [Long pause] "Well?"

M: "Well, what?"

This is a man who's playing games, and a woman who's training him to play them.

Suggestion for Him: This is absurd. You do know that your line (after "I guess so. Sure.") is "How did you sleep?" If you suspect that this is a grammar rule honored primarily by women, and not one you'd follow with a male friend, you're right—but that's irrelevant. She's *not* a male friend. The fact that you're aware of the rule difference is a clear demonstration that you understand what's going on here.

Suggestion for Her: Give him the benefit of the doubt. Tell him, without sarcasm, "When I ask you how you slept and listen to your answer, I'd be pleased if you then asked me how I slept. That's fair." If that doesn't help—if he doesn't return the courtesy the next time you ask how he slept or how he feels, or whatever—stop asking. This is a game he can't play without your cooperation.

DIALOGUE THREE

M: "Are we going to your mother's for Easter?"

F: "Do we have a choice?"

M: "How would I know? She's your mother!"

F: "Well, you don't have to get nasty about it!"

When she says, "Do we have a choice?" he knows she's not happy about it; furthermore, his reminder that they're discussing *her* mother is clearly sarcastic. The dialogue above can only go in one direction. He'll say, "Who's getting nasty? Can't I even ask a simple question?"; she'll say, "You were getting nasty, and YOU KNOW it! As if I didn't feel bad enough already. . . .'' And so on, far into the night. I suggest this rewrite:

M: ''Are we going to your mother's for Easter?''

F: ''Do we have a choice?''

M: ''I don't know, honey. You know her a lot better than I do. What's your honest opinion?''

F: ''I think we have to go.''

DIALOGUE FOUR

F: ''Why didn't you call me?''

M: ''I meant to.''

F: ''Then why didn't you?''

M: ''I don't know.''

F: ''That's not a reason!''

M: ''Look—I told you . . . I meant to. I just didn't, that's all!''

This is silly on both sides. If he had a good reason for not calling, he would have told her immediately. She would have said, ''Why didn't you call me?'' and he would have said, ''Because all the phone lines in my building were out,'' or ''Because I was stuck in traffic,'' and she would have said, ''Oh! Okay.'' When no good reason is forthcoming, pursuing the issue is a waste of time and is unlikely to lead to anything pleasant. For example, she risks having him tell her the truth, as in ''Because I'm not a child and I don't HAVE to call you every five minutes!,'' or something similar. An open challenge like that is difficult to respond to without a fight, or an intense and uncomfortable discussion, or a serious loss of face for one or both of the persons involved.

Suggestion for Him: Just say ''I meant to, and I had no good reason for not following through. I'm sorry you were worried.'' Notice: you don't say you're sorry you didn't *call*, which would be a lie; you say, truthfully, that you're sorry she was worried. (If you *are* sorry you didn't call, of course, say that.)

Suggestion for Her: This man resents being pressured to call you. The more pressure you use, the less often he will call, and the more you'll fight about it. If it's important to you to make the point, go ahead, but respond to ''I meant to'' with a clear statement of your position. As in

"When you don't call me, I feel frightened, because so many people have accidents on that freeway."

DIALOGUE FIVE

M: "Did you do the laundry?"

F: "YOU KNOW I had to take the kids to the dentist!!"

M: "What did I say to deserve _that_?"

One of the major problems in family conversations is the one shown here: One person asks a question, and the other person answers some _other_ question. This woman is answering "WHY didn't you do the LAUNdry?"; he didn't ask that question. She should answer the question that he asked, with either yes or no, and then give him her reason if she feels that an explanation is necessary.

DIALOGUE SIX

F: "We were really lucky, you know, getting all those little trees for a dollar fifty apiece."

M: "A dollar fifty-_nine_ apiece!"

F: "_Why_ do you always do that?"

M: "Do what?"

F: "_You_ know what! WHY do you ALways CORRECT me like that?!"

M: "Why can't YOU ever get anything RIGHT?"

Again, the substance of this argument is trivial—but such arguments often occupy vast amounts of time and energy for couples. Either one of these people can avoid going down this dead-end road; it's a question of which one is willing. Two possible rewrites are suggested.

F: "We were really lucky, you know, getting all those little trees for a dollar fifty apiece."

M: "A dollar fifty-_nine_ apiece!"

F: "You're right—it was a dollar fifty-nine. What a terrific price."

—or—

F: "We were really lucky, you know, getting all those little trees for a dollar fifty apiece."

M: "We sure were."

DIALOGUE SEVEN

F: "I'm <u>sorry</u> I didn't send out any Christmas cards—but I just <u>couldn't</u>. A doctor's time is not his <u>own</u>!"

M: "Shouldn't that be 'A doctor's time is not <u>her own</u>'?"

F: [Pause] "Of course not! That sounds <u>ridiculous</u>."

M: "Well, you're a woman—and a doctor. I suggest you explain yourself. What's <u>ridiculous</u> about it?"

F: "You're trying to make me feel stupid because you're still mad about my not sending out those cards."

These two people are sparring, and he is *determined* to have a fight. He doesn't appear to care much what the fight is about, as long as he has one. She feels guilty about not sending the cards, which is apparently a responsibility she has accepted, and she throws out the "A doctor's time is not his own" platitude because it's an excuse that ordinarily works. After all, how can anybody ask someone whose time is spent saving the sick and the injured to do something as mundane as sending out holiday cards?

The excuse not only doesn't work with him, he uses it as a springboard for backing her into a corner and embarrassing her further. He certainly understands that the reason his revision of the excuse sounds strange to her is because it *is* a platitude, and she has always heard it said with the masculine pronoun. Her best move would be to stop sparring and say this: "You seem determined to have an argument. How about telling me what you're *really* angry about?" And his best move would be to do so.

DIALOGUE EIGHT

F: "Hello, darling."

M: "Is dinner ready?"

F: "Why don't you just go on back to the office?"

M: "What?"

There's no excuse for "Is dinner ready?" without so much as a greeting first; her response is understandable. All he has to say to avoid this unpleasantness is, "Hello! Is dinner ready?" That's just one additional word, and it's not enough effort to justify getting into an argument.

DIALOGUE NINE

M: "I really like Pittsburgh—it's a fantastic town."
F: "What's the matter with Wichita?"

If these two lines are in the middle of an ongoing discussion about Wichita and Pittsburgh, and she has been trying hard to make a case for Wichita, "What's the matter with Wichita?" is just fine. Otherwise, her line is an attempt to start an argument. His best move is to say pleasantly that so far as he knows Wichita's a great town, too, putting the ball back in her court.

DIALOGUE TEN

F: "That's a good-looking shirt, honey."
M: "You should have <u>told</u> me you wanted me to wear a jacket!"

This is the equivalent—for a statement—of answering a question you weren't asked. He's responding to a sentence she didn't say: "I wish you had put on a jacket instead of just a shirt." He may feel positive that that's what she *meant* by her remark, but the time to deal with that sentence is after it's actually said. Here are the possibilities:

F: "That's a good-looking shirt, honey."
M: "Thanks."
F: "You're welcome."

You see? This is a basic and pleasant exchange that leaves them both free to get on with what they're doing instead of involving them in a time-wasting and counterproductive altercation.

F: "That's a good-looking shirt, honey."
M: "Thanks."
F: "I wish you had put on a jacket too, though."

Now she has said what was actually on her mind, confirming his suspicions; now he can usefully respond to the sentence with whatever is appropriate for their situation.

CHAPTER 2

Some Basic Terms and Concepts for Discussing Language

Scenario Two

Mary didn't wait for Frank to ask her about her day; she just told him about it at dinner, straight through from beginning to end. How her presentation had gone well, with none of the glitches she'd been worried about and none of the strong objections for which she'd prepared detailed responses. How John Gellis had immediately expressed his own strong <u>positive</u> reaction—and then thrown in the remark about what a day-brightener it was to have her pretty face to look at! How Bill Cartwright had stopped by her office right after the meeting to tell her what a great job she'd done—and then thrown in the crack about her strategy in wearing the black sweater. She laid it all out for him, because she badly needed his sympathy and his advice about how she might have handled it better. But what he said when she came to the end of her story was very different from what she was expecting to hear.

"Hey, that's terrific!" he said. "I <u>told</u> you I was sure the presentation would fly, remember? Congratulations! Now what happens next?"

Mary set her knife and fork down carefully on her plate and stared at him, pale with both exhaustion and anger.

"What happens <u>next</u>?"

"Right! Do they start the project now or are there more meetings first or what?"

"You're incredible!" she told him, through gritted teeth. "You didn't understand a <u>word I said, did</u> you?! My boss and his buddies knock themselves out to make me look like some airhead that has to rely on batting her eyelashes because she hasn't got brain <u>one</u>—and all YOU can do is conGRATulate me! YOU'RE as BAD AS THEY are!''

Frank pushed back his chair, put down what he was eating, laid his napkin beside his plate, and folded his arms over his chest. ''Now, wait just a minute,'' he said. ''Hold on. Let me see if I've got this straight.''

''Frank—''

''No, wait. Just <u>wait</u>. Let me check this out. I come home from one of the worst days I've had in months, and before I can even eat my dinner you're telling me—in <u>excruciating</u> detail—about your latest triumph. Right so far? And I listen, right? And then when I tell you how terrific I think it is, you bite my <u>head</u> off! You don't make any sense at <u>all</u>, you know that?''

Mary took a long deep breath, and looked down at her plate.

''All right, Frank,'' she said wearily. ''I'm sorry I brought it up. Just forget I said any of it, and eat your dinner.''

''I've had all the dinner I'm interested in eating,'' he snapped. ''<u>You</u> eat dinner; you've <u>ruined</u> MINE!''

Silently, Mary watched him leave the table. It was hopeless; they didn't even speak the same language. And she was completely worn out. First the mess at the office; now *this*.

◆

What's Going On Here?

Frank's Point of View

If Frank had been listening carefully to what Mary was saying, he probably would have sympathized with her. Instead, he was thinking about the argument he'd had that afternoon after finally getting through to a telephone-tagging supplier, and he heard only two things: that her presentation had gone well and that it had earned compliments for her. He only learned what he had missed when she lashed out at him.

He understands that Mary resents the remarks about her appearance. He's sorry he didn't pay enough attention to pick up the right cues about that before she got angry. However, he does not understand *why* she feels the way she does. It seems to him that so long as she's also praised for her work she should be glad her male associates think she looks good, and are willing to tell her so. Like Bill, that seems to him to be her good fortune. And he considers it childish of her not to realize that it's an advantage she should be grateful for and make strategic use of.

Frank wouldn't have hurt Mary deliberately, especially not when she was already feeling so discouraged. But he's not about to apologize now. After all, he feels that she's the one who is *wrong*. He was only trying to be pleasant and to let her know he was proud of her. In spite of the rotten day he'd had, he was trying to show some genuine interest in her work. If she can't understand that and appreciate his good intentions, so be it; he's not going to struggle with her.

Mary's Point of View

As Mary perceives it, Frank should have been as outraged by the remarks John and Bill made as she was; even if he was a little preoccupied, he should have understood immediately. He knows she prides herself on doing the same kind of good solid work a man would do, and on never taking advantage of the fact that she's physically attractive. He knows she would like to have been given compliments on the soundness and thoroughness of her work instead of on her looks; she has explained that to him a thousand times. She can't imagine how he could have failed to give her the sympathy and support she needed—if it had been the other way around, and he had been insulted at the office, she would have sympathized with *him*. She feels betrayed, and she feels foolish. It hurts more coming from him than from anyone else, because she feels she has a right to expect him to understand. After all, he's her husband; he *lives* with her. Frank knows her better than anyone else ever could. How could he misunderstand her so completely?

◆

Here we have two people who love and respect each other, who are doing their best to make a life together, and who would never deliberately cause each other pain. But they seem to have only two kinds of conversations: Either they talk about trivial, safe topics like the weather and the traffic, or they have arguments like the one above. Is it perhaps true, as Mary was thinking, that they don't even speak the same language? Is that what's wrong? If it's true, what would it *mean*? Let's take a look at some basic terms and concepts that are needed in order to answer these questions.

Basic Facts about Language and Communication

What Is a Language?

Language is far more than the words people write and the words people say. ANYTHING A HUMAN BEING DOES THAT TRANSMITS A <u>MESSAGE</u> IS LANGUAGE. "*A*" language comes into being when a group of people has a set of shared rules (called a *grammar*) for transmitting messages. The difference between a language and a set of signals— traffic lights, for example, or the twelve words a parrot has learned to say—is that a human language is always an *open* set. Nobody could ever list all of the possible sentences of any living human language; nobody could ever demonstrate that any living human language is "finished." Another new sentence could always be added; another new word could always be coined.

Four information barriers stand between most of us and our potential for maximum understanding and use of our language. First: We aren't sufficiently aware of three important facts:

* Language is a *system*.
* Language is a *technology*.
* Every one of us has a *flawless internal grammar* of our native language.

In addition, we *are* aware of a set of misconceptions, distortions, and outright myths about language. The need to *un*learn that set makes matters even worse.

We tend on the one hand to take language for granted, which is a serious mistake. As Robin Lakoff says on page 13 of *Talking Power*: "Language is powerful; language is power. Language is a change-creating force and therefore to be feared and used, if at all, with great care, not unlike fire." We tend on the other hand to believe that real *skill* with language is something possessed only by experts, people with advanced degrees, and those lucky enough to be "born with a silver tongue in their mouths." This is also an error. We are all experts in our native language and potentially highly skilled in its use.

Much of our difficulty is due to the way we *store* our linguistic knowledge. We don't learn it as a well-organized system for which we have ready access to detailed inventories and directories. Much of what we know is far below the level of our conscious awareness. It's like a large library with no card catalogue or other index, where finding a particular book would be a matter of blind luck or of dogged persistence over long periods of time; everything we need is probably in there, but we have no way to find it quickly or efficiently or reliably.

Varieties of Language: Idiolects, Dialects, Registers, and Genderlects

Idiolects and Dialects

It's obvious that even people who do speak the same language don't all speak it in the same way. Every human being has a grammar that is different from the grammar of every other person speaking the same language. The language behavior that results from using that idiosyncratic grammar is called an *idiolect*. Words in your idiolect will inevitably have slightly different meanings from words in other idiolects, because the experiences that are associated with the words differ from one individual to another. We have no reason to believe that any two idiolects of a language are ever identical.

When a group of idiolects are so much alike that people using them ordinarily don't realize that they're different, we call the set a *dialect*. Popular ideas about dialects—none of them accurate—include the following:

- A dialect is a funny way that other people talk.
- Only uneducated people speak dialects.
- Only people who come from specific geographical areas—New York City, for instance, or "the South"—speak dialects.

In fact, everyone speaks at least one dialect, and that dialect is the sum of the idiolects of all the individuals who share *nearly* identical grammars.

Sometimes it's hard to tell whether two ways of using language are two different languages or two dialects of a single language. Navajo and Apache are very much alike, for example; a strong argument can be made that they are one language. In other cases the dialects of a single language are so drastically different that it's tempting to call them two different languages. But the differences really must be substantial before that can happen; it must be genuinely almost *impossible* for speakers of the two dialects to understand one another, in the way that it's almost impossible for a native speaker of French to understand a native speaker of German.

Registers

In addition to speaking an idiolect and at least one dialect, everyone speaks one or more *registers* of a language. We all know that lawyers talk differently in the courtroom during trials than they do at lunch with close friends. A father talks differently to his three-year-old son than he does to his sixteen-year-old son. A small child talks differently on the playground ("Hey, guys!") than to an elderly grandmother he sees only two or three times a year ("Hello, Grandmother!"). When language behavior can be systematically described, and when it is clearly tied to a specific *role* of the speaker or writer, it is called a register—not a dialect. The more registers a person can use skillfully, the more successful that person is likely to be. Registers are essentially independent of gender except in the sense that "mother" is a role of women, "father" a role of men, etc. Most roles, and their registers, are open to both sexes.

Here's a typical example of the *academic* register:

> *Culture clash*, a phrase intelligible to most Americans, presupposes a society conversant with the idea of multiple cultures coexisting uneasily. (Lakoff 1990, p. 165)

There's nothing that makes "a phrase intelligible to most Americans" better than "a phrase most Americans understand." The meaning difference, if there is one, is trivial. But when Lakoff uses language in this way she is instantly recognizable to other academics as a member of their group, and that has significant advantages.

Genderlects

Finally, we come to the *genderlect*. The term is transparent; it means "a variety of a language that is tied not to geography or to family background or to a role, but to the speaker's sexual gender." There are languages that may well have genderlects, at least on a minor scale—Japanese, for example. In a column titled "Women's Talk" (*New York Times Magazine*, 1 September 1991, p. 8), Ellen Rudolph writes of the language difficulties faced by Nobuko Yotsuya, the first woman ever elected to serve as vice chairman of the powerful Metropolitan Assembly in Tokyo: "But for all the power that was suddenly hers, she was unable to break through a formidable barrier: the linguistic one. She couldn't bring herself to use a simple three-letter suffix, *kun*." Previous vice chairmen of the group had addressed other members as "So-and-So-kun" rather than "So-and-So-san"; but women do *not* use the honorific "-kun." Ever. There are many more examples of this kind for Japanese. Lakhota Sioux also has sets of specific forms that are used only by men, and others used only by women.

In these two languages, female/male language differences aren't just a matter of differing vocabulary choices. Male use of the female forms, or vice versa, is an error in the same sense that saying ''growed'' for ''grew'' is an error in English. Whether there really are genderlects of American English or not is a matter of controversy; certainly there are no examples like those we find in Japanese or Lakhota Sioux.

What Is Communication?

The traditional model of communication seems like simple common sense. It proposes that communication takes place when people follow four steps:

1. I, the speaker, have something in my mind that I want to say—a chunk of meaning I want to pass on to my listener.
2. I use words and body language to *say* that chunk of meaning.
3. My listener hears and observes my words and body language.
4. The listener then has in his or her mind the same chunk of meaning that I wanted to pass along.

If I'm writing the message instead of speaking it, I will write the words instead of saying them; if my language is a sign language, I will use signs rather than words. The model remains the same.

This model claims that a message is basically the same as a package. Suppose I put a rose in a box and hand it to you: I can be sure that when you open the box it will still contain a rose and not a frog. If communication really worked this way, life would be far simpler. I could be sure that when I put my message for you into a ''box'' of language, the message you understood would be the same message I intended to give you.

Unfortunately, communication isn't like that. THE ONLY MEANING A SEQUENCE OF LANGUAGE HAS IN THE REAL WORLD IS THE MEANING THE LISTENER (OR READER) UNDERSTANDS IT TO HAVE. Suppose my message is ''Here's a rose for you'' but you understand me to mean ''Here's a frog for you.'' My intentions are irrelevant to your understanding, and your behavior toward me will be based not on the rose I intended but on the frog you understood.

People on the receiving end of your communication base their understandings not on your intentions but on a long list of other factors that make up the *context*, including:

- What they expected you to say.
- What other people have said to them in the past in the same situation.
- What they believe it is polite to say.
- What they would have said if they were you.
- What they, in your situation, would never say under any circumstances.

Add to all this the fact that your communication is filtered through such things as how well they can hear or see you, how tired they are, whether they are worried or frightened or sick, how similar factors have affected *your* communication skills, and many other real-world variables. There's nothing wrong with the internal, mental grammar of the listener or speaker. The problem is that so many things outside that grammar can interfere with performance.

Under the circumstances, what's amazing is not that communication so often breaks down but that it works as well as it does. And it will work for you more often, and more reliably, if you discard the inaccurate "A message is a package" model.

What Is Translation?

Again, there is a popular traditional model for translation; again, it is a flawed model. It claims that when you want to translate a sentence of Language X into a sentence of Language Y, you substitute the words of Language Y for the corresponding words of Language X, make a few adjustments for the differences in such things as word order, and you're done. Sometimes this works, especially when the two languages are closely related. You can take the English sentence "I see you," substitute the French words ("je" for "I," "vois" for "see," and "vous" for "you") for the English ones, adjust the word order for French—where the verb will come last in this sentence—and end up with the accurate translation "Je vous vois." But that is the exception rather than the rule. Most of the time, it won't work; and even when it works for an isolated example, it won't work for a sequence in context.

To translate a sequence of Language X into a sequence of Language Y, what you really have to do is this:

✦ Find in Language Y the sequence that a native speaker of Language Y would have used *in the same situation* . . . in the same real-world context.

The two sequences may be radically different. One may be only a few words, while the other requires several sentences. The two sequences may have few or no words in common. The two sequences may refer to different chunks of time or space. One sequence may have to contain many things that don't appear in the other at all. The translation of English "I am sitting down" into Navajo is approximately "I have ceased to move around and have taken up a sitting position," plus some details about *precisely* how that has been done.

The same principles hold for "translations" of dialects, registers, and genderlects. In an article titled "Power: Are Women Afraid of It—or Beyond It?" (*Working Woman*, November 1991, pp. 98–99), Maureen Downs quotes a line from former White House Chief of Staff John Sununu: "I'll chainsaw your balls off." In the traditional model, although "chainsawing" might be tricky, translation to a female genderlect would presumably be "I'll chainsaw your ovaries off." But it's very unlikely that that is what a woman would say in the same situation, and "ovaries" has no informal corresponding word that pairs up the the way "balls" pairs with "testicles." Similarly, it's unlikely that a female boss in a meeting would tell a man that the opportunity to look at his handsome face as he presented a proposal had brightened everybody's day.

Put It All Together . . .

Now let's take this information and consider how it applies to the current theories about communication between male and female speakers of American Mainstream English.

It's clearly a distortion to say that "men and women speak different languages." A great deal of the time the two genders understand one another perfectly. If what is being communicated is an item of fact—like "It's twenty minutes after six" or "This shirt costs forty-three dollars" or "The train leaves at midnight exactly" or "My birthday is on September 29th"—the meanings at both ends of the transaction will almost always match. WHEN TWO PEOPLE SPEAK DIFFERENT LANGUAGES, THIS IS NOT THE CASE. The "different languages" idea can be set aside without any hesitation. It is in any case primarily a distortion spread by mass media, and not something that was presented in the original sources. It represents a typical example of a communication breakdown between scholars or scientists and the media.

The idea that male/female communication requires translation between two *dialects* is not as easily discarded. Speakers of different dialects understand each other much, even most, of the time, because their grammars are similar and their vocabularies are largely shared. In addition, they have a resource that speakers of different *languages* do not have: When a communication breakdown occurs, they're able to use their shared language to find out what has gone wrong. It may take a while, but it can be done. One speaker can say things like "Wait, I don't understand what you mean by that!" and "What's head cheese? I never heard of it!" so the other speaker will know an explanation is needed and provide it.

Suppose we were to decide that there *are* genderlects of American Mainstream English—a male dialect and a female one. I don't believe that case can be made, frankly, and there certainly isn't sufficient evidence to make it at the moment. But even if genderlects of AME exist, both genders have the resource of that process for *negotiating* meaning available to them. That's a vast improvement over "speaking different languages."

However, there are two major problems with the process of communication by negotiation when it takes place between AME-speaking women and men.

First: The two varieties are so much alike on the surface, so much alike in the words used and the rules applied to the words with regard to things like word endings and word order, that the speakers tend to *assume* no nontrivial differences exist. Men and women can go to a meeting, carry on a discussion, and go away with quite different perceptions of what went on there and what decisions were made—*without being aware that the different perceptions exist*.

Second: Speakers of both dialects tend to feel that they shouldn't have to *worry* about communication in this way, that the other speaker *ought* to understand without a struggle. Particularly when the man and woman involved are a couple, they feel that communication between them *ought* to be easy. When it's not, there's a strong and dangerous tendency for each half of the couple to suspect that the other one isn't trying—doesn't really want to communicate; is deliberately obstructing communication; has some kind of secret agenda; and so on. The better the two know each other, and the longer they have spent much of their time together, the worse this problem tends to be.

Whether there are AME genderlects, or there is only a dominant variety and a subordinate variety, these same two conditions will apply.

The question is, then: Assuming, as I do assume, that most men and most women would prefer to communicate effectively with each other, what can they do to achieve that goal?

There are many simple techniques that can be used to work toward satisfactory cross-gender communication; it's not true that nothing can be done. I will be presenting some of the techniques to you in this book. They are easy to learn, easy to remember, easy to put into immediate practice, and thoroughly tested. We can turn immediately to the first one: Using Miller's Law.

Technique #1
Using Miller's Law

George Miller is a psychologist with an extraordinary ability to construct clear and compelling statements about language. One of those statements is so critically important to communication, in my opinion, that I call it *Miller's Law*.

> In order to understand what another person is saying, you must assume that it is true and try to imagine what it could be true of. (Interview with Elizabeth Hall, *Psychology Today*, January 1980, pp. 38–50 and 97–98)

A great deal of the time, when people hear someone say something they don't immediately understand, they assume that it's false and try to imagine what could be wrong with the *person saying it* that would cause him or her to say anything so ridiculous. This is a kind of Miller's-Law-In-Reverse, and a guaranteed recipe for communication breakdown.

Remember that package on page 23 that started out as a rose and was understood as a frog? Let's extend that just a little further, in the context of Miller's Law. Suppose I thought I put a rose in the package, and I've handed it to you, but when you look inside you're quite sure you see a frog. Suppose I then say to you, "Aren't you going to put it in a vase?" Applying Miller's Law to this otherwise very strange question, you will assume that I'm speaking *what I believe to be the truth* when I suggest putting the contents of the package in a vase. And you will have no trouble understanding that in that case I must have *thought* the package contained one or more flowers, since that's what gets put in vases. You are then less likely to throw the box away and walk off angry.

Suppose what I say to you is not quite that illuminating. Suppose I say, "Aren't you going to put it in water?" Both flowers and frogs could reasonably be put in water, which means you have to entertain the possibility that I *intended* to give you a frog all along. But if you apply Miller's Law in that case, you'll realize that a world in which I would do that, with a smile on my face and a polite question to follow it up, is a world in which for some reason I thought you *wanted* a frog. You may wonder where I got such a wild idea. You will certainly realize that our communication has broken down. You may want to start the process of communication by negotiation, if the circumstances allow for that. But you are *still* unlikely to throw away the box and walk off in a rage.

You will have read and heard many times the suggestion that you should try to "share the other person's perceptions" or "understand the other person's worldview." Applying Miller's Law is a straightforward, practical method for doing that. Suppose you've heard someone say something that baffles you, something that you find outrageous or illogical or difficult to understand. Then—

1. Assume (not *accept*, just assume) that what you heard is true.
2. Ask yourself: What could it be true *of*? In a world where it is true, what *else* would have to be true?

    The results will be well worth your trouble, for two reasons.

- Because you haven't responded with instant annoyance, you'll avoid the hostility that an irritated response is sure to provoke, as well as the unpleasant interaction that typically *follows* an irritated response.
- Because you can't answer the question in Step Two without paying attention to what was said, the speaker won't feel ignored or cut off without a hearing.

This improves your chances for successful communication, not only with the person to whose language you applied Miller's Law this one time, but for those you talk to later, who won't find you already in a bad mood.

Another Look at Scenario Two

The communication in Scenario Two broke down at the point where Frank thought he was being most supportive of Mary—when he had told her how terrific it was that her presentation had been a success and encouraged her to continue talking by asking her what would happen next. Let's look again at the relevant lines from the scenario.

Frank: "Now what happens next?"

Mary: "What happens <u>next</u>?"

Frank: "Yeah. Do they start the project now or are there more meetings first or what?"

Mary: "You're incredible! You didn't understand a <u>word I said, did</u> you?! My boss and his buddies knock themselves out to make me look like some airhead that has to rely on batting her eyelashes because she hasn't got brain <u>one</u>—and all YOU can do is conGRATulate me! YOU'RE as BAD AS THEY are!"

There are two places in this sequence of lines where following Miller's Law would have prevented the communication breakdown.

The first is when Mary reaches the end of her account and expects to hear Frank respond with a statement of outrage at the way her male colleagues treated her, plus a little sympathy. When she heard his calm "Now what happens next?" she should have applied Miller's Law. She would then have realized that he responded as he did only because all he'd understood from her account was that the presentation had gone well.

The second is when Frank asks what will happen next and expects an answer to that question, and instead he gets a furious "What happens <u>next</u>?," with Mary's body language clearly indicating anger. If he'd asked himself what else would have to be going on in order for her response to make sense, he would have realized what had happened: She would only have said what she did if he'd misunderstood her so badly that his question was totally inappropriate.

Let's rewrite the dialogue to show the effect of using Miller's Law in each case.

If Mary Had Used Miller's Law

Frank: "Now what happens next?"

Mary: "Frank, if you had heard everything I said I don't believe you would be asking me that question. Tell me what you think happened to me today."

Frank: "Your presentation was a smash hit and you got a lot of compliments, right? Or did I miss something?"

Mary: "You missed the most important part."

Frank: "I'm sorry—my mind was still at the office. Tell me again, and this time I'll pay attention."

If Frank Had Used Miller's Law

Frank: "Now what happens next?"

Mary: "What happens <u>next</u>?"

Frank: "Wait a minute, honey. I must have missed something important in what you were saying, or you wouldn't sound like that—or look the way you do. I spent most of the day playing telephone tag and I'm still frazzled; I'm sorry. Tell me again, and this time I'll pay attention."

Mary and Frank each had an opportunity to avoid the ugly fight that made an already unpleasant day far worse. All they needed was a conscious awareness of Miller's Law and a willingness to put it into practice.

Dialogues for Analysis

DIALOGUE ONE

F: "Golly, it's hot in here!"

M: "You could at least <u>try</u> to get along with these people! Or do you <u>want</u> me to lose this account?"

This is what happens when you apply Miller's-Law-In-Reverse. The message she wants to transmit is that she finds it too hot in the room for comfort. He doesn't think it's hot, and his immediate reaction is to reject what she says as false. We can summarize what he says to *himself* roughly like this:

"She says it's hot in here. That's ridiculous. It's not hot at all. What's <u>wrong</u> with her to make her say something that stupid? . . . Oh, yeah! She didn't want to come to this cocktail party, she <u>never</u> wants to do the social stuff that's important to my job, and she's working up an excuse so we'll have to leave. Well, it's not going to <u>work</u>."

When he starts talking, he responds not to what she said, but to his own ideas—an excellent way to start a fight.

Let's assume for the sake of argument that he's right, and she really *is* just tooling up to insist that they leave. His best move is nevertheless to assume that what she says is true and try to imagine what it could be true of. For example: It could be true of someone whose tolerance for heat is lower than his, or someone wearing clothing heavier than his, or someone having one of the hot flashes typical of menopause. I suggest a rewrite:

F: "Golly, it's hot in here!"

M: "I'm sorry you're uncomfortable. Maybe it would help if we moved closer to the window."

This is completely nonconfrontational, it's courteous and considerate, and it puts the ball back in her court. If she plans to ask him to leave, she'll have to say so more explicitly.

DIALOGUE TWO

M: "Sheeeeesh! What a day!"

F: "I know. Me, too."

M: "Oh, sure. What'd you do, break a fingernail?"

He'll have no trouble applying Miller's Law here. He's familiar with the kinds of crises she has to deal with at home every day, and what she says could be true of any day when one or more of those crises had occurred. Responding with "What'd you do, break a fingernail?" is just snarling and spitting. It's totally counterproductive, and it's guaranteed to ruin the *rest* of his day.

Suggestion for Him: When she says "I know. Me, too," say, "I believe you. Me first, though." Tell her as much about your day as you feel inclined to tell. Then tell her it's her turn, and listen to what *she* has to say.

Suggestion for Her: Answer his opener with "I know. Me, too. But you first. What happened?" And then listen carefully until he's ready to listen to you. If you can't do that because you have an emergency on your hands, proceed like this:

M: "Sheeeeesh! What a day!"

F: "I know. Me, too. And I want you to tell me what happened— just as soon as we catch the snake that's in the garage."

DIALOGUE THREE

F: "Why are you just sitting there staring off into space?"

M: "I'm not awake yet."

F: "That's ridiculous!"

M: "Mmmmph."

F: "I might as well go out to breakfast with a potted plant! For heaven's sakes, make an effort!"

If she goes on like this, she will eventually wake him up, but he won't be pleasant company. She's a person who, once her eyes are open in the morning, is awake and ready to function; this in no way justifies her conviction that every normal human being shares that characteristic. There are many people—like this man—who wander in a fog for a while when they first get up. Her proper move is to assume that he's speaking the truth. Here's the rewrite.

F: "Why are you just sitting there staring off into space?"

M: "I'm not awake yet."

F: "That must be a real nuisance."

M: "Mmmmmmmph."

F: "Tell you what—I'll read the paper. You let me know when you feel conscious enough for conversation."

DIALOGUE FOUR

M: "Hey, you look terrific in that black sweater! I wish I could go into a meeting with that kind of an advantage!"

F: "If you think your smart cracks are going to rattle me, buster, you're going to be VERY disappointed!"

M: "But all I said was—"

F: "Don't TRY it! Just put it out of what passes for your mind!"

This is a serious communication breakdown, and is likely to cause bad feeling for a long time. Her move is not well chosen. Suppose she uses Miller's Law and assumes that he's telling the truth; she can simply thank him and go on into the meeting. Then she should make an opportunity to talk to him privately in a casual setting—over coffee, for example—where she can explain that although she appreciates a sincere compliment, she would prefer to be complimented on her work. She can also explain that most women in the workplace agree with her.

And if that's *not* the situation? It's possible that this woman's instant hostile reaction is justified. Maybe what he says is false; maybe he's saying it only in an attempt to sabotage her performance; maybe she has solid evidence that that's the case. If that's what is going on, he isn't entitled to an application of Miller's Law. But even then, her response in Dialogue Four is poor strategy. I suggest this rewrite.

M: "Hey, you look terrific in that black sweater! I wish I could go into a meeting with that kind of advantage!"

F: "No reason why you can't. You can get a sweater just like this one at Dillard's."

DIALOGUE FIVE

M: "Good morning. Tell me why you came to the emergency room."

F: "It's my gallbladder."

M: "Wait a minute, please. Tell me where the pain is."

F: "My Aunt Grace had exactly this same problem, and it was her gallbladder. She—"

M: "Ma'am, I'm not interested in your Aunt Grace. If I'm going to help you, you have to answer my questions. I need to know where your pain is, when it starts, how long it lasts, and anything you can tell me about what seems to set it off, so that I can find out what's wrong with you!"

F: "I told you what's wrong. It's my gallbladder. My—"

M: "Never mind your Aunt GRACE! Please—try to cooperate! You're not the only patient we HAVE, you know!"

What this man is doing is guaranteed *not* to accomplish his goals. The more he orders the patient not to talk about her Aunt Grace's gallbladder attack, the less she will be inclined to cooperate with him and the longer it will take him to get the information he needs. This is bad not only for the two people in the dialogue, but also for the other patients he says are waiting for his attention. Applying Miller's Law would look like this:

F: "My Aunt Grace had exactly this same problem, and it was her gallbladder. She had to have an operation."

M: "I understand. Now tell me—when your Aunt Grace had this problem, where was her pain?"

And so on, through each of the questions he needs answers for.

DIALOGUE SIX

F: "I'm sorry. I can't give you your check in person; I have to <u>mail</u> it to you. That's the rule."

M: "That's the most ridiculous thing I ever heard in my <u>life</u>! It's <u>my</u> money, and I'm <u>here</u>! I suggest you hand it <u>over</u>!"

F: "We don't hand out checks in person, sir."

M: "But that check is LATE! I see no reason why MY life should be disrupted because YOU people aren't capable of doing your JOB! I demand—"

F: "NEXT!"

One of two things is going to happen here. One: he'll have to leave without his check and wait until it arrives in the mail. Two: he'll make a scene, waste thirty minutes fighting with this woman's supervisor, and—maybe—get his check. And from that moment on the people in this office will delight in losing his checks, delaying his mail, and sabotaging his life in every way legally available to them. Suppose he applies Miller's Law instead, and proceeds to function in the clerk's reality . . . the one where everybody has to follow the rules, no matter how stupid the rules may be. . . .

F: "I'm sorry. I can't give you your check in person; I have to <u>mail</u> it to you. That's the rule."

M: "I understand. And I'm sure <u>you</u> understand that the rules say that check has to be in my hands no later than the third day of the month. This is the <u>fifth</u>. Good thing I had time to stop by and pick it up!"

DIALOGUE SEVEN

F: "Your secretary is really <u>angry</u> with me this morning!"

M: "Mother, you're imagining things. My secretary doesn't even <u>know</u> you."

F: "When I called and asked for you, she was angry. I could tell by her tone of voice. And she didn't want me to talk to you, either. I had to <u>insist</u>."

M: "Mother, please. <u>Trust</u> me. My secretary was not angry with you.

She has nothing to be angry with you <u>about</u>. Where do you <u>get</u>
these crazy ideas, anyway?''

F: "You know, I may be getting <u>old</u>—but I'm NOT SENile!''

M: "Mother, nobody said anything about senile! Do you want me to
meet you for lunch, or <u>not</u>?''

F: "Crazy ideas, you said. <u>Crazy</u> ideas.''

M: "Well sure, but it's just a figure of speech. It doesn't mean
<u>crazy</u>!''

F: "REALLy. Well, what DOES it mean?''

(And so, lengthily, on.)

Two of this man's sentences—"you're imagining things" and
"where do you get these crazy ideas, anyway?"—should be eliminated
from his language behavior on general principles. Both sentences transmit
this message: "I have no respect for your perceptions of reality." His
problem is, of course, that he doesn't want to be bothered with the
conversation right now, and he thinks that if he lets his mother start
talking he'll have trouble getting off the phone. What he doesn't realize
is that the conversation would in fact be over sooner—and he would not
have insulted his mother—if he would apply Miller's Law. Here's a
rewrite.

F: "Your secretary is really <u>angry</u> with me this morning!''

M: "No kidding? What did she say to you?''

F: "She didn't actually <u>say</u> anything . . . it was just her voice. She
sounded cross.''

M: "Mother, she's answered forty calls this morning, and most of
them have been a hassle. I don't think the way she sounded had
anything to do with you.''

F: "You're probably right; you know her a lot better than I do.''

M: "Okay! Now, where shall I meet you for lunch?''

If, on the other hand, the secretary *did* say something cross to his
mother, this rewritten dialogue will give her the opportunity to tell him
what it was, so that he can deal with it in whatever way he considers
appropriate.

CHAPTER 3

◆

"Oh, That's Only
Semantics!"

─────── Scenario Three ───────

Paula Gellis stared at the television set in horror, wishing it would do some good to throw something through it. "Damn!" she said. "_Damn_ him!"

Her husband and son looked at each other with raised eyebrows. For Paula to say "damn" once was a rare event; twice was out of the question. Why would a mild little science fiction movie like _Dreamscape_ provoke her so?

"_You_ ask her, Dad," Larry said. "This is out of my league."

John nodded, and turned to his wife. "Honey," he asked, "what are you swearing about? Whatever it was, Larry and I missed it."

"Didn't you see what he _did_?"

"What _who_ did?"

"The so-called male hero!"

"Sure. Standard seduction scene, in a dream. Hearts and flowers. Very touching. Not even very steamy. What's to swear about?"

"John," Paula said grimly, "she _told_ him she wanted nothing to do with him sexually, remember? She told him in no uncertain _terms_. And he agreed not to bother her about it again—he gave her his _word_!"

"But Mom," Larry broke in, "he backed off! He kept his word. It was only in the _dream_ that he went after her!"

"This is a science fiction movie," Paula insisted, her voice trembling. "With _shared_ dreams! Everybody that works in the lab has access to that dream. Everybody knows what—"

"Oh, honey, come on!" John scoffed, interrupting her. "Admit it—you're being ridiculous."

"I am <u>not</u>! It's horrible. Here she is, working with all these people, and with <u>him</u>, every single day, and they all <u>know</u> about it—IN DETAIL!"

"Mom . . . come on! Nothing really happened. The guy didn't really <u>do</u> anything to her!"

Paula looked from son to husband and back again, and when she spoke this time her voice was steady. "Am I understanding this correctly?" she asked quietly. "Do you two really agree on this— that 'nothing really happened' and he didn't do anything wrong?"

"Absolutely," said John. "No harm done! Frankly, I don't know how you manage to make such a big deal out of something so trivial, Paula."

"Yeah, Mom," Larry agreed. "What's the problem?"

Paula walked out on them without another word, and in a few seconds the two men heard her close the bedroom door behind her.

"Hey," Larry said slowly, "that was weird. It's only a movie, for crying out loud! Do <u>you</u> understand what Mom's all upset about?"

"No," John admitted, "I don't. It makes no sense at all to me. But you know, Larry, it's <u>impossible</u> to understand women; don't even try. Whatever it is, she'll get over it. Want some popcorn?"

"Shouldn't you maybe go talk to her?"

John laughed. "Now you're sounding like a seventeen-year-old kid," he said.

"Well, I <u>am</u> a seventeen-year-old kid!"

"My point exactly. Believe me, humoring her would only make it worse."

———————————————— ✦ ————————————————

What's Going On Here?

John's Point of View

As John perceives it, two things matter here:

•   The woman in the movie has not been so much as *kissed* by the man she asked to leave her alone, and she therefore has not been harmed in any way. In John's opinion, she should in fact feel a sort of amused admiration for the hero's cleverness in getting around her objections while still honoring them, and she should be complimented by his continued interest and passion.

• No matter *how* the movie is analyzed, it's only a movie. For Paula to ruin the evening for the whole family over something that's not even real is, in John's opinion, childish and petty.

He's sorry this incident happened, because they don't have a lot of time for evenings together at home. But he's glad Larry was there to observe his mother's behavior; it will be useful experience for the boy, down the line. He might as well start getting used to the crazy way women react to things.

Larry's Point of View

Larry agrees with his father about the argument at issue. He perceives the same "facts" his father perceives, and he is genuinely baffled by his mother's reaction to the movie. But he's in a bind. He knows John will use the incident as yet one more piece of evidence that women are emotional and immature and incapable of functioning successfully in a man's world—an idea that Larry feels is true of some women, but not all. He knows his dad will bring the incident up again and again, any time he finds it useful, and Larry dreads having to serve as witness. He feels caught between his mother and father, knowing that they both expect his agreement and support; there's no way he can take both positions at once. Like John, he resents Paula's spoiling everybody's evening over something that happened only in a fictional world.

Paula's Point of View

As Paula perceives it, the woman in the movie suffered serious harm. If the man's sexual experience with her had been in a dream only he had, that would be different, but this dream was available to everyone. Every time the woman sees him, she'll have to face the fact that he remembers the episode, that he knows her body and its responses intimately, and that he gained that knowledge over her clearly stated objections. Furthermore, others who watch the dream are going to assume that she was a willing partner. This is a terrible position for her, made worse by the fact that since in "the real world" the man hasn't touched her, she has no redress.

He's put her in the same social position she'd have been in if the encounter had taken place outside the dream, with none of the penalties he would have had to deal with in that case.

Paula *understands* that this is only a movie. If John and Larry had reacted to it as she did and had shared her outrage, she would have set it aside. But for both her husband and son not only to watch what happened and feel *no* outrage, but to remain baffled even after she explained? That *hurts*. The knowledge that their feelings are so alien to her is a shock, and incomprehensible. If she'd stayed in the room she'd have had to argue the issue through; she couldn't have just pretended everything was okay. She walked out not to demonstrate anger but to keep from spoiling the evening for Larry and John.

──────────────── ✦ ────────────────

Here we have a family, husband and wife and teenage son, who love each other and would like to get *along* together as a family. These are not people struggling with poverty and crime in an inner city, or hiding shameful secrets of domestic violence. The Gellises are an unremarkable American family living a basically uneventful life in a typical, pleasant suburb. They share the same values and goals, except for the normal differences arising from the gap between two generations.

Nevertheless, they have just gone through an experience in which they observed the same set of data, but the meaning the woman took from it is so different from what the men understood it to mean that they might as well have been watching two entirely different movies. Not only that, both men perceive Paula's leaving the room as a move to spoil the family evening, while she perceives it as a move to avoid that very thing.

The incident was provoked by fiction in this case, but it's not unique. When John tells his son it's impossible to understand women, it's because there have been many other similar experiences in his life based on data that weren't fictional. If Paula were asked, she would also report similar experiences. What we have here is unfortunately a *common* phenomenon: a cross-gender communication breakdown over meaning—over semantics.

The Trouble with Semantics

Reality Gaps and Reality Bridges

We are forever hearing in disagreements that the point of contention is "only semantics," as if semantics were a minor spelling difference or something equally trivial. That's very wrong. Differences in semantics can be as dangerous as missiles, and are often as well hidden. Much of the time the problem can be summed up like this: Two (or more) people are making the same verbal noises—saying "the same words" in the same language—but in their *minds* those words have different meanings. The greater that difference is, the greater the potential for communication breakdown and associated negative real-world consequences for everyone involved.

Nobody knows what "reality" is. Respected philosophical and scientific positions range from the idea that everything is really "out there"—and would still be out there even if there were no living creatures to perceive it—through less rigid positions, to the claim that nothing is "out there" at all and our entire universe is composed entirely of our perceptions. Still, we have to interact with reality, whatever it may be, and we have to do it in something approximating a consensus, in order to carry on our daily lives.

We know, intellectually, that the earth is round and is spinning in space at a rate of 66,700 miles an hour, but we have to *behave* as if it were flat and motionless. We know that most of what we call "solid matter" is really empty space with particles hurtling around in it, but we have to *behave* as if it were as solid as we perceive it to be. We have to agree, somehow, on what we will call real and how we will deal with it, so that we can survive in the world. People who are unable to go along with the rest of us to any substantial extent find themselves labeled "mentally ill" and are not allowed to live as others live. The reality consensus is as important to us as oxygen, and language is the only tool or mechanism we have for creating and maintaining it.

When we talk to other people who are speakers of our language, we rely on them to base what they say on consensus reality; we take it for granted that they will always have almost the same chunks of meaning attached to their words as we have. We know there might be small differences now and then due to dialects or registers or idiosyncratic experiences, but we don't expect them to interfere with communication, and we know how to fix things when they turn up. The idea that there might be *major* semantic differences, differences of meaning large enough to cause serious communication breakdowns within a family or other close group, seems improbable to us. We're much more likely to conclude that the breakdown is due to some flaw in another person's character or background or motivation, or to some outside circumstance beyond anyone's control.

I call such semantic differences—which can perk along undetected for years, creating chronic misunderstandings and presumed "personality conflicts"—*reality gaps*. There is only one way to get rid of them or repair them: You have to build reality *bridges*, using language.

The semantic difference responsible for the conflict and confusion described in Scenario Three is a common source of trouble in American Mainstream English, and will serve us well as an example of the power such differences have to affect our lives. It has to do with a gender-linked meaning difference for a set of words and statements, all related to the hurt one human being can cause another human being or living creature. As a cover term for discussing this reality gap, we can use one word from the set: the word *violence*. And we can use a *Gentle Art* version of semantic analysis to explore it and to make it more comprehensible and manageable.

Technique #2
Semantic Analysis
Using Semantic Features

One of the mechanisms linguists have used for analyzing the meaning of words is the *semantic feature*. Semantic features can be thought of as "particles" of meaning, in the old-fashioned sense of being chunks too small to break down into any smaller pieces. One way to define a word— and to compare your definition with someone else's—is to list the set of semantic features that would separate it from everything else in the world. For example, if you want to define the word "bird," you need only two semantic features, as shown in Figure 1.

It's true that birds are warm-blooded and that they have wings, and so on through a long list of other characteristics. But they share those characteristics with many other creatures. Bats are warm-blooded and have wings, but they're not birds. However, birds are the *only* living creatures that have feathers, and all you need to know to be able to classify

bird
|
[+LIVING]
[+FEATHERED]

Figure 1

a "thing" as a bird is that it is alive (or was alive in the past) and is feathered. This definition is part of the reality consensus that speakers of English agree on.

For some English words, a semantic feature list is just this simple; two or three features will do it. For others, it's enormously complicated. (Try, for example, to define the word "sneaker" in a way that will unambiguously separate it from all other kinds of shoes!) It's especially hard for things that are abstract concepts, expressed in words like "liberty" or "democracy" or "love" or "justice." And when people have definitions for a word that are *almost* identical, they can go along using the word in their interactions without ever suspecting that a difference exists. *Until something like the disagreement in Scenario Three happens and it all blows up in their faces.*

The word "violence" is a reality gap word for AME speakers, and the difference that causes the gap has been shown to be a *gender* difference. If AME has genderlects, this is one of the spots where the two varieties diverge. For both genders, the definition of human violence includes four semantic features that we can summarize as [+FORCE], [+INTENSE], [+DELIBERATE], [+NEGATIVE]. For most AME-speaking men, however—but not for most women—it also has to carry the feature [+AVOIDABLE]. And for most AME-speaking women, but not for most men, it has the feature [+HARMFUL]. The result is the reality gap shown in Figure 2.

This gender difference was discovered when researcher M.D. Blumenthal, investigating attitudes toward violence in American men, had a baffling experience. She'd asked a thousand men from varying backgrounds to classify certain things as violent or nonviolent, and to rank them on a scale for their *degree* of violence. To her bewilderment, most

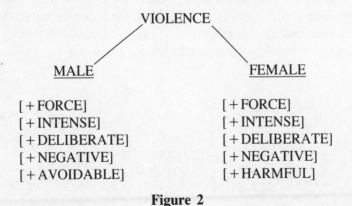

Figure 2

of the men in the study classified the burning of draft cards as violent, but they classified the shooting of looters by police as *non*violent. Her followup research eventually made their position clear.

To the men, burning a draft card is something illegal and significant and dramatic and so on, it's something much of society objects to strongly, and it is never something a person *must* do. It could always be avoided. Therefore, it is a violent act. Shooting looters, on the other hand, is perceived as an ugly job the police sometimes have to do in order to carry out their duties and fulfill their roles as law enforcers; it cannot be avoided. Therefore, it's not violence. (Blumenthal et al. 1972)

Whether harm is done to some other human being in the course of either act is important to men. Of course. But it is not *relevant* to them for the purpose of defining the word "violence."

For Paula Gellis the hero's sexual encounter with the woman in the science fiction movie was violence. It was force; it caused the woman pain; therefore, it was violence. For John and Larry Gellis, no violence was involved. The man wooed the woman in a dream; in the course of the wooing she gave in and yielded to him, and what happened next was natural and unavoidable. Furthermore, no "harm" was done; the man did not "hurt" the woman. Clearly, "harm" and "hurt," both words from this same semantic class, are also defined differently by the two genders.

When I discuss the fact that "violence" (and many words in the same semantic class) are defined differently by most men and most women in America, my audiences almost always express surprise. But the effects of the difference are easily observed all around us. When Mike Tyson, accused of raping Desiree Washington, insisted that he hadn't hurt her because no bones had been broken, it was that semantic difference in operation. The argument raging today over the definition of rape brings the difference clearly home to us. Much of the wrangling over what precisely constitutes "sexual harassment" is the result of this difference.

A More Subtle Reality Gap

Not all the reality gaps between the genders are so obvious. Take the word "game," for instance. On page 129 of *You Just Don't Understand*, Deborah Tannen makes this statement:

The game women play is "Do you like me?" whereas the men play "Do you respect me?"

I disagree with Tannen about this, but she is entitled to her opinion. For the present discussion, the important thing to notice about the sentence is that nowhere does it so much as hint that when men and women say the word "game" they usually *mean* different things.

I consider "game" one of the most significant reality gap words in American Mainstream English. It is responsible for massive amounts of failed communication. It leaks onto other words and phrases associated with game playing—important ones like "cheating" and "winning" and "being fair"—and guarantees semantic confusion for them also, especially when several items turn up in a single conversation.

For most women, the word "opponent" is essentially equivalent to the word "enemy," but not for most male AME speakers. For most women, the word "cooperation" usually refers to situations in which everyone involved pitches in and does *whatever needs doing* toward a shared goal. A familiar example is the process of preparing for and cleaning up after a big family meal such as a Thanksgiving dinner. For most men—accustomed to team sports in which you tend to your assigned role and expect everyone else to do the same—"cooperation" most often means doing *your* job and letting other people do theirs, a very different way of proceeding.

Few men today have much experience with situations where men cooperate in the women's sense of the word, as they once did for tasks like the old-fashioned barn raising or harvesting. The result is predictable. Mixed-gender attempts at "cooperation" all too often end in male irritation at the way women "butt in" and "get in the way," and female annoyance at the way men "refuse to do their fair share" and "only do the parts they like."

Most AME men treat many language interactions—especially public ones—as games; most women don't. There are of course exceptions, like Texas governor Ann Richards, but generally speaking, this is a male sport. Men want to be liked just as much as women do, but for them the need to be liked is for after the game. While it's going on, wanting or not wanting to be liked has nothing to *do* with anything. Playing the game, and playing it well, is what matters.

We see this demonstrated in meetings (often to the amazement of the women present) when groups of men who've just spent hours cutting one another to pieces verbally go off to lunch together, the very best of buddies, as the meeting ends. This behavior is learned by men in childhood, and it starts early. Nancy Arnott (in "Trouble Spots," *Executive Female*, 6 May 1988) writes of a woman who listened to her teenage son complaining bitterly about a boy on his basketball team who bullied and abused him. When the mother asked why on earth he went on playing with this person, "He looked at her in disbelief and said, 'Because he's *on my team*,' as though that were the most obvious reason in the world." Men functioning in the AME culture who for some reason do not fully absorb this male concept suffer consequences as grave as those suffered by women.

For most AME-speaking men, anything that involves negotiation, and that is not literally a matter of life and death, is a game. This includes many interactions that fall into the "romantic interlude" category. For women, whose childhood games were usually hopscotch and jacks and jump rope and dolls and the traditional playground games, the word "game" carries the semantic feature [+ TRIVIAL]. This is a major reason why women who hear their male colleagues discussing projects with sports metaphors and sports vocabulary often react by complaining that the men "aren't being serious" about the matters at hand.

When women decide to play a game and define it as men do, they are as intensely determined to be respected for their ability as players, both of that game and of games in general, as men are. (For a detailed discussion of an area of life in which women are deeply concerned about being respected rather than liked, see Chapter 13.) The semantic breakdown point is twofold; it includes:

- What each gender defines *as* a game.
- What each gender defines as "time out."

There are few couples for whom a careful exploration of their personal definitions for these two items would not be valuable.

Using Reality Statements

A second device that you can use for semantic analysis is the *reality statement*. Some reality statements—"A bird is a feathered, living creature"—are like traditional dictionary definitions. Facts about the items defined—"Almost all birds build nests"—are also reality statements. These statements are so much a part of our lives that we take them for granted. We shouldn't, because the collected *set* of such statements is a major component of our consensus model of reality. It is the need to include that set that makes programming computers for tasks such as registering students for college courses—tasks human beings find tedious, but easy to do—so difficult.

All the features that make up the definitions of words and phrases in your native language are stored in your brain; however, like so much other linguistic information, these features aren't stored and indexed in a way that lets you just go "look up" what you need. Let's consider a typical example. Suppose you suspect, after a series of communication breakdowns with your spouse, that the two of you have different definitions for the word "jealousy." Comparing the two definitions would tell you whether your suspicion is correct. How do you get at them so that you can do the comparison?

Begin by just asking yourself "What are the semantic features I use to define the word 'jealousy'?" and writing them down. That may be sufficient. But your brain can't always be counted on to provide an immediate tidy and complete list, especially when the item to be defined is an emotion or other abstract concept rather than something concrete like a bird or a desk or a restaurant. Often you have to "prime" the brain as you would prime a pump. Reality statements are one of the most efficient devices for that purpose. A simple and practical way to proceed is to write down a set of *partial* reality statements like those shown below and then try to complete them.

1. Jealousy is a(n) . . . .
2. People feel jealousy when . . . .
3. Jealousy is caused by . . . .
4. Jealousy causes . . . .

More statements will come to mind as you do this, providing you with additional data. It's important to remember that whether the statements you write down are *true* or not is irrelevant for this task. Language is not like math; there is rarely any single "right answer" for the definition of a word. Your goal is to get your own *personal* definition out into the open where you can examine it. Suppose your personal definition of "bird" included the feature [+ HORNED]. That would be a false definition, but the information would be no less valuable to you. When you compared it with others' definitions, you would suddenly understand why you and they so often disagreed about whether some creature was or was not a *bird*.

Once you have completed your own definition for "jealousy," your next step is to ask your partner to go through this same process. The two of you can then compare your definitions and discuss them, to find out whether they are a chronic source of conflict and confusion for you as a couple. You can carry out exactly the same process in the workplace, to investigate suspected cross-gender conflicts for definitions of key words in business situations. In any environment where arguments that are "only semantics" can arise, the procedure is the same.

At first you will have to do even minor semantic analysis step by step as described above, and you'll need to write down or tape every detail as you go along. But as you become skilled in the technique you'll find that—as long as all parties involved speak a single language—you can often achieve the same results just by a thorough discussion.

You may find that the analysis of one key word or phrase leads immediately to another. For most male AME speakers, combining the reality statements that define "violence" produces something like "Human violence is intense, deliberate, and *avoidable* force used wrongfully." For most American women, however, the result is, roughly, "Human violence is intense, deliberate, and *harmful* force used wrongfully." If you were trying to pin the meaning down tightly for each gender, you would next have to do semantic analysis for at least the meanings of "intense" and "deliberate" and "harm." What one man or woman considers intense (or fierce, or excessive) force may strike another as trivial or moderate; that's one of the reasons why people disagree about whether spanking is child abuse or good parenting. Does the blow of a boxer in the ring—or the blocking maneuver of one football player against another—*harm* his opponent, or is it just part of the game and all good fun? If a man's passions are fully aroused and he pressures a woman for sex, is that a deliberate act or is it unavoidable?

It is the way these words are defined by the two genders that causes men and women to disagree so strongly about the question of rape—especially marital rape and date rape. It is this group of words and definitions that lies beneath the extraordinary disagreement about what constitutes sexual harassment. We will be coming back to the topic of sexual harassment later; for now, let's just establish three summarizing points.

1. Semantics is not "only" semantics; it's critically important.
2. Just because people use "the same words" does not mean the same meanings are attached to those words.
3. Practical methods exist—semantic analysis, for example—for investigating meaning differences when they are large enough to cause communication breakdowns.

Just one question remains: How can you *tell* when a semantic conflict has occurred, so that you'll know an analysis would help? Certainly Paula and John and Larry Gellis, if asked, would have agreed on the following statements:

- Rape is wrong.
- Men should not force sex upon women.
- Men should not do women deliberate harm.
- Women have the right to refuse unwanted sexual partners.

That agreement would not have given them or anyone else a clue that although they were using the same words they were not saying the same thing at all.

Most of the time you won't be aware of reality gaps; that's the nature of human communication. You have to behave, most of the time, as if you can rely on the words you use having the same meanings when other people use them, just as you have to behave, most of the time, as if the earth stands still and matter is truly solid. You couldn't function in your daily life if you didn't. But there is one rule that you can apply, and that is particularly appropriate for communication between women and men:

✦ SUPPOSE THE OTHER PERSON IN AN INTERACTION WITH YOU IS SOMEONE WHOSE BEHAVIOR ORDINARILY MAKES SENSE TO YOU, SOMEONE YOU KNOW TO BE IN NORMAL HEALTH AND NOT UNDER THE INFLUENCE OF ANY DRUG. WHEN THAT PERSON SUDDENLY SEEMS TO YOU TO BE BEHAVING IN A WAY THAT MAKES NO SENSE, YOUR FIRST SUSPICION SHOULD BE A REALITY GAP.

That is: Suppose you've always respected someone—we'll call her Marian—and you believe her to be in a normal state of health and mind, and suddenly her behavior strikes you as absolutely incomprehensible. In that situation, suspect a reality gap. If possible, do a semantic analysis to find the gap and add the potential for repair to the interaction. Do this first. Do it *before* you decide that Marian is being deliberately uncooperative or hostile. Before you decide she's trying to spoil everybody's evening or sabotage somebody's project. Before you decide that she has a private agenda and is now an enemy. Before making any of those assumptions about someone and basing your behavior toward that person upon them,

LOOK FOR THE REALITY GAP. If you don't find one, the assumptions (with all their unpleasant consequences) are still available to you.

This is basic Miller's Law procedure. Assume that what Marian says, however unlikely or outrageous it seems to you, is true; then what would it be true of? It would be true of a world in which the word [X] is defined as Marian defines it. An investigation of that world may make it possible for you to discard your negative assumptions and proceed on a positive footing.

Semantic Features, Reality Statements, and Presuppositions

If we couldn't take for granted most of the information in semantic features and reality statements, talking to other people would be unbearably cumbersome. When I say the word "bird" to an English-speaking adult, I assume that I can take for granted "birds are living creatures" and "birds have two legs" and "birds have wings" and the feature [+FEATHERED], etc. Such information, which is part of the underlying meaning of a sequence of language and is understood by fluent speakers whether it is stated openly or not, is said to be *presupposed*.

If I tell you that your boss just slithered in, I don't have to tell you explicitly that I consider your boss a snake—you'll know that because "slither" presupposes it. If I tell you that "EVen TRACY could pass THAT class!", I don't have to say aloud that the class is absurdly easy or that I have little regard for Tracy's academic abilities; the sentence presupposes those things. People who are skillful with language and want to say negative things don't use obscenities and epithets—they use *presuppositions*. It's hard to deny that you've been verbally abusive if you call someone a bitch or a bastard, with body language to match; presupposed negative language is easier to get away with.

In Scenario Three, John Gellis uses presuppositions this way three times, by choosing sequences that I call "Trojan Horses"—because they look and sound okay, but in a context of conflict they conceal something unpleasant. Here are the lines.

> "Honey, come on," John scoffed. "Admit it—you're being ridiculous."

The word "admit" presupposes that what is admitted is something unsavory, illegal, immoral, embarrassing, etc.

"I don't understand how you manage to turn something so trivial into such a big deal."

The phrase "manage to [X]" presupposes that the person had a lot of trouble doing X, put a lot of effort into it, and was able to do it only after considerable hassle.

"Humoring her would only make it worse."

The word "humor" presupposes a feature we could summarize roughly as [+APPROPRIATE FOR CHILDREN].

In the context laid out in Scenario Three, John Gellis is too skilled in communication to say to Paula directly that she should be ashamed of her behavior, or that he feels she has deliberately *worked* at making a fuss that will spoil the evening. He is too skilled to say directly to his son that Paula is childish. He can be reasonably sure that his meaning will have been understood in all three of these examples, but he retains a certain amount of "deniability." For example: Suppose Larry, in a careless moment, tells Paula that John said "humoring her would only make it worse." Suppose Paula then challenges John about it and claims that he insulted her. He can claim in return that she's oversensitive, makes mountains out of molehills, reads meaning into words that aren't there, and so on. If he had just said "Larry, your mother isn't an adult—she's a child," and Larry had let *that* slip, John wouldn't have had a prayer of denying the insult.

It's easy to use Trojan Horse sequences without being fully aware of what they presuppose, in the same way that you're unlikely always to think of feathers when you talk about a bird. It's worth making an effort to avoid them unless you specifically *want* to convey their presupposed negative messages.

Another Look at Scenario Three

The communication breakdown point in Scenario Three wasn't in the initial argument over what happened in the science fiction movie. The breakdown came when Paula asked her husband and son, "Am I understanding this correctly? Do you two really agree on this—that 'nothing really happened' and he didn't do anything wrong?" The language she used made it clear that she was finding it very hard to understand the words they were saying to her. The two men couldn't have been unaware that something had gone seriously wrong in the interaction. But at that point, they both made an error. Here are the answers they gave to Paula's question.

John: "Absolutely. No harm done! Frankly, I don't know how you manage to make such a big deal out of something so trivial, Paula.'

Larry: "Yeah, Mom. What's the problem?''

These answers *insult* Paula. John's use of "managed" makes his sentence an accusation: that she has taken something trivial and, although it was difficult to do, has deliberately *worked* at blowing it up into a major issue for argument. And Larry has backed his father up in that accusation. Paula has been put in a position where any attempt to defend herself will require her either to insult the men back or to insist that they turn their attention to a serious discussion. She knows the plan for the evening was a casual, relaxed good time; neither of these alternatives will allow that. Unwilling to spoil things for her family and seeing no other choice available, Paula leaves the room, deeply hurt.

You may or may not agree with Paula's decision. You may feel that she should have stood her ground and insisted on settling the issue, regardless of whether it ruined the evening. That's what would happen in any soap opera, and it would make for heady drama. But let's set that question, which is a personal decision for anyone in a situation of this kind, aside. Let's instead focus on how easy it would have been to keep matters from reaching this sorry pass in the first place. For example:

Paula: "Am I understanding this correctly? Do you two really agree on this—that 'nothing really happened' and he didn't do anything wrong?''

John: "Yes—you're understanding us. But it's obvious to me that we're not understanding <u>you</u>. We're all too tired to start thrashing this out tonight, but I want you to know I don't think it's trivial. The first chance we get in the next few days, Paula, I'd like to sit down and talk this over.''

When this discussion actually came to pass, it might have been very heated indeed. It might have been lengthy and emotional. Using the technique of semantic analysis (either formally, as presented in this chapter, or in the informal way that such discussions are often carried on), Paula and John—and Larry, if he took part—could have discovered which of the key words in the argument they had differing definitions for. They could have explored those differences in detail. The resulting airing of the issues would have strengthened their understanding of one another and made them aware of areas they needed to be sensitive to in the future.

The response I've suggested here for John would have made it possible for Paula either to stay in the room or leave, whichever she preferred, without all the resentment and misunderstanding and bad feeling described in Scenario Three.

Alternatively, Paula could have responded to the men's lines like this: "I'm glad to know I'm understanding you; it's clear that you're not understanding me. I know this isn't an appropriate time to start thrashing things out. However, my feelings on this matter are important to me, and I want a chance to clear the air. Just let me know when you're ready for that discussion."

Dialogues for Analysis

DIALOGUE ONE

M: "Look, there's no <u>way</u> we can afford to get a new printer right now. I know we need it, but we'll just have to manage with the one we've got."

F: "I don't understand. . . . We could probably double our business if we bought one. It would pay for itself the first year."

M: "I know that; I agree with you. But when you can't afford something, you have to do without. That's just the facts of <u>life</u>."

F: "But I <u>still</u> don't understand! <u>Why</u> can't we afford it? We're making very good money, we're excellent credit risks, we—"

M: "Come on—we're in debt up to our <u>ears</u>!"

F: "We are <u>not</u>!"

M: "We <u>are</u>! I keep the books—I know what I'm talking about!"

F: "Listen, you may keep the books, but I'm part of this business, too, and I keep <u>track</u> of things! We have <u>never</u> been behind on a payment, not once!"

M: "What the heck has <u>that</u> got to do with it???"

The problem here is in the way these two people define the phrase "in debt." For him, you're in debt if you owe people money; the more you owe, the more deeply in debt you are. For her, you're not "in debt" as long as all the payments you owe on borrowed funds are paid right on time and you're earning enough money to keep them that way.

The clue that should alert this couple to their difference in definitions is the "Katydid!/Katydidn't!" exchange. When two adults go through a sequence like this one—

X: "We're in debt!"

Y: "No, we're not!"

X: "Yes, we are!"

Y: "No, we're not!"

—only two possibilities exist:

- They're basing their judgments on different facts, and one set of facts is incorrect. In this case, and if the issue is important to them, they can check to find out where the error is.
- They're basing their judgments on identical facts, but they define being "in debt" differently.

Any exchange of this kind between adults, no matter what its subject, indicates a probable reality gap. If the two people in the dialogue above agree on the total sum of money they've borrowed, then the first step toward bridging the gap is for one of them to say, "Hey, wait a minute! Before we go on with this, tell me what the words 'in debt' mean to you." They have all the language resources necessary to investigate this semantic difference and find a way to deal with it.

DIALOGUE TWO

M: "You look like the cat that ate the canary, honey—what's going on?"

F: "I won!"

M: "You won?"

F: "Right, I <u>won</u>! You know the award they give for bringing in the most new accounts? I <u>got</u> it this quarter!"

M: "How did you manage <u>that</u>?"

F: [Long pause] "I should have known you'd act this way."

M: "Hey, I think it's terrific! Congratulations!"

F: "Thanks for nothing."

M: "Oh, come on—I said it was terrific, didn't I?"

This man could of course make it worse. He could finish with "Oh, come on—I said it was terrific, didn't I? What do you want me to do, give you a <u>medal</u>?" But it's bad enough as it is. The source of the problem is the Trojan Horse "manage" in "How did you manage <u>that</u>?", which lets him take away his compliments with one hand as he gives them to her with the other.

Suggestion for Her: It's conceivable that this man is innocent. Maybe he really does have a definition for "manage to X" in his idiolect that makes "How did you manage <u>that</u>?" only an indication of his interest in your sales strategy. It's extremely unlikely, but it's conceivable. Instead of reacting with anger, you can use Miller's Law to give him the benefit of the doubt, answering his "How did you manage <u>that</u>?" with "I'm not sure I understand your question. Can you make it a little more clear, please?" Then pay very close attention to his body language as he responds.

If it's clear to you that he's sincere in his compliments and honestly bewildered by your reaction, explain to him what most people mean when they say "manage to X," so that he'll be aware of the potential for trouble in similar situations in the future.

DIALOGUE THREE

M: "Okay, let's get started! Who's got the ball?"

F: "Sorry?"

M: "Who's going to carry the ball on the first play?"

F: "You know, there's a lot of money involved in this project—this is very serious business. I'd appreciate it if you'd make an effort to keep that in mind."

She knows enough about sports to recognize what he says as coming from the sports vocabulary. But she doesn't understand that to most AME-speaking men sports *are* "very serious business." As a result, she behaves as if he'd worn Mickey Mouse ears to a formal dinner. At the end of the dialogue she considers him a lightweight and a clod, while he considers her a typical example of the female executive: If you forget yourself and stop tiptoeing around on eggshells, she turns into your mother.

Suggestion for Him: Add a line to the dialogue. Say to her, "Women sometimes think that men who use sports language aren't taking things seriously. I assure you, that's false. In this country, football players make millions of dollars a year. You can't get much more serious than that." This should get at least an "I see" from her, and perhaps "I should have sense enough to know that without you pointing it out to me; I apologize." Note that "Women often think that men who . . ." is in Computer Mode. This is a wise move. It eliminates the possible confrontational aspects of "You probably think that because I'm using sports language I'm not taking things seriously."

DIALOGUE FOUR

M: "Did you enjoy making a fool of me in there?"

F: "I don't know what you're talking about."

M: "When I said you have a degree in physics and you jumped right in like Little Miss Muffet with [falsetto] 'It's only a B.A.!' "

F: "But honey—it is only a B.A.! The way you were talking, they would have thought I had a Ph.D."

M: "Exactly! That's exactly the point!"

F: "But I don't have a Ph.D. Are you saying I should have lied?"

M: "I'm not talking about anybody lying! Did I say 'she has a Ph.D.'? Did I ask you to say that?"

F: "No . . . But I don't understand. If you weren't interested in lying to them, why was I out of line when I said I had a B.A.? That doesn't make any sense."

If a child of three asked them whether Santa Claus really exists, both of these people would say yes. If an elderly female acquaintance wearing a dress they thought was ugly asked "How do you like my new dress?" neither one would answer with "I think it's ugly." But this doesn't mean that they agree on the definition of words like "lying" and "honesty."

For him, it's okay to deliberately set up a false impression—to *mislead* someone—as long as you don't actually say any words that bring that false impression out into the open. He makes this pretty clear; he points out to her with considerable annoyance that he made no false statements whatsoever and he didn't ask *her* to. He just expected her to follow his lead and do nothing to *interfere* with his communication strategy. Such language behavior is not confined to men, and is the core of much business practice, as well as of politics and diplomacy. However, men tend to draw the line more loosely than women do, and the couple in the dialogue need to find out where their limits are.

In addition, for most AME-speaking men (but not women) neither false nor misleading statements are lies unless they can also be described as [+HARMFUL]. Both men and women agree that lies are wrong; their disagreement is over what *constitutes* a lie. As a department chairman once said to me after a meeting, "I know what I said wasn't true, Suzette, but it wasn't a lie. Not in that situation."

DIALOGUE FIVE

M1: "You're out of touch, buddy—you don't have a clue about where the sales figures are headed!"

M2: "Oh yeah? At least I know where they've been, which is more than anybody can say for you! You haven't looked at the database—really looked at it—for six months. And you know why? Because you're scared to, that's why! You don't have the guts to—"

M1: "Well, listen to the instant expert, will you? I happen to know that if you hadn't come in last weekend and spent four hours going over the data, you—"

M2: "Hey, you're way out of line! You don't have any way of knowing what I—"

M1: "Wait a minute!"

M2: "No, you wait a minute!"

F: "BOTH of you wait a minute! I'm calling time out here!"

You didn't know she was there until she spoke up? Neither did the two men.

She hasn't been part of the interaction up to now except in the role of spectator for the men. She's been listening to their tone of voice and watching their body language, and she's well aware that they're playing games. When it becomes clear to her that they've forgotten she's even on the field, she puts her foot down and calls for a time out. This is her proper move, and it should give her an opportunity to explain to them that she intends to take part in the discussion and she expects them to cooperate with her to make that possible.

On page 91 of *Talking Power*, Lakoff says that "The best protection against the abusive potential of a discourse genre are the rules of the genre themselves." That is: The best way for a woman to avoid being run over and trampled by men deeply involved in conversation-as-sport (or any other activity-as-sport) is by stepping into the reality of the game and using its rules on her own behalf. If the woman in Dialogue Five says, "Would you please let me talk once in a while?" or "I can't get a word in edgewise here!" the men probably still won't see or hear her. Making a formal demand for *time out* puts her inside the game they're playing, where the rules *they're* following require them to pay attention to her. This is more efficient, and much safer, than trying to out-bellow the men or trigger their chivalrous impulses.

◆

CHAPTER 4

The Role of
Body Language
in Communication

———— Scenario Four ————

"She's really ticked off at you guys about it," Louis said, chuckling. "Believe me when I tell you. . . ."—he paused, took a long drag on his cigarette, and exhaled, blowing smoke from his nostrils, before he continued—". . . this is no small thing with this woman! You know what I mean?"

John had sat quietly, listening without comment, while Louis Marin told him how much Mary Clayton had resented his remark at the meeting about her pretty face, and how Bill had upset her even more with a similar comment afterward.

"You through, Louis?" he asked, when the other man fell silent at last.

"Yeah, I'm through. I just thought you oughta know, buddy."

"Well, I appreciate your concern," John said, thinking to himself, *If you had a brain, Louis, you could play with it.* "And I want to tell you, right up front, that I'm astonished. Mary worked long and hard on that presentation, she let me know she wanted some positive and public support from me, and I gave her exactly what she asked for. She deserved it—she did good work. I find it very hard to believe that she doesn't have the grace to appreciate it, Lou."

"Believe it! She's—"

"In fact," John went on, right over whatever Marin had intended to add, "I'm insulted. Genuinely insulted. Offended."

"Well. . . ." Louis ground his cigarette into the ashtray on the desk, shaking his head. "You should've had better sense,

buddy. You should've had brains enough to keep your mouth
shut, you know what I mean?''

"No. I don't know what you mean.''

"I mean, any time—any time—you try to go along with some
female's request for public support, that's gonna backfire. It's
going to come right back around and zap you one, John! You're
old enough to know that.''

John gave him a long level look, and it got his attention.

"What?'' Louis said. "What are you looking at me like that
for?''

John spoke to him gravely, leaning back in his chair, his arms
folded over his chest. "I don't like to hear that kind of sexist talk
in my office, Louis. Not even from an old friend.''

"What?'' Louis spread his hands wide and turned to John's
secretary, who had said not one word throughout this exchange.
"Hey, Ann—did you hear me say anything sexist?''

John didn't allow people to abuse his staff. He cut this gambit
off abruptly, satisfied to see the look of panic fade from Ann's
face. She was a good secretary; he valued her highly.

"Cut it out, Marin,'' he said disgustedly. "I don't need a
ruling from my secretary on the matter. Now—if you're through
polluting the air in my office, how about getting down to
business? We've got a contract to work out, and I don't have all
day to play stupid games with you.''

"Hmph,'' said Marin, grinning at him. "That's the thanks I
get for trying to help you with . . . what do they call it? . . . Oh
yeah, with your Interpersonal Relations in the Workplace.
Right?''

"That's it,'' John said. "That's all you get. Now—Clause
One of this contract. I don't like it. Explain it to me.''

◆

What's Going On Here?

John's Point of View

As John perceives it, Louis is the one who ought to have brains enough
to keep quiet. For Louis to bring up this business about Mary Clayton in
front of anybody, let alone a member of his staff, is a rotten move. Ann
is sure to gossip about it and spread it all over the office, and it's the kind

of dumb story that gets distorted and blown all out of proportion. At the first opportunity, he intends to tell Louis exactly how he feels about it. For the moment, however, his concern is to be sure that when Ann starts the story down the office grapevine she has no justification for calling *him* sexist.

He's not at all surprised, of course, to hear about Mary's distress; it was the result he had in mind, and he's delighted to know that Bill accidentally gave him a helping hand. He *is* surprised to learn that Louis Marin has heard about it.

Louis's Point of View

As Louis perceives it, John worries far too much about his image. Louis runs his business, and his household, with an iron hand. He doesn't like women who aren't subordinate to men, he is scrupulously careful to hire only "old-fashioned" women, and he has no inhibitions about saying so. As for being careful what he says in front of the secretary, he *was* careful. He said just enough to get John's goat—deliberately—and chalked up the winning point for himself. Sometimes he wins these things; sometimes John does; this one was his. He wouldn't have talked about the incident in front of Ann if he'd had anything to say that could do John real harm, but this was just sport. Like John, he takes it for granted that the minute Ann is out of the room she'll be spreading the story all over the office. And he gets a kick out of what he thinks of as his friend's "liberal act."

Ann's Point of View

For her part, Ann is wary. She knows where she is with Louis, who is frequently in John's office. He's a hidebound traditionalist male who treasures and indulges his wife and his daughters, feels sorry for women who don't have a male to treasure and indulge them, and despises feminists. Ann's father was just like Louis Marin, and she knows exactly how to deal with him: by always playing the role of The Good Little Girl when she can't avoid interacting with him. But with John she has serious communication problems. She hears what he says, and he talks a good line about women being equal to men in every way . . . he says all the politically correct things. But there's something about the way he says them, and the way he keeps "accidentally" offending Mary Clayton, that doesn't ring true for her. She has a strong suspicion that John is putting them all on. Ann guards her back.

And she will not be discussing the exchange between Louis and her boss with anyone except a close woman friend she sees on weekends, who has no contact with anyone in the company. Contrary to the stereotype that both John and Louis subscribe to—in which she is sure to spread stories all over the office—she feels the same contempt for office gossip they do.

———————————————— ◆ ————————————————

What we have here is one of the standard patterns of male/female communication in the workplace. Two classic elements of the pattern are shown in the scenario.

First: The communication between the two men is essentially a *performance*. They're both playing roles, and they both know it. This is a common male sport, usually carried on for the benefit of others present, sometimes done just for the fun of it even without an audience. Male AME speakers ordinarily learn this game in childhood; women rarely do. John and Louis trust one another not to go too far and not to do anything with really serious consequences, such as causing the other man to lose an important account. Neither one would engage in this sport if it meant public loss of face for the other; that's one of the rules of the game.

Second: Ann, who has the spectator role in this scenario, does not trust either one of the men. She's not sure what they're up to, but she understands very well that something phony is going on, and she pays careful attention so that she won't accidentally get sucked into the action. She considers this to be part of her job, just like typing. She would never lower her guard and talk freely to either of these men except in the direst of emergencies, when she would know she could be sure they'd stop the game and respect the need for a "time out."

This is male-bonded rapport, and a near-total absence of rapport between the men and the women. It goes on in tens of thousands of workplaces in this country, day in and day out, and it does nothing to improve the male/female communication situation.

Mistrust, Misunderstanding, and Mistakes: The Need for Rapport between Men and Women

The word "rapport" is tossed around pretty casually, and has a number of different—and often vague—definitions. A person who says "I really didn't feel that I had any rapport with Paul'' may mean that she didn't like Paul much, or didn't find Paul fun to be around. Another person may say the same thing to mean that he didn't think he had anything in common with Paul, or that Paul didn't seem to understand *him* very well. All these reactions may be accurate, but they fail to make the crucial point clear. The *important* thing about rapport is that it refers to trust and understanding and good feelings that are *mutual*. You can't "achieve" or "establish" rapport by yourself.

If I understand you but you don't understand me . . . if you trust me but I don't trust you, that's not rapport. If I trust you . . . but I do so blindly, on the basis of faith alone . . . that's not rapport. Rapport is trust and understanding that go both ways, and that reinforce one another in feedback loops; few things are less *linear* than rapport. Suppose you and I succeed in building rapport—the process is easier to describe than it is to carry out.

✦ Because I trust you a little, I am open enough with you to make it possible for you to understand me a little. Which makes you willing to trust me a little, as a result of which you feel free to be open with me. Which helps me understand you more, so that I trust you more. And so on, around and around the loops.

Unfortunately, rapport is missing a great deal of the time in relationships between men and women, even in relationships that have gone on for years. The *initial* trust, the trust that goes only one way, isn't there. Without it, neither the man nor the woman feels safe. Both feel obliged to be wary and self-censoring; both guard their backs. As a result, neither one is ever granted access to the data needed for understanding the other. In that setting, rapport—which is essential to building any strong relationship—is simply impossible.

Where to Begin: With Body Language

Effective communication between men and women has to start with the establishment—perhaps the re-establishment—of mutual trust. And that task must itself begin not with words alone, but with nonverbal communication (usually called *body language*). People often assume that the distance between two human beings is established and maintained by the words they say, and that if they could just find the "right" words, the magic words, all would be well. Appealing as that idea is, convenient as it would be if it were true, it's false. It's body language that tells us what people *mean* by the words they say. It's body language that makes Ann, in Scenario Three, suspicious of John Gellis's carefully nonsexist language. She hears him saying all the right words, but the nonverbal channel tips her off that he doesn't believe what he's saying.

For English, at least 90 percent of all emotional information, and at least 65 percent of all information whatsoever, is carried not by the words but by the body language that *accompanies* the words. Body language includes facial expressions, gestures, body positions, and such things as clothes and hairstyles, just as the popular materials on the subject will tell you. However, those materials tend to leave out completely the most important and most powerful part of the system: *the tone and intonation of the voice*. This is a serious omission. No matter how well dressed you are, no matter how elegantly you sit and stand and move, if your voice is unpleasant your communication is not going to be as effective and satisfactory as it ought to be. And unless you can control your voice quality, you risk losing control of the messages you're transmitting to others.

The most important fact to remember is this one: Any words at all can have their meaning canceled by body language—but not vice versa. Unless you are an actor of the caliber of Laurence Olivier or Meryl Streep, it's almost impossible for you to cancel or conceal the meaning of your body language with your words. You can take a single word or brief phrase—"Darling . . ." "You monster . . ." "How nice . . ."—and use it to express affection or hatred or lust or any of a long list of emotions. Only your body language tells your listener which one you mean. Your ability to do this on the *telephone* clearly demonstrates the power of the voice alone to carry the message.

The Gender Difference

Body language problems between men and women who are speakers of American Mainstream English today begin at the most basic of nonverbal levels: with the *pitch* of the voice. The admired voice for the AME culture is the adult male voice; the deeper and richer it is, and the less nasal it is, the more it is admired. Women tend to pitch their voices higher than men do, and this is a strike against them in almost every language interaction. Not because there is anything inherently wrong with high-pitched voices, but because AME speakers associate them with children. A high-pitched voice that's also nasal is heard as the voice of a *whiny* child. People know, of course, that they're hearing an adult woman (or, for the occasional man with a high-pitched voice, an adult male). But at a level below conscious awareness they tend to perceive the voice as the voice of a child. This perception, however much it is in conflict with reality, affects their response to and their behavior toward the speaker.

The contrast in voice pitch isn't really a *physiological* matter; the difference between adult male and female vocal tracts is too minor to account for it in the majority of people. In many other cultures, male voices are higher than those of AME-speaking men, although the physical characteristics of the males are the same. When American adults speak to infants, they pitch their voices lower as they talk to boys, and the infants respond in the same way. Females learn, literally in the bassinet and playpen, that they are expected to make higher-pitched sounds than males are.

In addition to the difference in baseline pitch, AME-speaking women's voices have more of the quality called *dynamism*: They use more varied pitch levels, they move from one pitch to another more frequently, and they are more likely than men's voices are to move from one pitch to another that's quite a bit higher or lower. In other situations the term "dynamic" is a compliment, while "monotonous," its opposite, is a negative label. But not in language; not in the AME culture. The less monotonous a woman's voice is, the more likely it is that her speech will be described by others as "emotional" or "melodramatic." Monotony in the male voice, however, is ordinarily perceived as evidence of strength and stability. (For a detailed discussion of these differences, see McConnell-Ginet 1983.)

Certainly male/female body language differences go beyond the voice. There are positions and gestures and facial expressions that are more typical of one gender than of the other. But the effect one gender achieves by learning to use such items of body language from the other gender is rarely positive. A woman who hooks her thumbs into her belt, spreads her feet wide, and juts out her chin usually looks foolish, as does a man who carefully crosses his legs at the ankles. There are a few stereotypically feminine items that reinforce the "childish" perception which a woman can be careful *not* to use, such as giggling behind her hand or batting her eyelashes. But the most useful thing any woman—*or* man—can do to get rid of the perceptually filtered "I'm listening to a child" effect is to make the voice lower, and less nasal, and more resonant, so that it will be perceived as an *adult* voice.

This is something that anyone not handicapped by a physical disability that interferes with voice quality can do. One way to do it is to put yourself in the hands of a competent voice *coach*. If you have the time and money to do that, and you live where such experts are available, that's an excellent idea. On the other hand, it's also something you can do by yourself, using an ancient technique that in the *Gentle Art* system is called *simultaneous modeling.* You'll find simultaneous modeling described in detail on pp. 68–71 of this chapter.

Let me make one thing clear, however, before we go on. I'm not suggesting that anyone, of either gender, "should" try to change the quality of their voice. As is true for many linguistic questions, this is not a moral issue but an issue of cultural fashion. Low voices are not "better" than high voices. In the same way that some people insist on their right to wear jeans in an office where everyone else dresses more formally, people have every right to take the position that the voice they have is the voice they prefer to have. I approve of that, one hundred percent. However, because that decision can have grave consequences, people need to be aware that the consequences exist and that the choice is theirs to make.

It's unacceptable for someone to be unaware that the primary reason for his or her communication problems is a high-pitched voice, and to assume that the problems are caused by the lack of a "powerful vocabulary," or a thin enough body, or a sufficiently expensive blazer, or some such thing. It's also unacceptable for those who do realize what the problem is to believe they're helpless to do anything about it. Except in cases requiring medical attention, *anyone*, working alone, can change his or her voice to make it closer to what our culture perceives as the ideal and adult voice. When a medical condition complicates the issue, the potential for improvement may be less, but even limited change toward the ideal can bring about significant positive effects.

The facts about body language and its critical importance to communication can be frightening. We don't study body language in school, and few of us are given formal training in the subject. We read everywhere that "a more powerful vocabulary" is our ticket to communication success, and that seems easy—just buy a book or a software program and learn some new words. Improving our body language skills seems mysterious and difficult by contrast. But there's no need to be intimidated; it's simpler than you think.

Your internal grammar, the same one that you use to put the right endings on your words and arrange your words in the proper order in your sentences, contains all the rules for body language in your culture. You just haven't had convenient *access* to that information that would let you use it consciously and strategically. The sections that follow will help you establish that access.

Improving Your Body Language Skills

Developing Your Observational Skills

The first step in developing observational skills for nonverbal communication is simply learning to PAY ATTENTION to the speaker's body and voice. Men in the AME culture tend not to do this, and to be unaware that it matters; when they do pay attention they usually follow a rule that tells them to pay attention only to the speaker's face. Women do somewhat better, not because they have any built-in biological advantage, but because it is universally true that those having less power pay more attention to the body language of those having more power. (In the most primitive situations, this means being alert to the movements of the powerful person so that you will be able to get out of the way before the powerful person grabs or hits you.)

This gender difference is well known. In 1975 a footnote in the *Virginia Law Review* suggested that perhaps women should be excluded from jury duty, because their skill at observing and interpreting nonverbal communication might make them excessively vulnerable to body language effects, interfering with the defendant's right to an independent and unbiased jury. ("Notes: Judges' Nonverbal Behavior in Jury Trials: A Threat to Judicial Impartiality," *Virginia Law Review*, 1975, 61:1266–1298. For a review of research and an account of experiments proving that the body language of trial judges has a significant impact on jury decisions, see Blanck et al. 1985.)

Sometimes this language skill is an advantage for women; sometimes it's not. Like any other skill, it depends on how it is used. Nobody likes the idea that another person is able to read his or her mind. The woman who expresses in words what a man's body language tells her—with claims such as "I can tell by the look on your face that you don't want to go to St. Louis" or "Don't try to tell me you want to go to St. Louis; the way you keep wiggling your index fingers gives you away every time"—is almost sure to provoke hostility. Such remarks are equally counterproductive coming from men who have well-developed body language reading skills.

The only way to learn to pay attention to body language is to *practice*. You have to work at it consciously until you become so skilled that you do it automatically, just as you would work at your tennis or your golf or a favorite handicraft. If you're not accustomed to body language observation, you'll find it extremely difficult at first. You'll keep *forgetting* to do it.

You've probably had the experience of "coming to" as you take the last highway exit on your drive home and realizing that you have no memory of your previous ten minutes on the road. In the same way, you'll start out carefully observing someone's body language and then suddenly realize that it's been five minutes since you were consciously aware of anything but the words, and perhaps the facial expression, of the speaker. If you continue to work at it, however, you'll get past this stage. As a first practice partner, I strongly recommend your television set. Unlike living persons, the tv set doesn't get tired, doesn't wonder why you're staring at it, is always available at your convenience, and—best of all—never gets its feelings hurt.

Establishing Baseline Values—and Spotting Deviations from Them—in Body Language

Body language baselines are profiles of people's speech when they're relaxed, as in casual conversations with close friends. Baselines include such information as the typical pitch of the voice, rate of speed for speech, frequency of eyeblink, body posture, number of hand gestures, etc., for the individual you're interacting with, during *relaxed communication*. This information is important because a *deviation* from the baseline—a move away from these typical values—is a signal to be alert. It indicates some sort of emotional involvement, positive or negative; it indicates that something is happening; sometimes it indicates an attempt to deceive or mislead you.

You will have read books or listened to tapes telling you that when you see a person cross his arms or scratch her nose it *means* a particular thing. You'll read that crossed arms signal defensiveness and disagreement with what you're saying; you'll hear that scratching the nose signals anxiety. Sometimes that's true, of course; but much of the time it means the person you're observing is cold or has a nose that itches. When such items *are* reliable, they hold for a restricted population in specific circumstances—usually for the middle class or upper class dominant white male in a business situation. Learning to establish baseline values for the other person and spotting deviations from that baseline is a great deal more reliable, and will be useful to you in every communication situation, including interactions with people from outside your own culture.

For example, one of the most reliable clues to anxiety, a lack of sincere commitment to what's being said, and a possible intention to deceive is a change to a higher voice pitch. But you won't know there's been a change unless you have first learned what pitch the speaker uses in normal everyday conversation. The same thing is true for other deviations from baseline values. Here are two simple and practical ways to get the necessary information:

- Make a phone call to the individual in advance of your meeting and discuss something entirely neutral, like how to get to the meeting site.
- When you're with the other person, don't begin by talking about anything important. Instead, spend five minutes—or as long as it takes—making small talk on neutral subjects.

Now we can move on to improving your body language *performance* skills, as opposed to observation alone.

Technique #3
Simultaneous Modeling

When students learn t'ai chi, they learn not by watching the teacher and then trying out the posture or movement by themselves but by watching and then moving *with* the teacher. This technique has been successful for thousands of years. If you've studied a foreign language, you're familiar with the traditional procedure: Listen to a sequence of the foreign language, and then, during the pause provided, repeat what you've just heard. At the University of California San Diego, instead of repeating the foreign language sequence *after* the recorded model, students listen to it several times to become familiar with the content and then speak simultaneously *with* the model. This technique (developed at UCSD by linguist Leonard Newmark) consistently produces results far superior to the traditional method. And there are many cultures in which people learn to do things (weaving, for example) by first watching someone who already knows how and then sitting down beside that person and working along with her or him.

These are all examples of *simultaneous modeling*. They take *advantage* of the way human brains work instead of fighting against it. When you change your behavior to make it like someone else's you have to make many small adjustments all over your body, all at once. You can't do that very well *consciously*. But your brain can do it competently and successfully, if you just stay out of its way. You can use this information and your brain's built-in skills to improve the quality of your voice, by adapting Newmark's foreign language teaching method.

Changing voice quality requires an array of small but crucial adjustments. You have to change the tension of the muscles of your tongue and throat and chest, you have to move the parts of your vocal tract in ways that you're not used to, and so on. When you listen to a foreign language sequence and try to repeat it afterward, you not only have to make all those adjustments but you have to *remember* the sequence. The final result is that you change your speech to match the sequence you *remember* instead of the one you actually heard. When you speak *with* the model voice instead of repeating on your own, this doesn't happen. Your brain takes over and does all the adjustments, matching your voice to the model.

Working with the Tape Recorder

You need a tape recorder (an inexpensive one will do), a few blank tapes, and a tape about thirty minutes long by someone of your own gender whose voice sounds the way you'd like to sound. For men, I recommend television anchorman Peter Jennings, or one of the male announcers on National Public Radio's regular news programs ("Morning Edition" or "All Things Considered," for example). For women I recommend a tape of Diane Sawyer or one of the female NPR newscasters. If you prefer someone else, either a public figure or someone in your own circle, that's fine. Just be sure the voice you choose as your model is one that you and others perceive as strong, resonant, pleasant, compelling, and—above all—the voice of a *mature adult*. Then follow the steps below, at your own convenience, at your own speed, and in privacy.

1. Make a twenty- to thirty-minute *baseline* tape of your own speech, write down the date on which it was made, and keep it for comparison with tapes you make later on. Don't read aloud, and don't say something memorized—just *talk*. Talk about your childhood, or why you have trouble communicating with people of the opposite sex, or anything else you can talk about easily and naturally.

2. Listen to the tape you've chosen as a model, all the way through, to get a general idea of its content. Don't write it down, and don't try to memorize it—doing either of those things just gets in the way and keeps you from succeeding.

3. Choose a sentence of average length to work with, from any point on the tape. Listen to it a couple of times, to become familiar with it. Then repeat it, SPEAKING ALONG WITH THE TAPE, SIMULTANE-OUSLY. Rewind the tape and do it again, as many times as you feel are necessary—ten times is not in any way unusual. Your goal is to be able to speak smoothly and easily with the model. Don't *struggle*. Trust your brain and let it carry out its functions without interference.

4. When you're bored with the sentence you chose, pick another sentence and repeat Step #3. You should also move on whenever you realize that you know a sentence so well that you've stopped needing the model voice; you aren't interested in learning to *recite* the tape. Continue in this way until you've finished the tape or achieved your goal, whichever happens first. (And go on to another model tape if you find that you need one.)

5. After about ten hours of practice (and after every additional five or six hours), make a new baseline tape of your own speech. Listen to it, and compare it with the earlier ones. When you're satisfied with the change you hear, STOP. The point of this technique is to improve your *own* voice. You don't want people to think you're doing Peter Jennings or Diane Sawyer imitations when you talk; if you go on too long, that's exactly what will happen.

How long this will take will depend on the amount of time you have for practice, how tired you are, whether you are a person who learns well by listening, and other individual factors. Try to make each practice session at least fifteen minutes long; thirty minutes is even better. Try to practice every other day, roughly. If all you can manage is ten minutes once a week, put in those ten minutes—just be prepared for it to take you much longer to achieve results on that basis. Remember: It doesn't make any *difference* how long it takes. You're not paying by the hour when you use this technique, and there won't be a final exam. Relax and let it take as long as it takes. Some of my clients have noticed substantial improvement in six weeks; others have needed six months or more for the same results.

The fact that you can't just take a Voice Quality Pill and change instantly is actually a good thing. The people you interact with regularly (and especially the person or persons you live with) need to be able to get used to the change in your voice gradually. You don't want your partner to leave in the morning, accustomed to the voice you've always had, and come home that night to someone who sounds like an entirely different person. A pleasant adult voice is a powerful tool for improving your relationships, but it shouldn't come as a *shock* to those around you.

Note: You can also use this procedure to learn to speak other varieties of English—other dialects or other registers—at will. If you feel that your native accent sometimes holds you back in the American Mainstream English environment, simultaneous modeling is a good way to learn a variety of English that's more helpful. Moving back and forth among varieties—called *codeswitching*—is a valuable skill.

Working with the Television Set

A voice coach (or an ''image'' coach) may be beyond the financial limits for many of us. It's fortunate that we have our television sets available to use as free coaches. In exactly the same way that you can improve your voice quality by speaking along with a tape recorded model, you can improve the rest of your body language by *moving* simultaneously with a model on videotape. Ideally, you will also have a VCR, so that you can work with a single tape over a period of time. If you have a video camera (or can rent one), to let you make a baseline video of your body language, that's also a plus. But if those items aren't available to you, choose as a model someone of your own gender that you can see on television several times a week, and practice moving simultaneously with that person at those times. As with voice quality, stop *before* you find yourself doing impersonations of your model.

I don't recommend that women try to learn ''male body language'' by working with a videotape of a male speaker, or that men work with a videotape of a woman to learn ''female body language.'' (The fact that the latter alternative is wildly unlikely outside the entertainment field is consistent with the power relationships in our society.) Cross-gender modeling is a bad idea, full of hidden hazards and boobytraps, and it almost always backfires. If you're gifted with the sort of superb acting ability that would let you do this *well*, like Dustin Hoffman playing the heroine in the movie *Tootsie*, you're not someone who needs improved body language anyway. You will be far more successful with the body language of a strong and competent adult of your own gender.

If you believe you have a long way to go in acquiring satisfactory body language skills, if you feel self-conscious trying to acquire them, if your opportunities to practice them are few and far between, by all means rely on the tv set. You can move on to practice with live partners when you feel more at ease.

Another Look at Scenario Four

There's a good reason why Ann is confident about her personal assessment of Louis but uneasy about what John Gellis may be up to. Louis openly talks of women in sexist terms, and his body language carries the same message. With John, on the other hand, there is a conflict between what his body language is saying and what his words are saying. Such conflict should always make the listener/observer alert, and—until it can be clarified—wary, as it does Ann. One of the most basic principles of communication is:

✦   WHEN THE WORDS BEING SAID AND THE BODY LAN-
    GUAGE ACCOMPANYING THEM DON'T MATCH, BELIEVE
    THE BODY.

Whether Ann is consciously aware of that rule or not, she is following it. She hears John say, "I don't like to hear that kind of sexist talk in my office, Louis. Not even from an old friend." But she's not convinced that the words are true, and it's not because John hasn't chosen the best or most eloquent words for the purpose. No matter how he phrases that sequence of language, it will not be convincing if it's contradicted by his tone of voice and the rest of his body language.

We can't hear the tone of voice in this scenario or see the body language in detail, because the printed word doesn't provide that kind of information. A writer can describe a gesture or a facial expression here and there and can add the occasional phrase like "he said disgustedly," but this provides only *hints* at what would be observed if the medium were film instead of print. I can't get around this problem; no writer can. But I want to call your attention briefly to specific items of language— especially body language—that in a context like Scenario Three are identifying characteristics of the *dominant* variety of American Mainstream English.

1. Louis uses one of the most domineering items of nonverbal communi-
    cation available: He begins a sentence, then pauses and goes through
    a lengthy and elaborate ritual with his cigarette, keeping John and
    Ann waiting as he does so, before completing the sentence. The tactic
    would not have to be done with cigarettes; many other objects—
    telephone books, cosmetics, food items, etc.—can be used in this
    way. Any sequence of language in which the speaker pauses in mid-
    sentence to go through some voluntary process that is irrelevant to
    the interaction—keeping listeners waiting all the while—is a blatant
    power trip.

2. John and Louis interrupt each other and cut each other's speech off abruptly.

3. Both men make openly aggressive comments about the other's behavior. John says rudely, "You <u>through</u>?" and criticizes Louis's language as sexist. Louis tells John he "should've had brains enough to keep his mouth <u>shut</u>" and asks, "What are you looking at me like <u>that</u> for?"

It's the tone of voice and the assumed facial expressions and postures that make these comments aggressive, not the words they contain. Similarly, it's the body language that lets both men know this is sport rather than combat. When it's combat, the signals are different. For John and Louis, that would mean stiffened shoulders and spines, fists rather than open palms, narrowed eyes, and tightened jaws.

4. The men give each other open commands, presumably with the same aggressive intonation.

5. Both men initiate and maintain lengthy direct eye contact.

6. John leans back in his chair with his arms crossed over his chest and speaks "gravely" to Louis.

In the midst of such a display of linguistic dominance from her boss and his male friend, it's not surprising that Ann felt safer saying nothing. Nor is it surprising that she was dubious about the sincerity of John's overtly nonsexist words.

Because I'm the one writing the scenarios, I can say arbitrarily that both John and Louis are well aware of the effects of their body language and that they create those effects deliberately; I suspect that this is usually the case. But not always! Some men seem to be genuinely unaware of the impression they make. Men routinely stand up in my medical seminars, or approach me afterward, to tell me they're concerned because patients seem *uneasy* around them or frankly *afraid* of them, often making it difficult for them to carry out medical procedures. They're puzzled by this, they say, because they're careful to use *only nonthreatening words*. But their body language as they talk to me carries excessively strong messages of dominance and power. I advise them to watch a videotape of themselves interacting with others—so that they can see and hear why they're perceived as intimidating or hostile—and then to do simultaneous modeling with a video of someone who is perceived as strong and competent but not threatening.

Dialogues for Analysis

DIALOGUE ONE

M: "Honey, you don't have to work. We don't need the money."

F: "I want to."

M: "WHY the HELL would you want to go to WORK?"

Let's give this man the benefit of the doubt; let's assume he is a good and caring man who wants his wife to be happy and is baffled at the very idea that she'd want to work when he earns a good living and she doesn't have to. Let's assume that he's genuinely interested in hearing her explain this to him. In that case, he's shot himself in the foot. Not because of the words he's said, but because of the tune he's set them to. He hasn't a prayer of finding out why his wife would like to get a job, because he hasn't really asked her. His words aren't a question, they're an *attack*.

She's unlikely to be willing to talk to him after that Blaming line full of emphatic and abnormal stresses. She's most likely to say something like "I don't want to talk about it," or "It's no use talking about it; you wouldn't understand," or "Oh, just leave me alone!"

Suggestion for Him: Ask her the question, and leave out all the extra melodic frills. Ask, "Why do you want to go to work?" or "Why the hell would you want to go to work?" or "I'm sorry, I don't get it. Would you explain to me why you want to go to work?"

It's not the word "hell" that's carrying all the negative messages in the dialogue. "WHY on EARTH would you want to go to WORK?" would be just as bad, because it's set to the same angry melody. Like many women of my generation, I'd rather men (and women) would save swearing of all kinds for occasions of real crisis. But that's a matter of personal taste. Women are fully capable of distinguishing between swearing that's intended to offend and swearing that's just a characteristic of an individual's ordinary speech.

DIALOGUE TWO

F: "If you'll tell me what you have in mind for the conference, I'll try to figure out where we might find the money. For example, how many people do you expect to need travel money for?"

M: "Well, I . . . [HE PAUSES; HE TAKES A LONG SLOW DRAG ON HIS CIGARETTE; HE HOLDS HIS BREATH; VERY SLOWLY, HE EXHALES SMOKE THROUGH HIS NOSTRILS] . . . don't see any way to do it without travel funds for at least the top six, maybe seven, speakers."

The woman is clearly in the dominant position in this interaction, and the male speaker, equally clearly, doesn't like that much. The long by-play with his cigarette inserted into the middle of his sentence is a demonstration of power called a *dominance display*. You probably found it tedious to read about; it's equally tedious in the flesh. It's a way of saying, "You may be able to tell me whether my conference will be funded or not, but YOU don't boss ME around—you have to sit there and WAIT, silently, until I am good and READY to talk to you!" He knows this is a relatively safe tactic, because an objection from her would give him an opening he'd love to have. Take a look at Dialogue Three.

DIALOGUE THREE

F: "If you'll tell me what you have in mind for the conference, I'll try to figure out where we might find the money. For example, how many people do you expect to need travel money for?"

M: "Well, I . . . [HE PAUSES; HE TAKES A LONG SLOW DRAG ON HIS CIGARETTE; HE HOLDS HIS BREATH] . . ."

F: "I wish you wouldn't do that."

M: ". . . [VERY SLOWLY, HE EXHALES SMOKE THROUGH HIS NOSTRILS. HIS EYEBROWS GO UP, AND HE ASSUMES AN EXPRESSION OF TOTAL INNOCENCE]. You wish I wouldn't do <u>what</u>?"

F: "I wish you wouldn't stop in the middle of your sentences and go through that business of dragging on your cigarette and blowing smoke out through your nostrils, while I sit here and <u>wait</u>."

M: [HE NARROWS HIS EYES AT HER; HIS EXPRESSION IS ONE OF CONSIDERABLE SATISFACTION.] "If you'll tell me what you have in mind for the rules on talking while I'm smoking, I'll try to figure out whether I can follow them."

He could say a lot of other things that would give him the same amount of pleasure. "Wow . . . it really <u>doesn't</u> take much to fluster a lady administrator, <u>does</u> it?" Or "It must be <u>hard</u> to run a department when a piddly little thing like <u>that</u> can get you all upset!" And so on. The whole point of his cigarette display is to provoke her to admit that it bothers her; on the other hand, if she ignores it, he has proved that he can do this and get away with it.

Suggestion for Him: Don't do this. Deliberately annoying someone who outranks you, for no reason other than to prove that you can do it, is counterproductive. She will remember, and the first time you badly need her cooperation or support she'll hang you out at the end of a limb and watch you twist in the wind.

Suggestion for Her: You have to decide whether you want to invest any of your resources in dealing with such petty nonsense. If you don't, classify his behavior as you classify poison ivy and heavy traffic—as irritating facts of life to be avoided if possible, but not worth any emotional investment. (This would be my recommendation.)

If you *do* feel that struggling with him is required, prepare for a lengthy campaign. Each time you talk to him: Put him on hold by pausing in mid-sentence; pick up your phone; give one of your staff some "forgotten" instructions; hang up the phone; and then finish your sentence—while *he* waits. Or start a sentence, stop in the middle, take out your mirror and lipstick, repair your makeup, put away the mirror and lipstick, and finish the sentence—while he waits. You should think this over carefully. It could go on for years, and he may switch to a pipe or cigar for his own performance. A rule against smoking in your office would be a good move.

DIALOGUE FOUR

M: "Are you going to wear <u>that</u>?"

F: "What's wrong with it?"

M: "I didn't say anything was wrong with it."

F: "Yes, you did."

M: "I did <u>not</u>. You're <u>imag</u>ining things."

F: "I de<u>TEST</u> you!"

M: "Hey . . . what'd I <u>say</u>, for crying out loud?"

He does know what he said, of course, and he said it deliberately. This is a standard example of an activity that adult AME-speaking males refer to as "teasing" and seem to enjoy enormously.

Suggestion for Her: Answer his "Are you going to wear that?" with a neutral "Yes" and nothing more. That puts the ball back in his court. If he decides his next move should be to ask, "Are you sure?" give him another neutral "Yes." And *stay* neutral, no matter how ingenious he gets. Teasing is no fun if you don't get an outraged reaction from the person being teased.

Suggestion for Him: If it's actually the case that you don't like what she's chosen to wear for the evening, just tell her so. Say, "Honey, I don't like that dress much. Would you be willing to wear something else instead?" It may start an argument, but at least it will be an *adult* argument. If, as is more likely, you don't care what she wears and you only commented on it because you like to play this game, please consider giving it up for golf or poker. Women (and children of both genders) dislike male verbal teasing *intensely*. The kick you get out of it isn't worth the trouble, or the pain, it causes.

DIALOGUE FIVE

F: "I made five hundred dollars in the market today—isn't that great?"

M: "Hey . . . [HE CLASPS HIS HANDS IN FRONT OF HIS CHEST; HE LEANS HIS HEAD TOWARD HER; HE SMILES AS HE ANSWERS HER.] You made five hundred dollars! In the stock market!"

F: "Yes, I did. Are you pleased?"

M: "Sure! [HE CONTINUES TO SMILE, MOVING HIS HEAD FROM SIDE TO SIDE.] That's terrific!"

F: [SHE FROWNS SLIGHTLY, WATCHING HIM.] "You're not pleased."

M: "Whadda you mean? I said I was pleased, didn't I? I'm pleased. I'm smiling, okay? See? See the smile?" [HE POINTS TO THE SMILE, JABBING THE AIR WITH HIS INDEX FINGER.]

F: "Why aren't you pleased? I don't understand."

M: "Oh, for crying out loud! Why are you trying to pick a fight?"

Until the very end of this interaction, when he shows his irritation, he has not said one word that she could complain about. If the words represent his feelings, he's more than *justified* in being irritated. However, she is basing her reaction not on his words but on his body language, which—except for the smile—is uniformly negative. She is following the rule on page 72. His body language clashes with his words, so she doesn't believe them.

He moves his head in a way that ordinarily means "no"; he jabs the air with his index finger; he clasps his hands and leans toward her as if he were an aristocratic salesman forced to sell to a grubby peasant. If we could see his smile, we would probably recognize it as too broad and too long-lasting to be genuine. She's right that he isn't pleased about her five-hundred-dollar profit.

Suggestion for Her: Let it *go*. Don't answer his question about picking a fight; don't go on insisting that you don't believe the words he's saying to you. And don't, for heaven's sakes, try to start a long investigative discussion. Obviously he does *not* want to talk about this; maybe you'll have an opportunity at a later time, when it's not so fresh in his mind, to discuss his reasons for that. But not now. For now, just say "I'm glad you're pleased; I certainly am!" And change the subject. Immediately.

Suggestion for Him: Because your body will betray your intention to deceive, this is a poor strategy. You'd be far better off answering her "Isn't that great?" with "I wish I thought so; I don't." Then either explain your reasons or tell her in a neutral tone that you aren't willing to discuss it. That may lead to an argument, yes; but the language in the dialogue absolutely *guarantees* one.

DIALOGUE SIX

M1:   "How come Mom hasn't got a beer?"

M2:   "I didn't know she wanted one. She didn't say anything about wanting a beer."

M1:   "Well, she shouldn't have to make a speech, just to get a beer!"

M2:   "I don't think she wants one!"

M1:   "Of course she wants a beer! What's the matter with you?"

If you've noticed that the woman in this dialogue hasn't had any lines, you're way ahead of her two adult sons; they don't appear to have noticed. This bit of language behavior—talking about someone as if he or she were not there, or were incapable of talking—is one that both genders are guilty of, especially when the person being talked about is an elderly person or a child. I suggest a rewrite.

M1: "How come Mom hasn't got a beer?"

M2: "Mom, do you want a beer?"

F: "Thanks, I'd like one."

It's that simple.

DIALOGUE SEVEN

F: "She said it <u>deliberately</u> to insult me!"

M: "Oh, come on, now . . . what's the big deal? So she said we have a nice little house—what's wrong with that?"

F: "It was the <u>way</u> she said it! 'A nice little house'! The <u>nerve</u> of that woman!"

M: "Darling, only neurotics go around reading mysterious secret motives into every word people say. She said it was a nice little house—that's not an insult, and it's an accurate statement."

F: "You don't understand!"

M: "I certainly don't."

F: "<u>You</u> wouldn't know an insult if it BIT you!"

He may be right; she may be right. She was there when the "nice little house" was mentioned; he wasn't. Few things are a bigger waste of time and energy than arguing over something that's impossible to prove either way. He's wrong when he insists on making his judgment on the basis of words alone. She's wrong when she keeps trying to get him to agree with her even though he doesn't have the necessary information about the other woman's body language. He's doubly wrong when he makes the crack about neurotics; she's doubly wrong when she makes the crack about his inability to spot insults. This is a silly argument. Here's one possible way to avoid it.

F: "She said it <u>deliberately</u> to hurt me!"

M: "I'm sorry your morning was ruined; maybe the rest of the day will be better."

F: "I certainly hope so."

Notice: He hasn't questioned the accuracy of her accusation, nor has he accepted it. Instead, he's expressed his sympathy about something that's *not* a matter of dispute, in a way that's appropriate in this context.

DIALOGUE EIGHT

M: "Okay! <u>Next</u> item on the agenda is that damn contract with—
Oops! Sorry—my mistake. I keep forgetting there's a lady present."

F: "Hell, <u>I'm</u> not a lady!" [SHE FOLDS HER ARMS OVER HER CHEST.]

M: [PAUSE; HE STARES AT HER HARD.] "Just one of the guys, are you?"

F: "Damn right!"

M: "Funny . . . I don't remember anybody issuing you a uniform."

When a man says a word as innocuous as "damn" and goes into an elaborate apology about ladies being present, we know that one of two things is true:

• One: He is a very old-fashioned, courteous, chivalrous man who is truly apologetic at having said "damn" in front of a woman in public.

• Two: He is a sexist man who is determined to grab every possible opportunity to demonstrate that he doesn't think women belong in a business setting.

Neither of the men described will react positively when the woman responds with aggressively male body language. All the woman in this dialogue accomplishes by this tactic is to cancel the rules that would ordinarily protect her from public humiliation by a colleague. Telling her she doesn't have a uniform—isn't on the team—in front of everybody is vicious and cruel. It's also a demonstration. He's saying: "You want to be treated like a man? You <u>insist</u> on being treated like a man? <u>Fine</u>! You asked for it, I'll give it to you! Here's how I treat men I have no respect for!" I suggest a rewrite:

M: "Okay! Next item on the agenda is that damn contract with—
Oops! Sorry—my mistake. I keep forgetting there's a lady present."

F: "That's quite all right; I've heard the word before. Please go on."

And what if the woman had been able to get away with the lines in the original dialogue? What if her rank in the company, or her skill as a communicator, or both, made it possible for her to shove her male body language down this man's throat? That would be a very bad outcome in the long run, because she would have caused him to lose face—in public—and that would affect every subsequent interaction between them. The chances that those effects would be positive are nearly zero.

DIALOGUE NINE

F: "I want to <u>talk</u> to you, Mr. Andrews."

M: "Certainly, Mrs. Norton. What's on your mind?"

F: "I want you to know that I am <u>shocked</u> by this company's shoddy treatment of its female employees! I think it's time we all stopped relying on phony manners and started interacting like a community; I'm here to get that process under way."

M: "Go on."

F: "For example, you have no day-care facilities here, and you don't have adequate parking. That means I either have to wake my kids at dawn to take them to the sitter or I have to walk six blocks because the parking lot is already full when I get here."

M: "Mmhmm. Is that it?"

F: "No. There's more. Because you have no family-leave policy, when my kids are sick I'm really in a <u>bind</u>. You have to understand—"

M: "Wait. I <u>do</u> understand. I have always thought that the office was no place for a woman who has children. Listening to you, I am more convinced of that than ever. And I want <u>you</u> to know that you don't have to put up with it. You don't even have to give me notice. You just go right on home and look after your kids and put all this annoyance behind you."

F: "But that's not what—"

M: "No problem! I'm 100 percent on your side in this matter. We'll mail you your check."

The trouble with written dialogues is that they have almost no context and there's no nonverbal communication data to clarify them. This dialogue is a perfect example.

In the real world we'd be able to tell from his body language whether

Mr. Andrews is a sincere but over-fatherly man who has just badly misunderstood Mrs. Norton. In the real world, that possibility exists; on the printed page it's impossible to tell. The other alternative is that he's using a classic technique I call a "You Poor Little Thing" maneuver, and that the woman has seriously misjudged him.

Presumably she was prepared to carry on a vigorous debate with him about whether the company should change its policies to make life easier for its working mothers. Instead, she dug a deep hole for herself and leaped in. In *either* case, she is now in an embarrassing position. There's no dignified way out of this; far better not to get into it in the first place. The cue she missed was when he said only "Go on," instead of defending himself and the company against her accusations.

CHAPTER 5

◆

Breakdown Point: Hostility Loops

―――――――――――― **Scenario Five** ――――――――――――

"Sit down, please, Mary," John said courteously. "Thanks for coming in."

Mary smiled at him. "That's all right," she said. "What did you want to see me about?"

He leaned toward her, his elbows on the desk, his hands folded. "Mary," he said, "we've got a serious problem here, and it has to be taken care of. Everybody in the office is at the end of their <u>rope</u> over it."

"I'm sorry to hear that. Tell me about it; maybe I can help."

"Mary," he said, his voice suddenly stronger and louder, "you certainly can help, if you <u>choose</u> to, because <u>you're</u> the <u>problem</u>."

"What?"

"<u>You</u>. And your attitude. Not to mention your vivid imagination."

"I beg your pardon?"

"Would you explain to me, please," he said, "how you can <u>al</u>ways manage to find something offensive in every word people in this company <u>say to you</u>? No matter how hard they try to rise to your lofty standards?"

"Now wait a minute, John!"

"No. I'm not going to wait a minute. This has gone on too long. I'm <u>sick</u> of it. We're <u>all</u> sick of it!"

"There is no way," said Mary icily, "that I can contribute to this discussion unless you <u>stop</u> making vague moral <u>judg</u>ments and tell me specifically what you're ob<u>ject</u>ing to."

"You got it!" John agreed. "We'll start with the fit you threw after I told you you'd done a good job in last week's meeting—and the little extra fit you threw for Bill's benefit. I'm grateful to Louis Marin for bringing this particular example to my attention, because I missed this one. But it's not the first time it's happened."

"I don't know what you're talking about!"

"Yes, you do! You always say that—but we both know better. Apparently you live by some bizarre code that says it's immoral to tell you you're attractive, and vicious to tell you that you dress well. . . . That's pretty warped, Mary! Why do you always have to be such a prima donna?"

"Why do you always have to do everything you can to put me down?" Mary shot back at him. "Why can't you ever just say my work is good—which is true—and save your flowery remarks for your wife? They're wasted on ME, and I don't appreciate them!"

John straightened, and looked at her hard; distaste was clearly written on his face. "Oh, I know that, Mary," he said, very quietly. "I know, and everybody knows, that you have no appreciation whatsoever for the efforts we make to support you around here and to let you know that you're a valued colleague. We couldn't possibly be unaware of that fact, because you make it crystal clear to us, day after day."

"John," Mary said, floundering now, "that's not fair! That's not what I meant! I didn't mean that I don't appreciate the support I get here . . . you know I do! I'm sorry if . . ." She stopped for a second to catch her breath, and then went on. "What I mean is, of course I appreciate the support I get here. What I don't appreciate—"

John cut her off sharply. "You don't appreciate people trying to be nice!" he snapped. "Because they aren't sophisticated enough to be nice according to your rules. Correct?"

"No, John, it's not like that! I know I didn't express myself very well . . . you caught me by surprise, I wasn't expecting any of this! I'm sorry I said it so badly. But—"

She stopped again, and looked at him. He had folded his arms over his chest and settled back in his chair; his face was stony with anger and grim disgust; his jaws were clenched as he waited for her to continue. To continue making a fool of herself, obviously.

"Never mind, John," she said, with as much dignity as she

could muster. "You wouldn't understand anyway. There's no point in even trying to explain it to you. Once again—I'm sorry."

And she stood up and walked out on him.

◆

What's Going On Here?

Mary's Point of View

Mary is reasonably sure John's playing games with her—but she doesn't know what game. And she wasn't expecting game-playing from him this time. She thought he was going to give her the schedule for the new project, and his attack caught her off guard. Then came the shock of learning that her distress on the day of the meeting is now common knowledge—and realizing that her husband, who plays golf with Louis Marin, has to be the source of the leak.

Badly rattled, she finds herself in the middle of an undignified row with John before she can recover her composure. Everything he says twists her words and distorts her actions, and she is quite sure he's doing it on purpose. She knows that attacking him back is the wrong move, and invites even more distortions; she knows that if she starts trying to explain why she was so upset things will only get worse, because it would take such a long time to establish even the most basic points. She tries to bring the encounter back to a more neutral level by apologizing, but in her anger and distress she overdoes it. And when this brings on John's Great Stone Face act, she knows that if she doesn't get away from him she will *really* lose her temper. She's not about to give him that satisfaction.

Mary is proud that she made a dignified exit; she's proud that she didn't cry. She's disgusted with herself for having said she was sorry when she had nothing to be sorry about. And she wonders whether giving Frank hell for talking about her private affairs will be worth having to listen to him tell her that she's getting more paranoid all the time. He'll ask her how she could possibly have managed to turn something so trivial into such a major *mess*—and what can she say? There doesn't seem to her to be any way to explain that won't make her sound . . . as John said . . . like a prima donna.

John's Point of View

As John perceives it, every time he gives Mary a chance to save herself she throws it away, making one foolish strategic error after another. He is amazed at how easy it is to "get her going," how little effort it takes before she loses control of a language interaction . . . how helpless she is before what he knows very well are crude techniques. There were a half dozen ways she could have handled the situation and backed him down—she didn't use any of them. Her performance this time confirms his previous opinion: Mary can't handle herself in "man-to-man" situations, and he wouldn't be able to trust her to represent the firm competently on her own. He hopes that this time she will be discouraged enough to give up and resign; if not, he's prepared to schedule additional sessions like this one until she does.

Unless, of course, she surprises him and demonstrates that he's misjudging her. He prides himself on being fair, always. Should that happen, he would stop trying to drive her out and back her all the way, as he would any other valued employee. But he would be *very* surprised.

◆

Scenario Five is an unpleasant example of a typical verbal confrontation between a skilled verbal abuser and a victim he outranks; between an individual good at playing language games and a person who not only doesn't know the rules of the game but isn't sure which game it is. It has a Winner and a Loser, and the *facts* involved are completely irrelevant to the outcome.

It doesn't have to be like this. There's a better way to deal with such confrontations, starting with one of the *Gentle Art* metaprinciples—

◆ ANYTHING YOU FEED WILL GROW.

—and using a technique based on the work of therapist Virginia Satir. (Satir 1972) Let's take a look at it.

Technique #4
Recognizing and Responding to the Satir Modes

People use language differently when they're tense than when they're relaxed. When we're upset or angry, when we're under stress, when we're frightened . . . when we're feeling any strong emotion . . . our language behavior changes. Everybody knows that. What we usually fail to realize, however, is that our language behavior doesn't just change *randomly*. Our grammars continue to function, although they may switch to emergency rules; the changes are in many ways predictable. Knowing this, and understanding the system involved, can make a tremendous difference in your language environment and in your life.

One of the most predictable changes was discovered by therapist Virginia Satir, who found that when people communicate under stress their language behavior falls into the patterns I call the *Satir Modes*: Blaming, Placating, Computing, Distracting, and Leveling. She also found that although none of the patterns is a part of anyone's *character*, people do have strong preferences for one Satir Mode over another, depending on the type of situation in which they find themselves. You may not be familiar with the names Satir gave to these patterns, but you will recognize the language that goes with them, because they are part of your internal grammar.

Recognizing the Satir Modes

If you have trouble "hearing" the language of the examples below, I suggest that you read them aloud, putting extra stress (emphasis) on the sections that are underlined or all in capital letters. The sequences all in capitals should get the *strongest* emphasis.

Blaming and Placating

The most obvious features of Blaming are hostility and anger. In addition, it has the following characteristics:

1. Frequent use of *personal* language—"I, me, you, my, your," etc.
2. Frequent use of strong stresses on words and parts of words.
3. Frequent use of "absolute" words such as "always, never, everybody, nothing," and so on.
4. Body language that is threatening and hostile: fists that pound; fingers that are shaken or jabbed at people; scowls and frowns and clenched teeth; *looming* over others; etc.

People who are using Blamer Mode say things like these:

"WHY can't you <u>ever</u> do anything RIGHT?"

"You ALways let the grass get THREE FEET HIGH before you mow it!"

"You <u>never</u> think about <u>any</u>body but yourSELF!"

Placating, like Blaming, can be recognized by its frequent use of "I/ me/you" language and its strong emphasis on words and parts of words.

However, the Blamer (shorthand for "someone who is using Blaming language") appears obviously angry; the Placater (shorthand for "someone who is using Placating language") gives a very different impression. Placaters appear desperately anxious to *please* other people. The body language of the Placater, Satir said, will remind you of a cocker spaniel puppy. Placaters wiggle and fidget and blink; they lean on people; they pick lint off others' shoulders. Here are some typical Placating utterances.

"YOU know how I am! Any̲thing YOU want is okay with ME!"

"Oh, heavens—I̲ don't care! Anything you say̲!"

"I know̲ this is going to make you mad̲—I'm so SORry! But. . . ."

"You KNOW I'd never tell you what to DO, sweetheart, but. . . ."

Because Placating is a behavior that trumpets apologies and a desire to please, it is a *subordinate* behavior; Blaming, on the other hand, is a *dominant* pattern. However, it would be unwise to leap to the conclusion that this means Blaming is always abusive and Placating is only irritating. Suppose you and your spouse have to go out to dinner and you've been unable to find a sitter, so you ask one of your in-laws to help you out and stay with the kids. Here's what a mother- or father-in-law given to Blaming might say to you:

"Oh, of course̲! Just leave̲ the kids with me̲! Never mind̲ what I̲ might want to do! WHY do you two ALWAYS try to take adVANTage of me this way?"

That's hostile; that's abusive. No question about it. Now compare it with what you might hear from the in-law who prefers Placating for verbal confrontations in the home:

"Oh, of course̲! You two just go right̲ ahead and have a nice̲ dinner! You̲ know me—I'm always̲ glad to help in any̲ way I can̲! I'll just make̲ do with whatever you've left in the refrigerator̲ . . . I̲ don't mind!"

Is that any better? Notice, the words themselves are pleasanter, and there are no open accusations. But the intonation—THE TUNE THE WORDS ARE SET TO—is unmistakably unpleasant to any native speaker of English. This is a person who doesn't want to stay with your kids, doesn't want you and your spouse to enjoy your dinner, and is determined to spoil your evening if possible.

Notice also that these two sequences could come from someone of either gender. I am often asked about the gender-linked distribution of the Satir Modes, but no large studies researching that question have yet been done; I can answer the question only in a very general way. Because Placating is a more subordinate style, and women find themselves in subordinate roles more often than men do, it may be somewhat more common in women than in men. Blaming, with its surface aura of dominance, might be a bit more common in males. But I have observed many male Placaters and many female Blamers. Furthermore, many women and men rely on *both* of these modes. A person who prefers Blaming for workplace confrontations may Placate when things get tense at home, or vice versa. People who typically use Blaming Mode in most other situations often switch to Placating in an argument with a doctor or a police officer.

The choice of Satir Mode is essentially independent of gender, and where gender differences do show up they will ordinarily be in the body language rather than in the words. Adult males who are Placating are less likely to bat their eyelashes than women are; adult females who are Blaming are less likely to pound their fists on the furniture than men are.

Computing

Computing is very different from Blaming and Placating; it is the most *neutral* of the Satir Modes. It can be recognized by the absence of personal language, and by the flat intonation that stresses only those words and parts of words that English grammar *requires* stress for. All English statements, for example, are required to have at least one stressed item, usually at or near the end of the sentence; people using Computer Mode obey their grammar and provide that stress. But their sentences lack the hills and valleys of Blamer and Placater sentences. In addition, Computing has these characteristics:

1. Frequent use of generalizations and abstractions and references to hypothetical items.
2. Body language that is as neutral as possible, with very little change in posture and expression and very few gestures. (The flat intonation already mentioned is part of this body language style.)

People using Computing language say things like these:

"There is undoubtedly a good reason for this delay."

"Reasonable people would not be alarmed by that noise."

"People who are unable to handle their share of the workload often find themselves looking for other jobs."

Distracting

You don't need to learn any new characteristics to recognize Distracter Mode. Distracters cycle rapidly through the other modes—a Blamer sentence, a sentence or two of Placating, another Blamer sentence, a Computer sentence, maybe a little Leveling thrown in—and their body language switches from mode to mode right along with the words. As the name says, it's distracting. Here's a typical example of a Distracter talking:

"WHY IS it that every time I come here I have to wait for THREE HOURS? Not that I have anything else to do . . . you know me, I don't care! I might just as well be waiting! But responsible people should make an attempt to keep their appointments on time. And I'm NOT going to put UP with this much LONGer!!!"

Leveling

Finally we come to Leveling, which is the behavior left over. That is: If what you're observing isn't one of the other four Satir Modes, it's Leveling. Levelers may use *any* of the words and sentences used in the other Modes, at any time—it's very important to remember that. But the accompanying body language, especially the intonation of the voice, will be different. Compare the following two sentences:

BLAMER TALKING: "WHY do you eat SO MUCH JUNK food?"

LEVELER TALKING: "Why do you eat so much junk food?"

If we had an efficient method for printing intonation, you'd be able to see that the Blamer's voice goes up on "why" and "so much junk" and falls on "do you eat" and "food"; the capital letters make this clear, after a fashion. And you would also be able to see that the Leveler sentence has only one pitch change. From the word "why" on, it is pitched slightly higher than a statement would be; the change occurs at the point where the pitch of the Leveler's voice *falls*, on the word "food." The words are exactly the same; the tunes are radically different. This matters, because Levelers, most of the time, mean what they say. Blamers, most of the time, don't. Let me explain.

Inner Messages and Outer Messages

Everyone has three channels for spoken communication: the words that are said; the body language that goes with the words; and something we have no very good word for, sometimes called "vibes," that reflects the speaker's inner feelings. When all three channels match, we say that the speaker's message is *syntonic*, or *congruent*. The speaker who can't stand the sight of you, and who says so, with appropriate body language, is presenting you with a syntonic message in which everything matches. That speaker is *Leveling*.

The message on the outside of a Blamer, carried by the words and most of the body language, is "I have ALL the power!" But the inner message, the one the Blamer *feels*, is "I don't have <u>any</u> power." People use Blaming language because they feel that others don't respect them; Blamers are afraid nobody will do anything they ask unless they throw their weight around. They are trying to win by force in situations where they're very afraid they'll lose. This is a serious mismatch among channels.

Placaters say they don't care because they care so *much*. The outer message is "I don't care"; the inner one is "I care! I care! Please don't get angry with me!"

Computers present "I have no emotions; I'm completely neutral here" as their outer message because they feel one or more emotions that they prefer to conceal.

Distracters, on the inside, feel that they don't know what to say; on the outside, they say everything and anything, on the off chance that the "right thing to say" may accidentally turn up. Distracting is a linguistic expression of panic.

Only with the Leveler do the inner feelings—so far as the Leveler is accurately aware of them—match the words that are said and the body language that accompanies the words.

This means that when the Leveler threatens someone, it's *serious*. The Leveler will probably carry out the threat. The Blamer is unlikely to do so unless pushed into a corner and panicked. It means that when the

Leveler says "I really don't care; you decide," that's exactly what the Leveler means. But the Placater who says "I really don't care! You decide!" will resent any choice you make unless it happens to be the one the Placater would have made. Remember this very basic fact:

◆   THE ONLY WAY YOU CAN TELL THE DIFFERENCE BE- TWEEN LEVELING AND THE OTHER SATIR MODES IS BY THE BODY LANGUAGE, ESPECIALLY THE TONE AND INTO- NATION OF THE VOICE.

This is what lies behind the classic "It wasn't what you said, it was the way you said it!" complaint, which is absolutely accurate. It isn't the words that are said in any of the Satir Modes that cause the resentment and hostility and other negative emotions; it's the *way* they're said. And "the way they're said" means the body language that goes with them. This is a potential source of much misunderstanding between the sexes, and is made worse by the fact that AME-speaking men tend to pay less attention to body language than AME-speaking women do.

Now, let's return to the metaprinciple—ANYTHING YOU FEED WILL GROW—and apply it to what we know about the Satir Modes, as a way of determining how to *respond* to these patterns after we have recognized them.

Responding to the Satir Modes

Nobody will argue if you say that a child or a pet or a plant that is fed will grow. We can see that happen; it's part of our reality. We tend to forget this reality statement when we think about language, however, with unfortunate consequences. ALL LANGUAGE INTERACTIONS ARE FEEDBACK LOOPS. (Another metaprinciple.) When you feed information and emotion into a communication loop, it grows. Look at this sentence from John Gellis, in Scenario Five:

"Why do you always have to be such a prima donna?"

That's Blaming. It's openly hostile; it's personal; it contains several extra chunks of stress on words and parts of words. And what does Mary Clayton say back?

"Why do you always have to do everything you can to put me down? Why can't you ever just say my work is good—which is

true—and <u>save</u> your flowery <u>remarks</u> for your <u>wife</u>? They're
wasted on ME, and I don't appreciate them!''

Right! She Blames right *back* at him. She feeds the Blamer loop that
John has set up. As will always happen, that makes it grow. Blaming at
a Blamer always guarantees a verbal confrontation.

Feeding a Placater loop gets you *this* kind of dialogue:

X: "Where do you want to go for lunch?"

Y: "Oh, <u>I</u> don't care! <u>You</u> decide!"

X: "No, really—I couldn't. Please. Where would <u>you</u> like to eat?"

Y: "<u>You</u> know me! <u>I</u> don't care! Wherever <u>you</u> want to go is just <u>fine</u>
with <u>me</u>!"

X: "But <u>really</u>. . . ."

And so, hungrily, on. Placater loops guarantee you just one thing:
undignified delay.

Computer loops guarantee delay, too, but it's *dignified* delay. Like this:

X: "There's undoubtedly a good reason for this delay."

Y: "There must be. People don't keep others waiting for no reason at
all."

X: "Sometimes it's difficult for those who are waiting to understand
that it can't be avoided."

Y: "On the other hand, sometimes those responsible don't realize
how much inconvenience they are causing."

Nothing much is happening here; not much information is being exchanged; it's not exciting or dramatic. The interaction is neutral and
unemotional and dignified. This is a typical Computer loop.

Distracter loops, which are panic feeding panic, are of course to be
avoided at all costs.

Finally, there's the Leveler loop, which is the simple truth going both
ways. It's the most efficient form of communication, and theoretically
the most perfect. That doesn't mean it will necessarily be pleasant. For
example, here's a flawless Leveler loop:

X: "You don't like me, do you?"

Y: "No, I don't. I never have. I can't stand you."

X: "I feel the same way about you."

Y: "Well, at least we agree on something."

Ideally, the speaker always speaks the truth and the listener always responds truthfully. In the real world, however, we know that isn't always appropriate or acceptable or safe.

You will have no trouble recognizing the Satir Mode coming at you. You've known how to do that since you were a small child. And from the information in this section, we can now put together the two simple rules for *responding* to these modes.

✦ **RULE ONE:**   If you want what's coming at you to grow, match that Satir Mode: feed the loop.

✦ **RULE TWO:**   Otherwise, go to Computer Mode, and stay there until you have a reason to change.

When you recognize the language you're hearing as Blaming, and a fight is what you *want*, Blame back. If you recognize it as Placating and you are equally determined to slow everything to a crawl and pretend to be a doormat, Placate back. When you recognize it as Leveling and you're willing and able to respond with the unvarnished truth, Level back. If you need time to decide what to do next, so that a dignified delay would be useful to you—or if you don't have enough information to make a reasoned choice of modes—Compute back. Because Computing is the safest and most neutral of the modes, it's the best fallback position.

It's important to make a distinction between using the Satir Modes as an unthinking reaction to tension and distress, and using them as strategic linguistic *choices*. The surgery patient who uses Computer Mode because he's afraid someone will find out how much the operation scares him isn't making a strategic choice; he is using a pattern that he has come to rely on when he's frightened, and is probably not consciously aware of what he's doing. By contrast, an executive may consciously decide to use Computer Mode in a meeting because she's concerned about sales figures and feels that it would weaken her negotiating position if others knew that. That *is* a strategic decision. In both cases, the goal is to conceal an emotion, but the executive is acting rather than *re*acting.

Many couples rely on a useless, ugly strategy in which, at the slightest sign of conflict or unpleasantness, one person moves into Blamer Mode and the other person Placates back, or vice versa. The dialogues below are typical examples of this counterproductive pattern:

Male Blaming; Female Placating Back

M: "<u>Why</u> do you <u>al</u>ways <u>hide</u> my BROWN SOCKS?"

F: "Oh, honey, <u>can't</u> you <u>find them</u>? I'm <u>so</u> sorry!"

M: "You <u>do</u> it on <u>pur</u>pose! You <u>want</u> me to be late to work, <u>don't</u> you?"

F: "I <u>don't</u>! <u>Really</u>, I don't! Here, wait, let <u>me</u> find them for you! Gosh, I'm so <u>sorry</u>!"

Blamers want a fight, but they want a fight which makes them feel that they do in fact have some *power*. They don't get that feeling when Placating is the only resistance they're facing. No one feels powerful stamping on a doormat. Placating doesn't calm the Blamer down or make the Blamer less angry; it has the opposite effect.

Male Placating; Female Blaming Back

M: "You <u>know</u> I don't expect per<u>fec</u>tion, honey. . . . I really <u>don't</u>. But still. . . . [HEAVY SIGH]"

F: "<u>Now</u> what can't you find?!"

M: "Oh . . . <u>it's</u> not important. Never mind. <u>I'll</u> manage."

F: "Will you <u>quit</u> whining, and tell me what your <u>problem is</u>?"

Placaters are angry, but they're also terrified of the open anger of other people. They're trying to avoid it. But Placating only infuriates Blamers . . . which frightens the Placater more and leads to more Placating . . . which makes the Blamer even more furious and leads to more Blaming . . . and so on.

Neither of these combinations will ever result in successful communication. In both dialogues, either Computing or Leveling would be a far better response. Let's rewrite them both.

M: "<u>Why</u> do you <u>al</u>ways <u>hide</u> my BROWN SOCKS?" (BLAMING)

F: "Nothing ever gets lost except when people are already late for work." (COMPUTING)

M: "Well, do you know where my brown socks are?" (LEVELING)

F: "Sure. Try the second drawer down." (LEVELING)

M: "You <u>know</u> I don't expect per<u>fec</u>tion, honey. I really <u>don't</u>. But <u>still</u>. . . . [HEAVY SIGH]" (PLACATING)

F: "It's good that you don't expect perfection. That's very sensible." (COMPUTING)

M: "Well, do you know where my brown socks are?" (LEVELING)

F: "I think they're in the second drawer down." (LEVELING)

Notice what happened: In both cases, the person who had started the interaction with abusive language (Blaming or Placating) switched to Leveling when faced with a neutral response. This is a common result, and often does happen this quickly.

People tend to choose their Satir Modes on the basis of habit, often using patterns learned early in life by observing the language behavior of their parents or other adults. When the result is that they feed hostility loops, they get locked into interactions that don't work, that make all communication seem futile, and that destroy relationships. And they are at the mercy of skilled verbal gameplayers—like John Gellis—who make *deliberate* choices. Robin Lakoff (*Talking Power*, page 16) says of people like John that "It is not that they know things of which we are totally innocent, but that they are better at the tricks we all know." That is, both John and Mary used Blamer Mode; the difference was that he did it deliberately, to achieve his goals, while she did it blindly, as a reaction to his move.

To avoid problems like these, do two things:

- Be *aware* of the Satir Modes; actively watch and listen for them in others' speech, so that you will recognize them coming at you.

- Make your own choices among the Satir Modes systematically and strategically, based on the rules on page 94, your personal communication goals, and your knowledge of the situation in question.

Why Bother? The Fringe Benefits

A better language environment and improved communication with the opposite sex are not your only payoffs for using the Satir Mode technique and the other techniques in the *Gentle Art* system. There's much more.

Once in a while I run into people who have a "Why bother?" attitude about better communication. They usually fall into one of four groups:

- People like Louis Marin in Scenario Five, who think the idea of "improved interpersonal relations" is hilarious.

- People convinced that everybody is out to get them and that they can survive only by getting others *first*.

- People who've given up and who insist that nothing they could do could possibly improve this world and it's a waste of time to try.

- People who just have a *mean* streak and could care less whether they make everyone around them miserable.

To these people, and to the rest of you as well, I'm pleased to be able to say that using the *Gentle Art* techniques will bring you extra benefits— fringe benefits—that are valuable to you on the basis of pure self-interest alone. For one simple and uncomplicated reason: GOOD COMMUNICA- TION IS GOOD *FOR* YOU. Take a look at just two brief quotations that are representative of a very large literature on the subject:

> Angry, cynical people are five times as likely to die under 50 as people who are calm and trusting. . . . (Redford B. Williams, quoted by Sandra Blakeslee in the *New York Times*, 17 January 1989.)

> Scientists have long noted an association between social relationships and health. More socially isolated or less socially integrated people are less healthy, psychologically and physically, and more likely to die. (James S. House et al., "Social Relationships and Health," *Science*, 29 June 1988, pp. 540–44.)

Current research proves beyond all question that two kinds of people in our society are at serious risk: people who are hostile, and people who are lonely. (Often these are the *same* people, since few of us enjoy spending much of our time around hostile individuals.) Hostile and lonely people get sick more often, are injured more often, take longer to recover from illness or injury, suffer more complications during recovery, and die sooner. Exposure to chronic hostility is more likely to cause heart attacks than any other risk factor, including overweight, smoking, high cholesterol, and a genetic history of heart disease. Exposure to chronic verbal abuse doesn't leave you with obvious cuts and bruises, but it is a guaranteed recipe for ulcers, migraine headaches, high blood pressure, allergy attacks, accidents in the home and in the workplace and on the highways, colds, rashes, depression, and every sort of misery. (For a detailed discussion, see Locke and Colligan 1987, Ornstein and Sobel 1987, and Elgin 1991.)

These effects don't show up in the short term, which is why it took us so long to find out what was really happening. In the short term it often looks as if the meanest and angriest and least-liked people are the ones getting all the benefits. It took today's computers, which can find the patterns in the data from hundreds of thousands of health histories extending over lifetimes, to show us what the *real facts* are. They're not the "facts" you see on television.

When your language behavior makes other people enjoy being around you and look forward to talking with you, when you clean up your language environment so that verbal violence isn't a routine part of your life, you do more for your health and well-being than you could ever accomplish in any other way. If for no other reason, and no matter what your gender, *that's* why you should bother. It is our very good fortune that these results, which are so beneficial to each one of us as individuals, are also exactly what we need in order to establish and maintain good relationships.

Another Look at Scenario Five

Suppose Mary had gone into her confrontation with John in Scenario Five equipped with the Satir Modes technique. How would the scenario have developed? Let's explore some of the possibilities.

John's first move into Blamer Mode is with this sentence:

> "Mary, you certainly can help, if you <u>choose</u> to, because <u>you're</u> the <u>problem</u>."

The clue that would have alerted Mary—the characteristic that makes this a Blaming utterance—is the three strong stresses that occur in this one sentence. There's no sentence content that requires their presence for any reason other than to carry the Blaming message. Mary responded indignantly, with "What?" and "I beg your pardon?" and then "Now wait a minute!" And each of her responses gave John another opportunity to go on Blaming, with more hostile words and more hostile body language.

Instead of feeding the Blaming loop and watching it escalate, Mary could have moved to cut it off, by answering in Computer Mode:

John: "Mary, you certainly can help, if you <u>choose</u> to, because <u>you're</u> the <u>problem</u>."

Mary: "No one would make an accusation like that without a conviction that it could be supported."

John cannot now go on to say, as he did originally, "<u>You</u>. And your attitude. Not to mention your vivid imagination." That option is no longer available to him, and he'll have to think of some other way to continue.

Mary had many other opportunities of this kind, if she missed the first one. After every Blamer utterance from John, she could have answered with Computing or with Leveling, as in these examples.

John: "This has gone on too long. I'm <u>sick</u> of it. We're <u>all</u> sick of it!''

Mary: "Nothing is more frustrating than a problem that seems to go on endlessly." (COMPUTING)

—or—

Mary: "John, fighting about this is a waste of your time and of mine. Let's try discussion instead." (LEVELING)

One of Mary's most serious errors was her attempt to defend herself not just with Blaming but with an open counterattack, in these lines:

"<u>Why</u> can't you ever just say my work is <u>good</u>—which is true— and <u>save</u> your flowery <u>remarks</u> for your <u>wife</u>? They're wasted on ME, and I don't appreciate them!''

This gave John an opening he seized upon, in which he swiftly *agreed* with her that she didn't appreciate the efforts of her colleagues to support her, and assured her that she made that "crystal clear, day after day." His lines at this point, with the sudden quiet tone and the wounded words, are an example of the language behavior called Phony Leveling—given away by the extra emphasis he puts on words and parts of words, and by the context. His tactics worked, unfortunately, panicking Mary into a sudden and undignified switch to Placater Mode from which she was able to extricate herself only by fleeing.

It's crucially important to understand that when I refer here to errors and successes I am not making *moral* judgments. Everything about John's treatment of Mary in the scenario is morally wrong, in my opinion, and cannot be defended. I consider his behavior unacceptable from start to finish. But in theoretical terms—in terms of strategic skill—it's Mary who makes the mistakes, again and again, and John whose linguistic moves are consistently successful. She could have easily prevented that with a strategy of her own: consciously using the Satir Modes to make it impossible for him to carry out his plans.

Dialogues for Analysis

DIALOGUE ONE

F: "There's a pizza place! You want to stop for pizza?"

M: "Do you want pizza?"

F: "I don't know . . . Do you?"

M: "If you don't want pizza, honey, why did you bring it up?"

This is an ordinary example of casual and not particularly efficient communication, the kind we all participate in. At this point, two things can happen. Suppose her next line is "Darn, it's too late anyway—we've passed the exit!," and that ends the interaction. If that happens, everything is fine. There's no rule that says all conversation between couples must be significant, meaningful, and memorable. The other possibility, however, is *not* fine. Suppose what happens is the mess shown in Dialogue Two. . . .

DIALOGUE TWO

F: "There's a pizza place! You want to stop for pizza?"

M: "Do you want pizza?"

F: "I don't know . . . Do you?"

M: "If you don't want pizza, honey, why did you bring it up?"

F: "I brought it up because I thought you might want some PIZza!"

M: "Did I say I wanted pizza?"

F: "No, but—"

M: "Did I even suggest that I wanted pizza?"

F: "Wait a minute! Why are you BULLYING me about this?"

M: "Oh, come on, honey . . . you started it."

F: "I didn't 'start' ANYthing! I thought you might be HUNGry, THAT'S all! I was trying to be considerate of YOU, and as USUAL, I ended up REGRETTING it! Being nice to you is like—"

M: "Wait a minute! Let's go over this logically, one step at a time. First: you said you wanted to stop for pizza. Then—"

F: "I did NOT! You're IMPOSSIBLE! STOP it! Just STOP it!"

M: "Speaking of impossible, <u>tell</u> me something, sweetheart. I'm beginning to be seriously worried—I think we have to get to the bottom of this. We need to <u>know</u> why it's impossible for you to carry on an ordinary adult conversation."

This is ugly, and it will go on and on, mile after mile. He will quietly and gently explain to her what she does and why she does it; he will never sound sarcastic or upset. She will grow more and more frantic. By the time they get to their destination, she will be abjectly apologizing to him, and he will be graciously accepting the apology and telling her that he understands perfectly. And that will be the truth; he *does* understand perfectly.

This man is a Phony Leveler, and he's dangerous; fortunately, such people (of either gender) are rare. His inner feelings are that it's a lot of fun to torment this woman, for whom he has no respect and no consideration (although he may be very dependent on her for his emotional needs). But he's able to make his words and body language present a convincing facade of tenderness and concern—at least, he's good enough at it to convince *her*. Technically, he may or may not lie where "facts"—dates, times, prices, that sort of thing—are concerned. But emotionally, he's a liar.

Suggestion for Her: Assuming that you want to continue your relationship with this man, you must learn not to let him sucker you into episodes like this. That is distinctly *not* easy. Your cue is when he says, "If you don't want pizza, why did you bring it up?" You should recognize that as the opening line in one of his habitual interrogation sessions. Don't participate. *Change the subject.* Say "Can you read that sign up there? I can't quite make it out." He can't do this kind of thing without your help.

DIALOGUE THREE

M: "I guess we ought to get some lunch. Okay?"

F: "Well, do you want lunch?"

M: "Do <u>you</u>? I mean, if you're not hungry yet, I don't mind waiting a while."

F: "Well, <u>I</u> don't want <u>you</u> to be hungry, <u>either</u>! <u>You</u> decide!"

M: "Okay . . . I guess I could eat something."

F: [SIGHS] "Well, <u>you</u> know <u>me</u> . . . whatever <u>you</u> want is always okay with <u>me</u>."

M: "But wait a minute, we don't have to eat now . . . I'm perfectly willing to have lunch <u>later</u>. Tell me what <u>you</u> want to do."

He can waste a lot of his time this way. The basic steps in this Placating woman's game are extremely obvious.

- He will ask her for her preference in some situation.
- She will tell him she wants him to decide.
- When he makes the decision as she asked him to do, she'll make it clear to him that she will accept it, but she doesn't like it.
- Then he will ask her what she wants again. And they will go around and around this loop.

Suggestion for Him: When she tells you to make a decision, do it; and then follow through. When she says, "<u>You</u> decide!" your next line should be a firm and pleasant, "Fine, I'll be glad to. Let's go to Shoney's." And then *go*.

DIALOGUE FOUR

F: "Honey—are you busy?"

M: "WHY do you always do that? You can SEE that I'm busy!"

F: "<u>I'm</u> sorry. Just go back to whatever you were doing."

M: "You've already interrupted me—what did you WANT?"

F: "Oh, it wasn't important."

M: "Then why the hell did you INTERRUPT me?"

Let's assume that what she's saying is true—that she really could not tell whether he was too busy to talk to her or not. Let's assume that what he's saying is also true—he's busy, and he is of the opinion that she should be able to tell that he's busy, without having to ask. One of these people will have to change their language behavior.

Rewrite for Her:

F: "Honey—are you busy?"

M: "WHY do you always do that? You can SEE that I'm busy!"

F: "My mistake. I'll talk to you later."

If he then says that you've already interrupted and asks you what you wanted, *tell* him. Nothing is more infuriating to people who have—however grudgingly—stopped what they're doing to listen to you than to be told that you interrupted them for something you don't think is important.

Rewrite for Him:

F: "Honey—are you busy?"

M: "Yes, I am."

F: "My mistake. I'll talk to you later."

M: "Thanks."

—or—

F: "Honey—are you busy?"

M: "Yes, I am."

F: "I'm sorry to interrupt you. This can't wait, though."

M: "Okay. What's the problem?"

Her question—"Are you busy?"—is nothing but a neutral request for information. When you come back at her in Blamer Mode, you cut off all possibility of useful communication. Asking "What did you WANT?" will only make her reluctant to tell you, for fear of annoying you even more. Get rid of the Blamer language and you'll be able to get back to your work far more quickly.

DIALOGUE FIVE

M: "What's the MATTER with you? How can you POSSIBLY ask me for money when my wife is lying in there SUFFERing? DON'T you have ANY human feelings at ALL?"

F: "Sir, I only WORK here! I'm JUST doing my JOB!"

M: "Well, you ought to be ASHAMED! My wife could be DYING in there for all YOU know! YOU don't even CARE! You—"

F: "I do NOT have to take that kind of abuse, from YOU or from ANYONE ELSE!"

This is a man locked in Blamer Mode because he's so worried that he can't think straight. He knows the clerk isn't responsible for the

"Payment Is Expected at the Time Service Is Provided" policy, and under normal circumstances he wouldn't behave this way—these aren't normal circumstances. And he's right, of course; in a world run properly no one would be asking him for money at a time like this. On the other hand, she is correct in saying that she's not responsible for the world's imperfections. She has a right to be treated with courtesy, and his behavior is unacceptable. Nobody is "wrong" here, in a moral sense.

The error is one of communication strategy, not ethics. She should not Blame back at him, because that guarantees the fight presented in the dialogue. This is neither the time nor the place for a fight. Instead of setting up a Blaming loop, she should go to Computer Mode, as in this rewrite.

M: "What's the MATTER with you? How can you POSSIBLY ask me for money when my wife is lying in there SUFFERing? DON'T you have ANY human feelings at ALL?"

F: "People really have a hard time thinking about money when someone they love is in pain."

M: "That's what I mean . . . but I know none of this is your fault."

F: "Everybody wishes things were different, sir."

M: "Me, too . . . me, too. Okay—how much do I owe you?"

When people are Blaming not because they're vicious or angry but because they're in a crisis, Blaming back is absolutely the wrong way to go. The proper move is to get rid of all "I/you" language and talk about "people" and "everybody" and hypothetical situations, to give the distraught person a little breathing room. Usually a response in Computer Mode in such situations will lead the Blamer to switch from Blaming to Leveling. It doesn't matter whether the crisis is a major one, as in the dialogue, or something that strikes you as trivial—when it's clear that the *Blamer* believes it's a crisis, the strategy should be the one shown above.

CHAPTER 6

◆

Breakdown Point: Mountains or Molehills?

Scenario Six

"And I realized, finally, that I was going to have <u>do</u> something about this woman, before she does some serious damage."

Paula handed John another beer, and opened one for her sister. "What do you mean, 'before she does any serious damage'?" she asked him. "I thought Mary was one of your best people."

"She <u>is</u>," he said. "And that's exactly the problem. Mary Clayton is at the point now where, if she were a man, she'd be promoted to a senior executive position. I can't let that happen. Good as she is at her job, she's a hazard to the company. She cracks under pressure, and she doesn't understand how the game is played. She can't keep her personal feelings out of business situations. I can't trust her to handle herself properly in a crisis. But there's no way I can keep her on without promoting her."

"So what did you decide to do about it?" Heather asked. "I mean, you said you decided you had to do something."

John cleared his throat. "You sure you're interested?" he asked them. "And that nothing I say goes beyond this room?"

"Well, of <u>course</u>, John!" Paula said quickly. "Surely you don't need to ask either of those questions!"

"Okay," he said. "I'll explain." And he told them exactly what he'd been doing, how it had been progressing, and what his present assessment of the situation was. It didn't take long, and neither of the women interrupted him—but he didn't like the heavy silence at the end.

"Well?" he said encouragingly. "You said you were interested. How about some feedback?"

The scene that followed amazed him. He had thought they would ask a question or two, to clarify the situation in their minds. And then he'd expected sympathy. Because having to maneuver an employee into leaving, when she's somebody you like and would keep if you could, is a miserable situation. He hadn't thought he'd find himself involved in a row over whether Mary was justified in her behavior and whether he was justified in his. He certainly hadn't anticipated that the pleasant evening would turn into a shouting match. He hadn't expected to find himself facing a furious wife, or a sister-in-law so embarrassed at being in the middle of the fight that she was in tears.

"What's WRONG with you two women?" he heard himself bellowing at one point, knowing he was going to regret it later but unable to stop himself. "WHY do women always have to make a MOUNtain out of EVERY LITTLE MOLEhill? Why don't you BOTH GROW UP?"

◆

What's Going On Here?

John's Point of View

John feels that he ought to be able to relax in his own home and talk casually about problems at the office, without Paula and her sister making a federal case out of it. He can't imagine how the two women could create such a major scene from so little. He resents the fact that, as he sees it, they ganged up on him, and that Paula sided with her sister against him. He's hurt that Paula apparently doesn't understand either his motives or his strategies, and that she seems determined to *mis*understand them. He's embarrassed at having lost his temper when Heather was there; he's embarrassed by the things he remembers yelling late in the argument. It seems to him that Paula could and should have seen the blowup coming and done something to head it off. Before it was over, his heart was pounding, his stomach was in knots, and he had a blazing headache. He feels thoroughly *abused*.

Paula's Point of View

As Paula perceives it, it's awful for John to talk about Mary Clayton as if she were some sort of chess piece, to be moved around in any way that suits his purposes, and as if Mary's feelings are of no importance whatsoever. When he lost his temper and told her that if Mary were a man she wouldn't have reacted that way—and that that makes *her* sexist—she wasn't able to deny it. She suspects that he's right, she's uncomfortable with the suspicion, and she isn't sure why it seems to her that if the victim of John's strategy were a man it would be different. She is above all outraged that John would involve her in a fight like this, especially after it was obvious that she was terribly upset about it, in front of another person—even if that person *is* her sister. It seems to her that he could and should have done something to head off the row.

Heather's Point of View

Heather respects John Gellis and is a little bit afraid of him. She's been present a few times when he was maneuvering someone else into an uncomfortable corner in a conversation or discussion. She's observed that he has a knack for taking people's words and turning them into a noose for their speakers. But she has never before seen him lose control of himself. She has absolutely no idea how the fight got started, but once she was involved in it she felt she had to stand up for what she believes—and she agrees with Paula that John's behavior toward Mary Clayton is disgusting. She knows John is deeply angry; she knows her sister is embarrassed and hurt; she wishes she had stayed home. This, she thinks, is what always happens when you make the mistake of trying to have a serious conversation with a man instead of sticking to small talk and casual matters.

◆

This scenario presents one of the most typical of male/female communication breakdowns. A few people who are fond of each other, who come from roughly the same background and know each other well, are sitting around enjoying what they think is just a pleasant conversation about their daily affairs. And then suddenly, seemingly out of the blue, they're shouting at each other and everything has gone terribly, terribly wrong—and no one quite understands how it happened.

Clients who report an episode of this kind to me almost always ask just one question: "What on earth did I <u>say</u>?" And when they aren't able to identify any single utterance that they feel could have led to the fight—any one awful thing that somebody said—they tend to fall back on the stereotypes. "I guess women just don't have any sense of proportion." "I guess men just can't take criticism from a woman." "I guess women just don't understand anything about business.'' And:''I guess men and women just don't speak the same language.''

What to Do About It—Review

All of the techniques we've been discussing up to this point are needed in a situation like this one. The participants need to:

- Stop and apply Miller's Law before responding to things that sound irrational or outrageous or incomprehensible.
- Use their body language to make their meanings more clear and to alert others to the fact that things are beginning to get out of hand, so that the conversation can be cooled down *before* it blows up in their faces.
- Make an effort either to avoid words that are obviously triggering hostility or to clarify the meanings being given to those words.
- Recognize the Satir Modes being used and respond to them in ways that will keep the hostility from escalating.

This doesn't mean that the speakers must change the subject, or that they should compromise their principles and back down from positions they feel strongly about. It means that they need to use their linguistic skills to establish the kind of rapport and trust that will allow them to continue their discussion *as* a discussion—even when they strongly disagree with one another. They need to be able to tell when matters are beginning to get out of hand, and they need ways to defuse the hostility with no loss of face for anyone involved.

This is rarely *easy* to do when emotions are running high, but it's almost always *possible*. Let's look at another *Gentle Art* technique that can usefully be brought to bear in situations like these: using the Sensory Modes. It has two primary functions:

- Early recognition of situations in which intense verbal conflict is imminent.
- The speedy establishment of mutual trust and rapport.

Technique #5

Using the Sensory Modes

For the techniques introduced previously (using Miller's Law, simultaneous modeling, semantic analysis, and using the Satir Modes) firm information is available about original sources and history if needed. Technique #5 is different. The first source is as likely to have been a parent or kindergarten teacher as a scholar or scientist, and many fields have put the information to good use over time. The earliest references I've been able to find in print are in the books of Carl Jung and Edward T. Hall; you may have encountered the material in discussions of "visual, auditory, and kinesthetic persons" in the literature of Neurolinguistic Programming.

All human beings have to process information from both their external and internal environments. They have to filter the flood of data coming at them down to a quantity that can be managed without overloading their nervous systems. They have to recognize the data they pay attention to and sort it into two classes: those items that must be remembered and those that don't have to be. They have to organize the information they want to keep into a form that can be handled by the short-term (working) memory, and then index the items in such a way that—after transfer to the long-term memory—they can be retrieved when needed. All this, along with many more related tasks, has to be done while people carry out all the other responsibilities of their daily lives at the same time. It's an amazing performance.

The tools used for this processing are the *sensory systems* of the human body: sight, hearing, touch, taste, smell, balance, and so on. Everybody uses all of these systems that are in working order, because they need as much information as possible. However, by the time they are four or five years old (and perhaps much earlier) human beings establish a preference for one of the systems over the others—for the one that helps them the most in perceiving, understanding, learning, and remembering information from their world.

If you spend a good deal of time with someone and pay close attention, you'll be able to determine which sensory system that person prefers. However, there's a faster way to find out: by carefully observing the individual's language. Sensory preferences are often directly reflected in language, especially during communication under stress. In the *Gentle Art* system, this language behavior pattern is called a Sensory Mode.

Let me give you a quick example of how this works. Suppose someone has presented a plan for a new project and asked for your opinion. Suppose you think the plan is a good one, and that you're very impressed with it.

If your preferred sensory system is sight, you'll say something in Sight Mode, like this:

"That looks terrific! I see exactly what you mean—you've made it crystal clear. Let's do it."

If you're an ear person rather than an eye person, you're more likely to say, in Hearing Mode—

"That sounds terrific! It's music to my ears. Let's do it."

And if you are someone who prefers touch to either sight or hearing, you'll say something like this:

"That feels exactly right! You're really in touch with the situation—you've put your finger right on the solution. Let's do it!"

What if you think the presentation is completely unimpressive, and want to make that clear? Sight dominant people say "I don't see what you're saying" and "It doesn't look very good to me" and "Boy, was that a murky presentation!" Hearing dominant people tend toward "I hear you, but it doesn't ring any bells with me" and "It all sounds like a bunch of noise and static, in my opinion." Touch dominant people lean toward "I don't get it, frankly" and "That really rubs me the wrong way" and "I don't think you have a very good grasp of what's going on."

This doesn't work out perfectly, because there may not be a full set of sensory terms for a concept. I can write about an "eye person" and an "ear person," for example, but if I want an equivalent term for the person whose preferred sensory system is touch, I'm in trouble. A finger person? A palm and sole person? A skin person? None of those will serve. This is what linguists call a "lexical gap"—a chunk of meaning for which a language has no surface shape in the form of a word or brief phrase. English once had a word, "felth," which meant the same thing for touch that "sight" means for vision, but that word is no longer used, nor is there an analogous word for hearing. The AME-speaking culture is so strongly biased toward sight as the best of all senses that often a sight term will be readily available but corresponding words for one or more of the other senses will not. And once you get past sight, hearing, and touch, the vocabularies are truly impoverished. If there are people whose preferred sensory system is taste or smell (or one of the less-familiar others) they probably have no way to let the rest of us know that.

Under ordinary circumstances, in casual communication, people can and do shift from one Sensory Mode to another at will. But—as is true for the Satir Modes—people who are tense and under stress have a strong tendency to become locked in to their *preferred* Sensory Mode. The greater the tension and stress, the more likely this is and the tighter the lock will become. This causes predictable changes and predictable difficulties in communication; it also offers predictable opportunities.

- It provides us with a significant cue that tension is building in an interaction. Because when we notice that someone is relying on a single Sensory Mode to the exclusion of all others, we know that's evidence that the person is under stress—it doesn't ordinarily happen when people are relaxed and at ease.

- It provides us with a tool for increasing the trust and rapport we have with others, because it allows us to actively do our best to "speak the same language."

Suppose I suddenly began writing this book in Albanian. You might go on pretending to read it for a while, hoping I'd come to my senses and return to English. But you wouldn't trust me. There'd be no rapport between us. You'd be thinking to yourself, "This is a writer who cares nothing at all about whether she reaches me or not—she's only interested in showing off, or some other agenda of her own. She certainly doesn't care anything about communicating with me!" The same phenomenon occurs when people under stress encounter Sensory Modes other than their preferred ones. The Sensory Modes are all composed of English words, of course, and the difference between Sight Mode and Touch Mode is not equivalent to the difference between English and Albanian. But the problem is the same *type* of problem; it just has a very different scope.

Recognizing and Responding to the Sensory Modes

Recognizing the Sensory Modes is simplicity itself, because one of the ways your native language is cross-indexed in your internal grammar is by sensory vocabulary categories. When you hear "He's the apple of my eye" or "I can't see my way clear to do that" or "From my point of view, the prospects are dim" you don't have to ask yourself which sensory system the words come from. You don't have to go look the information up. You just *know*. The only effort involved in recognizing the sensory patterns is the effort of paying *attention* to them when you're not accustomed to doing so.

The rules for *responding* to the modes after you've recognized the one being used are almost as simple:

✦ **RULE ONE:**   Match the Sensory Mode coming at you.

That is: respond to "How does my plan look to you?" with "I see it as the perfect solution."

✦ **RULE TWO:**   If you can't follow Rule One, use as little sensory language as possible.

That is: if you're asked the same question and you can't think of a Sight Mode response, avoid sensory language altogether and answer with "I think it's terrific." This doesn't provide the advantages that come with Sensory Mode matching, but it lets you avoid a Sensory Mode *clash*. It's a more neutral response.

The simplicity of this technique often causes people in our "no pain, no gain" society to be dubious and to say things like "Nothing that easy could possibly work." That's false. The technique is extremely powerful. It has been working well all over the country in emergency departments and crisis centers. It has proved effective in literacy programs for people who had almost given up on trying to learn to read. It's fail-safe, because there are no situations in which increasing trust and rapport is a bad move. So many things are difficult to learn and use—be glad this is an exception.

The Problem of Touch Dominance

So far as we know, there's nothing *inherently* difficult about being a touch dominant person. There may be cultures in which touch dominance provides a significant advantage. But the AME culture is one in which every child hears from birth that touch is the sensory system we all *disapprove* of. We are a "Don't touch!" and "Keep your hands to yourself!" society. We would never ask children to attend school wearing blindfolds or earplugs, but we *do* expect the child who learns best with the sense of touch to learn standard school subjects alongside eye and ear dominant children while obeying the "Don't touch!" rule—the equivalent of learning to weave while wearing heavy mittens. Not surprisingly, this leads to problems. There are three major reasons why touch dominance is a handicap (usually an unrecognized handicap) in the AME culture.

• The everyday English vocabulary of touch is more limited than that of sight or hearing.

- Strong reliance on the body as a communication source is frowned upon or forbidden, and its expression is all too often misinterpreted as sexual or violent.

- The only high-status professions for which touch dominance is a plus are surgery, sculpture, and tactile arts, all open only to a few fortunate individuals.

As a result, an intimate relationship between two people, one touch dominant and the other eye or ear dominant, is almost certain to face special problems. By the time touch dominant persons are adults they have usually acquired negative labels such as "withdrawn," "difficult," "uncooperative," "hostile," and the like. Because of their communication difficulties and the negative experiences those difficulties inevitably lead to, touch dominant adults tend to *believe* the labels. Add to that the fact that communication between couples offers so many opportunities for intense stress—in which both parties are likely to become locked in to their preferred language behavior modes.

How You Can Help

If you are an eye or ear person paired with a touch dominant person, you have probably spent a great deal of your time baffled by his or her behavior. You are likely to spend time serving as a buffer between your partner and other people, with your role being to undo the tangles and misunderstandings. You may serve as a sort of interpreter, explaining your partner's mystifying behavior to others in an attempt to avoid social isolation. When your partner is a sculptor or a surgeon you may find that relatively easy to do (a familiar example is Ellen Craig, wife of the abrasive surgeon on television's "St. Elsewhere" series); otherwise, you may have to deal with embarrassments that drive you to distraction. *You* know that your touch dominant partner is a good and caring and competent person, but getting other people to believe it can be a major undertaking.

The *obvious* solution would be for the touch dominant person to switch to eye or ear dominance. Unfortunately, that appears to be as difficult as switching from left- to right-handedness, or vice versa. In casual interactions the touch dominant person often manages well, but under stress—which is usually the time when fluent communication is needed most—this coping skill frequently disappears, putting the burden on the eye or ear dominant partner. It's like the situation of a couple where one partner has no sense of direction and the other has normal spatial skills; it would be absurd for them to spend half their time *lost* in order to divide the labor of getting where they want to go "fairly."

If you are the eye or ear dominant partner, here are some things you can do to help.

- You can be aware that touch dominance, rather than negative personality characteristics, is the source of the problem. That in itself is a step forward.
- When you notice that your partner is becoming locked into Touch Mode, you can use all the techniques at your disposal to reduce the tension in the situation.
- You can try to use touch vocabulary more often yourself in your communication with your partner. (It's far easier for *you* to do this codeswitching than for your partner to do so. You're not the one with the communication handicap and the long history of negative reactions from others.)
- In all situations of tension and stress, you can do everything possible to follow the two rules on page 112 for using the Sensory Modes.

You will gradually acquire a larger touch vocabulary and begin to feel less awkward using it, over time. To get you started, here are a few suggestions to follow when the conversation is not casual and relaxed.

Items to Avoid:
"I don't see why . . ."
"Now look/Now listen . . ."
"It's perfectly clear . . ."
"Listen here/Look here . . ."
"Try to see it my way . . ."
"If you would just look at it rationally/calmly/like an adult . . ."
"Don't you see what I mean?"
"I see what you're saying."
"As I see it . . ."
"From my point of view . . ."

Items to Use:
"I don't feel . . ."
"Do you feel . . ."
"You've only scratched the surface."

"I don't think you have a firm grasp of . . ."

"If you were in touch with the problem . . ."

"One way to handle this would be . . ."

"How do you feel about . . ."

"This is really rough/hard/hard to handle."

"I don't understand your feelings."

"I don't get it."

"I can't seem to put my finger on the source of the problem."

"I can't seem to get a grip on . . ."

"Do you get what I mean?"

Another Look at Scenario Six

Most of the unpleasant language that would—in a novel or a play—have been part of Scenario Six was summarized on page 106. Let's go back and expand one likely sequence from that summary and take a good look at it in the context of the Sensory Modes technique. In the dialogue below, John is trying to defend himself and Heather is trying to stand up for her principles. They're both very angry, and elegance of expression is not on their minds.

John: "I don't see any reason for all these emotional reactions! It's only business—it's not anything personal!"

Heather: "It is personal! Mary's got feelings! She's not . . . she's not just a stick of wood! You've got no RIGHT to just push her around and manipulate her life for your own purposes!"

John: "Now look, Heather, you're completely in the dark here! You don't know anything about—"

Heather: "I know what's right! I know how I'd feel in her place! It's very slick for you to set yourself up as above everything and only dealing with issues, but it's hard on other people! You're out of touch with reality, John!"

John: "I'M out of touch with reality! Hey, you have the most distorted point of view I ever saw in my life! Do you really think I'm going to stand by and watch Mary Clayton wreck my business just because—"

Heather: "That's NOT what I was getting at! The point is, you should give it to her straight, John, instead of playing tricks on her and deliberately putting her in tight spots where you <u>know</u> she's going to have a hard time! Just give her the TRUTH!''

John: "Can't you see that if I did that Mary would sue me—and win? Can't you SEE THAT?''

This is a typical verbal confrontation in which Sensory Mode mismatch is making a bad situation worse. Heather is locked tightly in Touch Mode, John is locked in Sight Mode, and the interaction is out of control. The longer this goes on, the more their frustration with each other will increase and the fiercer the argument will become. At any point in the sequence, one of these two could switch to the other's Sensory Mode to reduce the level of hostility. For example, John could switch to the touch vocabulary:

Heather: "You're out of touch with reality, John!''

John: "I don't think that's the problem, Heather. The way I feel, <u>you're</u> out of touch with the cold hard facts about business in the United States today and that's why we're so far apart on this!''

Or Heather could switch to Sight Mode:

John: "It's only business—it's not anything personal!''

Heather: "It doesn't look that way to me, John. As I see it, it couldn't <u>be</u> more personal. And I believe you'd see it my way if you'd think about it <u>care</u>fully!''

Alternatively, either John or Heather could use the second Sensory Mode rule and just avoid using sensory language at all. Notice that these changes don't require either person to back down from the positions they're taking. They don't have to placate or compromise. Like speaking the other person's native language, matching Sensory Modes is a way to remove *unnecessary* barriers to understanding and make it possible to disagree without the discussion turning into a knock-down drag-out.

Dialogues for Analysis

DIALOGUE ONE

M: "I don't get it. Sorry.''

F: "You're not listening, <u>that's</u> why!''

M: "I'm sitting right here. You've got my full attention."

F: "But you're not <u>listening</u>! If you were, you wouldn't be telling me you don't get it!"

He is relying on Touch Mode; she's relying on Hearing Mode. They can go on like this, back and forth, getting more and more annoyed. Or they can attempt to communicate on the same wavelength, as in these rewrites.

She Switches to Touch Mode:

M: "I don't get it. Sorry."

F: "I don't feel like you're listening. It's hard to follow somebody else's words when your mind is a million miles away."

M: "You're right; I wasn't really paying attention. Could you go over it one more time?"

F: "Sure."

He Switches to Hearing Mode:

M: "I don't get it. Sorry."

F: "You're not listening, <u>that's</u> why!"

M: "I've heard every single word you've been saying; you've had my total attention."

F: "Then I must not be talking carefully enough. How about if I try to say it one more time?"

M: "Sure."

DIALOGUE TWO

M: "The way I see it, we need at least two more salespeople in here."

F: "You've got no grasp of the problem at all."

M: "Look, I've worked here as long as <u>you</u> have!"

F: "Yes, but you're completely out of touch with <u>reality</u>!"

M: "Just once, would you look at the big picture? <u>Just once</u>?"

Here we have a man using Sight Mode and a woman in Touch Mode, arguing over problems at work. Either one could switch modes to be more syntonic (more "in tune") with the other, and to slow down the growing

tension in the interaction. Suppose, however, that this man feels uncomfortable with the touch vocabulary, and isn't willing to make the effort
to use it. In that case, when he hears the woman say "You've got no
grasp of the problem at all" he can use the second Sensory Mode rule
and avoid sensory language altogether. In this rewrite, he chooses words
from the *cognitive* vocabulary to replace the sensory ones.

M: "The way I see it, we need at least two more salespeople in
here."

F: "You've got no grasp of the problem at all."

M: "You know, I've worked here as long as you have."

F: "Yes, you have. But I don't feel like you've got all the facts you
need to make this decision."

M: "I think what we have to do is consider the store as a <u>whole</u>
instead of concentrating our ideas on just this one department."

They will still disagree; the Sensory Mode technique isn't magic. But
it helps keep differences of opinion from becoming *fights*, and that's a
large improvement for so small an amount of effort.

Remember the last time you tried to carry on a serious discussion in
a noisy restaurant? The extra effort it takes to hear in a noisy environment
increases the difficulty of understanding and making yourself understood.
Sensory Mode mismatch is like that—a kind of ongoing noise. Fortunately, it's an easy noise to get rid of.

DIALOGUE THREE

M: "How did my mother look to you?"

F: "How did she look? I don't know. Okay, I guess."

M: "Was she wearing the robe we gave her, or what?"

F: "Honey, I don't remember. But she <u>sounded</u> absolutely great! Her
voice was strong, and—"

M: "I don't believe this! You spent a whole <u>hour</u> with my mother at
the hospital and you didn't even look to see what she was
<u>wearing</u>?"

F: "You don't have to <u>yell</u> at me!"

M: "<u>I'm not</u> YELLING!"

F: "You ARE yelling! If you don't like the reports you get from me,
you can just go visit your mother <u>yourSELF</u>!"

He prefers Sight Mode; she prefers Hearing Mode. The fact that she has a vivid memory of her hospitalized mother-in-law's voice, but no recollection at all of her appearance, is typical of ear people. The more genuinely concerned she was about the other woman, the more she would be likely to rely on the sensory system she trusts the most to give her important information. Her husband, on the other hand, feels completely in the dark about his mother's condition when he is only told how she *sounded*, and it worries him. The result is two people who care about each other and about his mother—but end up sounding uncaring, petty, and cross.

It's too late for her to pay attention to the visual information he wanted her to bring him, and it's too late for him to ask her specifically to make sure she'll be able to describe the way his mother looks and what she was wearing. He needs to remember that unless he does make it specific, his wife is likely to forget everything but what she hears, especially in a hospital setting where it's difficult to be anything but tense. She needs to remember, even if he forgets to be specific, that when her husband asks her to tell him about something he will always want to know how things *looked*. In the meantime, they might be less likely to get angry at each other if one of them would switch to the other's preferred mode at some point in the dialogue—and the sooner the better. Since it's *his* mother who's sick, it would be appropriate for *her* to make that effort. For example:

M: "How did my mother look to you?"

F: "Oh, dear—of course you'd want to know that! I'm sorry, honey, I was so concerned about her that I forgot. Next time I go see her, I promise you I'll bring you back a full report about how she looks."

DIALOGUE FOUR

F: "Now do you see what I mean?"

M: "So far, I haven't heard anything that even sounds <u>promising</u>."

F: "But you haven't even <u>looked</u> at the proposal! That's not FAIR!"

M: "Listen . . . YELLING at me isn't going to change my mind!"

When you pay attention to people's Sensory Mode preferences, you will probably be surprised at how often you hear exchanges like the first two lines in this dialogue. "How does it look?" And then "It sounds pretty good!" And neither person notices anything odd about that. The brain doesn't process language for understanding literally, word by word; what is stored is the extracted *meaning*. The shared meaning in "How does it look?"/"It sounds pretty good!" is something like "What is your perception of it?" and "My perception is pretty positive." As long as no one notices and the conversation goes smoothly, there's no reason to change. But that's not the situation in this dialogue, where a sight dominant woman and a hearing dominant man appear headed for a fight.

Suggestion for Him: Switch to Sight Mode and say "So far, I haven't seen anything that even looks promising." You will have transmitted essentially the same negative message about the proposal itself, but you're also sending a metamessage: "I perceive the world the way you do; we have that in common." That makes your criticism easier for her to accept. And she won't be able to respond with "But you haven't even looked at the proposal!" You will have removed that option.

Suggestion for Her: He obviously isn't responding with enthusiasm to your proposal, and irritating him further is unlikely to help you make your case. Try matching his Mode, as in this rewrite.

F: "Now do you see what I mean?"

M: "So far, I haven't heard anything that even sounds promising."

F: "Maybe that's because I keep trying to show you when I should be telling you. Let me put all this stuff away and just sit down and try to explain."

She has gone beyond word choice here and made a wise move. When you're facing a strong negative reaction from a person whose preferred sensory system is hearing, an array of impressive "visuals" is useless. You can show snazzy graphics and four-color glossies and animation as long as you like—you'll be wasting your time. The hearing dominant person will not be impressed, will probably be bored, and may even be annoyed. The proper strategy is to stop presenting visual information and start tailoring the message for the *ear* instead of the eye.

DIALOGUE FIVE

F: "Sorry—I don't get it."

M: "Well, of course not! You haven't even looked at it!"

F: "All that information is already in my head. I don't have to read about it."

M: "But you're not seeing it the way I see it at all!"

F: "Exactly! You put your finger right on the problem that time!"

M: "It looks to me like you're not willing to even try to understand what I'm suggesting!"

This is unlikely to get any better unless a change is made. Both of these people are irritated, and the hostility level is increasing. I suggest a rewrite.

F: "Sorry—I don't get it."

M: "Can you explain to me exactly where you started feeling that you didn't understand?"

F: "All that information is already in my head. My problem is that I don't understand how—using that information—you got to the conclusion you reached."

M: "I think you'll find that the data on pages fifteen and nineteen are brand new. If you had those missing pieces in place, I'm confident that you'd feel differently about the proposal."

DIALOGUE SIX

M: "These figures are music to my ears!"

F: "I see."

M: "Well, thanks for the vote of confidence!"

F: "How can I be excited over figures I haven't even seen?"

M: "You heard me say they were great, didn't you? Why do I always have to prove everything to you?"

For him, information for the ear—auditory information—coming from a source he trusts, is adequate information; he doesn't feel a need for anything more than that. She feels the same way about information that she *sees*; it's hard for her to understand and remember things on the basis of sound alone. (She's like my sight dominant husband, who can't understand a cassette tape properly unless he has his glasses on while he listens to it.) But this man is leaping to a false conclusion when he decides that she doesn't trust *him* personally. She needs to either explain that to him at the end of the dialogue or head off the misunderstanding before it happens. I suggest this rewrite.

M: "These figures are music to my ears!"

F: "I see."

M: "Well, thanks for the vote of <u>con</u>fidence!"

F: "You know me well enough to understand that things don't seem real to me unless I can see them; how about <u>showing</u> me those numbers so I can congratulate you properly?"

DIALOGUE SEVEN

F: "If you see anything you like, let me know and I'll pull over."

M: "How am I going to know whether I like it if all I get to do is look?"

F: "But we can't go through every single one of these model homes!"

M: "Then we might as well go on home; we're wasting our time."

F: "WHY do you always have to be like this?"

This man can't get enough information by simply looking at a house from the street even to know whether he's *interested* in going inside. The appearance of the outside of the house isn't information he values, and he can't use it to visualize the inside. He needs the data that he gets from having the house *around* him—from moving around inside it and "getting the feel of the place."

Presumably his wife would like to find a house that they both like well enough to want to buy it. She wouldn't buy a house without seeing it; she should realize that it's exactly the same for him—he's not going to buy one without "feeling" it. He wants to do the same process of gathering and comparing information that she is doing as she drives along the street and looks at each house in turn. Her best move when he says they might as well go home is to say "Tell you what—let's compromise. Let's start by going through every other house." Asking "WHY do you always have to be like this?" is like asking him why he "always has to" have brown eyes or be six feet tall.

◆
_____ ◆ _____

CHAPTER 7

How to Complain—
And Still Be Heard

_____ **Scenario Seven** _____

"I'm here today, John," said Mary, "because I feel that we
need to clear the air on a few things."

"Good enough," he answered. "What's on your mind?"

"First, I want you to know that I was very distressed by the
way our last meeting turned out. As I told you then, you caught
me by surprise and I handled the situation badly. It would be
helpful to me if—before you call me in for anything of that kind
again—you give me a little warning. You could call me and tell
me what the subject to be discussed is, or send me a quick
confidential memo."

"All right," he said. "I'll be glad to do that. And I agree
with you—that was an ugly meeting."

"Yes, it was."

"Next?"

Mary frowned, and looked at him carefully; he seemed
neutrally pleasant and attentive. She relaxed as much as was
possible under the circumstances, and squared her shoulders.

"John," she said, "I'm very concerned. Something has to be
done."

"About?"

"About the fact that I am constantly subjected to sexist
language in this company, from you, and from the other men as
well. It won't do, John; it's intolerable. It's <u>wrong</u>. It has to
stop."

"Uhuh . . . ." John cleared his throat. "I see. Okay, you give me a list of the sentences you don't want said in your presence, and I'll send everybody a copy.''

"John," Mary snapped, "please be serious. Don't trivialize this!''

"So far as I know," he answered, "it is trivial. That is: So far as I know nobody has fondled you. Nobody has ordered you to have sex with him or get fired. Nobody has used obscene language around you. Nobody has done anything—you correct me if I'm wrong—except tell you that you're an attractive woman. Politely.''

"It's not just that!" she protested.

"Oh?" John reached for a pad of yellow paper and picked up his pen. "You've got a formal complaint of sexual harassment? Somebody has laid a disrespectful hand on you? Told a dirty joke in front of you? Give me the details, Mary, and I'll deal with it immediately.''

"John," she said, "nobody here is that kind of person. You know that as well as I do. What I'm objecting to, because it makes it impossible for me to do my best work, is much more subtle than the kinds of things you're talking about.''

"Mmmhmm," he said. "You mean that if men compliment you you can't keep your mind on your work? You get upset, and it interferes with your performance? Is that what you mean? I've noticed that myself, a number of times, and it's worried me. I've wondered if you wouldn't perhaps be happier working somewhere where your colleagues were all women. Have you considered that option?''

"John! That's totally unfair! You're doing exactly what you always do! Twisting my words! Turning everything I say upside down! Flatly refusing to carry on an adult conversation! Acting like—''

"Mary," he interrupted, "I'm not the one acting like a child at the moment. I'm not the one who's shouting and jumping up and down. You are.''

"I am not jumping up and down!''

"All right; I withdraw that. You're only shouting.''

Mary stood up, hands on hips, and she spoke to him quietly, but she spat the words one by one between her teeth.

"Talking to you," she said, "is like talking to a brick wall! You ought to be ashamed!''

"Of telling you you're pretty? And not firing Bill for saying you looked good in your black sweater? Sorry. I don't follow you.''

"John, please.'' She sat back down and folded her hands in her lap. "Forgive me for losing my temper. Please . . . just sit there, without interrupting, and let me give you some specific examples of the kind of things I'm complaining about.''

He shifted to his Great Stone Face posture, but she had been expecting that; it didn't put her off balance this time. And she began telling him, in careful detail, about two incidents she was sure would make her position clear.

She'd been talking a good five minutes before she realized that not one word of her carefully rehearsed account was getting through to him.

◆

What's Going On Here?

Mary's Point of View

As Mary perceives it, she is constantly subjected to remarks and behavior from the men in the office carrying a single metamessage: YOU'RE A WOMAN, WHICH MEANS YOU'RE NOT ONE OF THE GANG, AND WE DON'T INTEND TO LET YOU FORGET IT. She feels that she has every right to complain and to demand that the behavior be changed. She knows that a formal complaint of this kind has to be supported with facts and detailed evidence, and she has taken great pains to be sure that her account meets those standards and cannot be described as "subjective" or "emotional." But John didn't give her a fair hearing; his mind was made up in advance. She could tell from his body language that his surface compliance hid inner contempt. The words he would have liked to say were written all over him: "Only a woman could take trivial little bits of normal casual behavior and turn them into insults the way you're doing! You're a FLAKE!'' It seems hopeless. It seems to her that there's no point in trying to make him understand. She can't go on working in an environment like this; it's time to admit that, and resign.

John's Point of View

As John perceives it, Mary really *is* being a flake, and the things she's complaining to him about are so trivial, so innocuous, that no normal person could consider them cause for a complaint to the boss. Sure, she might take offense and tell the person that she didn't care for what he was saying. But making a formal complaint? It seems to him that it takes an exceedingly fertile imagination to find cause for that in the examples she's offering him. He has been very careful to do nothing she could possibly find improper; it appears to him, listening to her examples of "subtle sexism," that the rest of the men in the firm have done the same.

Up to this point John has seen all of this as in many ways a game, but now Mary has made him angry. Who does she think she *is*, anyway, ordering him around? Trying to impose her own standards of behavior on everybody else, when they've bent over backwards to treat her fairly and courteously? He finds her arrogant and narrow-minded, and he wonders how she expects to get along in this world with an attitude like hers. It will be a relief to him, he realizes, when she's finally gone.

This is an unsavory demonstration of communication gone wrong. Mary hears John's words during their confrontation, but she tunes out much of his body language and overlooks signals she should pay close attention to. In addition, she is so concerned about saying exactly the right words that she fails to be careful about her own body language. Because "the way she says it" strikes John as so arrogant, he stops listening to her, closes his mind firmly against her, and acts not on the basis of her account but on the basis of his own feelings—especially his outrage at what he perceives as an attempt to give him *orders*, coming from someone who has no authority over him and, in his opinion, no acceptable reason to complain.

Mary may be correct in her claim that she's subject to subtle sexism from the men. John may be correct in concluding that she overreacts and reads imaginary insults into interactions where no insults exist. If they were communicating properly, they could probably sort matters out and come to some reasonable conclusion. But no useful communication is possible under *these* circumstances.

What to Do About It—Speech Acts

The theory of speech acts, first introduced formally by J. L. Austin in his 1962 book, *How to Do Things with Words* (London: Oxford University Press), has proved very useful in linguistic analysis. Every utterance exists both as its semantic content and as a speech act—as a command, a promise, a threat, a request, a question, etc. If every sentence had a marker identifying its speech act category unambiguously, communication would be simpler; there are languages that attempt to do that. But English isn't structured that way. Some of the most interesting problems in linguistics take up such issues as how we English speakers know, when someone says "Why don't you make some coffee?" that we're not hearing a question, and how we recognize "I wonder if you could open the window" as an indirect command.

Speech acts have a potential for causing trouble in at least three situations:

• When the speaker intends one speech act and the listener understands a different one (as when someone understands another person to have made a promise and no promise was intended)

• When the listener reacts not to the content of the utterance but to its speech act category (as when someone is angry not about what he or she was ordered to do but at having been given *any* order)

• When the listener has doubts about the qualifications of the speaker or of the utterance (as when someone who the listener believes is not legally empowered to do so says "I now pronounce you man and wife"— or someone who does have the necessary qualifications says "I think you're man and wife now")

All of these potential complications were factors in Scenario Seven. Mary didn't intend to give John direct orders, but he understood many of her sentences that way, and his negative reaction to what he heard as her commands and complaints made it impossible for him to understand their content properly. He also felt that she didn't qualify to give him orders and that her complaints failed to measure up *as* complaints.

Complaining is a normal part of human life; we all have to complain to other people from time to time. Few things are as counterproductive and as sure to guarantee a miserable relationship as feeling resentment about another's behavior and not expressing it, while neither forgetting nor forgiving. Such suppressed resentment *festers* and becomes a permanent barrier to communication. However, essential as they are, every complaint has two strikes against it before it's made:

• First: it contains a message that the other person's behavior has something wrong with it, which pleases nobody.

• Second: every complaint includes as a metamessage either the com-

mand "Change your behavior" or a request—an *indirect* command—
that it be changed.

Most adults have an automatic kneejerk negative reaction to the presuppositions that go with a command from another adult. Those presuppositions include: "I am telling you to do this, I have the right to tell you
to do this, and it's something I believe you are able to do." When that
negative reaction occurs, the person spoken to doesn't consider the actual
content of the complaint. It could be something the "complainee" has
no objection at all to going along with; that makes no difference. The
negative reaction is a response to the fact that a complaint is being *made*.
This is a waste of time for everyone involved; fortunately, a useful
technique is available for dealing with the problem.

Technique #6
Using Three-Part Messages

This technique began with a language pattern called the "I-message," as
in "I feel sad when you forget our anniversary." Thomas Gordon, whose
Effectiveness Training workshops have been so helpful to so many people,
developed the "I-message" concept into what he called the "three-part
assertion message." (Gordon 1977) In the *Gentle Art* system it is developed further and is called simply a "three-part message."

In my experience, assertiveness training, although useful for people
with minor communication problems, can be dangerous for those whose
difficulties are severe. *People who always say the wrong thing come out
of assertiveness training saying the wrong thing far more eloquently; this
is not an improvement.* The three-part message isn't a pattern for "assertion of one's rights" (although it may often serve that purpose); it's a
pattern for structuring complaints so as to bypass as much as possible of
the automatic negative reaction they provoke in most AME-speaking
adults. It looks like this:

✦   "When you [X], I feel [Y], because [Z]."

        1   2   3

The pattern must be adhered to strictly, because any monkeying
around with it inevitably ruins it. Each of the variables (X, Y, Z) must
be filled with something that is verifiable in the real world and about
which, as far as is possible, there cannot be any argument. Let's consider

the three parts separately, to see how each one is put together and what purpose it serves.

Constructing Part One of the Three-Part Message

[X] represents the item of behavior the speaker wants changed, and is verifiable because it can be directly observed. The goal should always be to fill it with just *one* item, unless there's no way to avoid including another one because the two are inextricably linked in some fashion. All of the sequences in #1 below meet the requirements for Part One.

1. a. "When you yell at the clerical staff . . ."
    b. "When you bring the car home with the gas on empty . . ."
    c. "When you overdraw our bank account . . ."
    d. "When you forget to water the tomato plants . . ."
    e. "When you say to me, 'You've got a terrific body' . . ."
    f. "When you don't give me a gift on our anniversary . . ."

But none of the sequences in #2—all of them subjective and subject to argument, and none of them verifiable—could be fit into the pattern.

2. a. "When you act like you're some kind of royalty . . ."
    b. "When you behave the way you do . . ."
    c. "When you mistreat the clerical staff . . ."
    d. "When you refuse to carry your share of the load . . ."
    e. "When you use sexist language in talking to me . . ."
    f. "When you act like our anniversary isn't even important . . ."

A man either yells at the clerical staff or he doesn't; a woman either brings home the car with the gas gauge reading "empty" or she doesn't; a person either presents another person with a gift or doesn't do so. The item of behavior that the speaker wants changed—an item observable in the real world—is made absolutely clear in #1a–f. This is not true for "When you act like you're some kind of royalty" or the empty "When you behave the way you do," or any of the other examples in #2. They are filled with undefined terms, moral judgments, personal ethical positions, and an abundance of material to be argued over.

Completing Part Two

Part Two is the weakest of the three parts, because it's impossible to *directly* verify another person's feelings, but it carries that process as far as it can be carried. [Y] should be filled with the emotion the complainer feels when [X] happens. It should meet three conditions:

- It's an emotion that the complainer considers to be appropriate to the context.
- It's an emotion that the complainer believes other people would consider appropriate.
- It's an emotion consistent with the body language that accompanies the words.

This is the closest thing to verification that's available for personal feelings.

Part Two should never be elaborated into unverifiable statements such as "I feel so angry that I just can't stand it" or "I feel so miserable that I know it has to be bad for me" or "I feel so ashamed that no decent person could be expected to put up with it." The wording should never be changed to "you make me feel [Y]." Just say "I feel . . ." and name the emotion. Here are some good examples:

3. a. "I feel angry . . ."
    b. "I feel distressed . . ."
    c. "I feel frightened . . ."
    d. "I feel frustrated . . ."
    e. "I feel embarrassed . . ."

And here are some examples that *won't* work, for the same reasons that the examples in #2 won't work:

4. a. "I feel like a second-class citizen . . ."
    b. "I feel like somebody in a soap opera . . ."
    c. "I feel persecuted . . ."
    d. "I feel as if you don't respect me at all . . ."
    e. "You make me feel foolish . . ."

The temptation to use "you make me feel [Y]" may be strong, but that change has serious flaws. For one thing, it says to the other person "you have the power to determine what emotion I will feel," and that's bad strategy. If it's true, for heaven's sakes don't admit it! For another, if it's true, it's a separate complaint, and complaining about more than one thing at a time reduces the effectiveness of the message. Finally, the idea that someone "makes" another person feel something is even less verifiable than the feeling itself. Stick to "I feel [Y]," with a single emotion filling the slot.

Completing Part Three

Part Three is where complainers most often run into trouble in constructing these messages. [Z] is the real-world consequence of the behavior being complained about. It must be directly observable and verifiable, not subject to argument, and it must serve as evidence that the complainer *does* have a right to complain. That is: Instead of "I have a right to complain about your behavior and ask you to change it because I'm more powerful and important than you are"—which is sure to provoke hostility, even when it's true—the message is that the right to complain exists because of real-world consequences that reasonable people would want to avoid. Here are some good examples:

5. a. ". . . because someone has to stop their work and turn it off."
    b. ". . . because the plants die afterward."
    c. ". . . because the wrong total appears on the screen."
    d. ". . . because it's too large for the baby to swallow."
    e. ". . . because it costs more than we have in our account."

Examples that don't fit the pattern and won't work are:

6. a. ". . . because no decent person would act that way."
    b. ". . . because it breaks my heart."
    c. ". . . because everybody knows that's a terrible thing to do."
    d. ". . . because it means you don't love me."
    e. ". . . because I can't stand being treated like that."

The Complete Message

Now let's put together a complete message, with all its parts properly constructed:

7. "When you yell at the clerical staff, I feel distressed, because people

who are upset and angry can't type properly and the work doesn't get done.''

This isn't as satisfying to the complainer as—

8. ''When you treat the clerical staff like slaves, you make me furious, because no decent person would behave the way you do.''

—but it's far more likely to be heard, understood, and acted upon. In #8 the behavior to be changed isn't specified, the real-world consequence that justifies the complaint isn't even mentioned, and all three parts of the complaint are subject to argument.

Communication rarely breaks down over differing meanings for words that are concrete, like ''restaurant'' and ''kick.'' When such differences occur, they're usually very obvious and an immediate repair attempt will be made, as in ''How can you call this place a restaurant?'' and ''Hey, you can't kick somebody with a fist! What are you trying to say?'' The three-part message pattern does everything possible to *restrict* complaints to concrete words. Trouble is already likely in complaints between adults because of the built-in power struggle, and when complaints are made across genders, it's even worse. The three-part message can't fix all this; it's not a magic cure-all. What it *can* do, however, is reduce the number of possible semantic boobytraps—and their associated potential for catastrophe—by keeping matters concrete rather than abstract.

I strongly recommend that you construct your three-part messages in advance when you have that option. There'll be times when you don't, because an immediate crisis requires immediate action, or because someone who outranks you has ordered you to deliver an immediate complaint, and you feel that you have to comply. Most of the time, however, you can sit down in advance of making your complaint and write out (or tape record) the message to be sure it has all its snaps and buttons on. This has a number of advantages.

- It provides you with practice, so that when you *do* have to construct a complaint off the top of your head, you're more likely to get it right.
- It gives you a chance to find out—*before* you say the words aloud—whether you'd be embarrassed to hear them coming out of your mouth.
- It gives you the opportunity to discover that you're unable to complete one or more of the three parts—which means one of three things:

1. You don't really have a complaint.
2. You don't understand the complaint well enough yet to construct it properly.
3. You have chosen the wrong speech act for dealing with the problem.

Suppose you start with "When you don't give me a present on my birthday, I feel sad, because . . ." and discover that you haven't the remotest idea what real-world consequence could be used to finish the sentence. "Because my father always gave my <u>mother</u> a birthday present" is one of those things you'd rather not hear yourself say, as is "Because none of the women I dated before I married <u>you</u> ever forgot to give me a birthday present." "Because it means you don't love me" obviously isn't directly verifiable in the real world and is *very* subject to argument. "Because no decent person neglects his wife/her husband that way" is out. "Because it breaks my heart" clearly won't do it.

Until you can complete that third part of the message, this is not the other person's problem—it's yours. It makes no difference how serious or trivial the problem is: If *you* don't know what real-world consequence gives you the right to complain, you can't expect the complainee to know. Similarly, if you don't know what behavior you want changed, or what emotion you feel about that behavior, it's absurd to expect the other person to have that information or act on it.

Another Look at Scenario Seven

In this scenario, just about everything that could go wrong did. The time Mary spent constructing careful and compelling arguments for her position was wasted, because John didn't listen to them. And the time both John and Mary spent in the interaction was wasted, because they only made their existing disagreements worse. Given the amount of tension and bad feeling between them, that's not surprising, but it wasn't inevitable.

Let's consider for a moment the often-neglected question of communication *strategy*. Mary initiated the meeting with John, and she didn't have small talk in mind. What she could have done to change the outcome of the scenario depends on which of three possible sets of goals she was working toward.

•   If Mary's goals were (a) to become involved in an argument with John, (b) to express her anger and frustration, and (c) to win the argument, that's one thing. We could say that she accomplished the first two goals but was unable to accomplish the third. Her tactics were almost guaranteed to provoke the argument she wanted and to provide her with opportunities to express her feelings. But once she made John so angry that he stopped listening to her, she lost any chance she might have had to *win*. He outranks her; he has the power to refuse to do what she wants done; and he can yell louder than she can. (And it must be pointed out that winning arguments in a situation like this, essentially by force, accomplishes nothing for the long term. The loser will resent the loss and seek future opportunities to get revenge.)

• If Mary's goal was to educate John about subtle sexism—to "raise his consciousness"—that's something else again, and we would have to say that she failed completely to accomplish it. *People who are too angry to listen cannot be educated*. Mary would have had to revise her words and her body language in such a way that John would be willing to listen to her and take part in a relatively calm *discussion* of the issues.

• If Mary's goals were to gain John's agreement that his own behavior and that of the other men in the office is sexist and should be changed, and to persuade him to take action toward that change—again, she failed.

In each of these cases, the anger Mary provoked in John made it impossible for her to achieve her goals.

What if her strategy had been different? What if she had paid attention to the clear warnings that John was becoming too angry to listen? What if she had changed her words and body language to avoid the impression that she was there to give orders? Could she then have used the three-part message technique to turn the scenario around?

Yes. But she would have had to do some preliminary work, because the consequences of "subtle sexism" are rarely concrete. She could easily have completed Part One of the message, starting with "When you and the other men . . ." and filling in [X] with one of the incidents that troubles her. Part Two—"I feel angry" or "I feel distressed"—would have been simple enough. But Part Three is harder to construct in this situation, because none of the behaviors that Mary is concerned about has an *obvious* real-world consequence that she can point to.

Suppose she wanted to begin with: "When you and the other men make comments about my physical appearance, I feel distressed, because. . . ." Because *what*? This is very different from "When you forget to water the tomatoes, I feel angry, because they die." She can complete this message, but only if she carefully prepares the ground first. For example:

Mary: "John, I'm here today because I have a problem that I'd like to talk to you about."

Notice: she hasn't said that "we" need to do anything; she says that *she* has a problem she wants to talk about.

John: "Good enough. What's on your mind?"

Mary: "I feel as if I were the only person on the team who didn't get a uniform—that's what's on my mind."

Notice: she has moved directly to the issue, instead of first reminding him of their previous argument. She has stepped inside the "game" framework that she knows he's comfortable with, by using an image framed in sports language to sum up her feelings. And she has refrained from issuing any "decrees" such as "It has to stop."

John: "I don't follow you."

Mary: "Suppose you worked in an office where you were the only man, John. Suppose that when you walked into a room where people were talking, there was an immediate silence—and then one of the women told you how handsome you looked and everyone else snickered. Suppose that when you were entitled to hear that you'd done a good job you were told that you owed your success to the shirt you had on. Would you be comfortable in that situation?"

John: "Is that what it's like for you around here?"

Mary: "Yes. That's exactly what it's like."

Now Mary has put in place a very different set of circumstances. She has told John why she felt she had to talk to him, without making him furious and shutting off all possibility of proceeding. She has bypassed the difficulty of finding exactly the right words by putting John in the *same* situation, hypothetically—where he would have the same difficulty clarifying and defending his feelings that she has. With that accomplished, she can go on to introduce three-part messages that end with statements such as "because feedback based on physical appearance tells me nothing about the quality of my work." She can safely assume that John will be able to verify such "because" statements, despite their slightly abstract character, because they are statements he could imagine making *himself* in the analogous situation she has described.

The final question is, of course: Is there anything John could have done to improve matters? We know *his* goal is to make Mary so confused and miserable that she'll resign. For that goal, the original scenario could hardly be improved upon, and he needs to make no changes. But if his goal had been to find a way to bridge the gap that's widened between him and Mary, what could he have done?

His proper strategy in that case would have been to stop Mary almost immediately, as soon as he began to feel angry, and to use either Leveler or Computer Mode to negotiate a major change in the language behavior being used.

If John Used Leveler Mode:

"Mary, this isn't going to work. Something about the words you're saying or the way you're saying them is shutting down everything for me except irritation. I want you to know that if we go on like this, I'm not likely to understand a word you're saying. Let's start this conversation over again from scratch."

If John Used Computer Mode:

"Mary, when the only reaction someone's words or body language set off in the listener is irritation, the chances that person has of being understood are very limited. Starting the conversation over from scratch is probably the best move in situations like that."

Either of those utterances would have given Mary an unmistakable signal that the interaction was headed for communication breakdown, before it was too late to try to head it off or repair it.

Dialogues for Analysis

DIALOGUE ONE

M: "I need to talk to you sometime this morning."
F: [PAUSE] "What have you done now?"

In this dialogue we see a woman deciding, on the basis of no perceptible evidence, that she's hearing a *warning* rather than a simple statement. She may be right, but consider the consequences of her choice. Suppose he *has* done something awful—wrecked the car, or overdrawn the bank account, or lost the dog. That in itself guarantees unpleasantness. He will already be on the defensive and his feelings of guilt will be interfering with his ability to communicate effectively. By pouncing on him in this way, as if no possibility other than disaster existed, she will increase both his defensiveness and his guilt; this can't possibly help matters. If, on the other hand, he's done nothing she could disapprove of and was only making a statement of the facts, she has accused him falsely, which also has no possible positive consequences. A line like the one she uses here is always a no-win linguistic move.

DIALOGUE TWO

F: "What a horrible thing to say to me! How <u>could</u> you!"

M: "Oh, come on! It wasn't <u>that</u> bad!"

F: "Wait a minute! You really <u>hurt</u> me, saying that! It WAS that bad!"

M: "Hey, I didn't mean anything by it! I was only KIDding, for crying out loud!"

One of the most common strategies used in verbal abuse is the one shown in this dialogue. The attacker says something abusive; then, when the person attacked reacts more strongly than was anticipated, the attacker claims to have been "only kidding." Typically, attackers deliver the "only kidding" line with body language indicating that *they* are the ones being abused. Far too often, this works; far too often, you could add the following final line:

F: "Oh, <u>I'm</u> sorry! I guess I shouldn't be so sensitive!"

Dialogue Two is entirely "unisex." You can switch the F's and M's throughout, with no need for any change.

As long as verbal abusers of either gender can get away with issuing verbal attacks and then claiming that a joke was the speech act they intended, this strategy will continue to pollute the linguistic environment. A better final line (from either gender) is this one, said firmly, with full eye contact, and without sarcastic intonation:

X: "You were kidding? All right, I'll give you the benefit of the doubt; maybe I misunderstood you. And I'm sure there will be no possibility of a similar misunderstanding in the future, because now you are <u>aware</u> that I find the sort of thing you said offensive, not funny. I'm sure it won't happen again.''

What if there is a *genuine* misunderstanding? What if the woman in Dialogue Two really is only imagining things? What if he had nothing but the best intentions and is astonished by her reaction? Then Dialogue Three would be appropriate.

DIALOGUE THREE

M: ''I've obviously offended you. I had no such intention—I really thought what I said was funny.''

F: ''Well, I didn't think it was the least <u>bit</u> funny!''

M: ''I understand that, and I apologize. However, in the same way that you insist on making it clear to me that you're not amused, I insist on making it clear that that amazes me. If you want to discuss it, I'm willing.''

The point of discussing the misunderstood attempt at humor is not to change either party's mind about what's funny. That's usually impossible. The point of a discussion is to find out, in a neutral interaction, where the *limits* are. She may consider all ethnic jokes offensive but enjoy sexual jokes that aren't just schoolyard humor. He may find jokes about his *own* ethnic group funny but object to all others; he may find all jokes about his personal appearance unacceptable. They may both find all religious jokes offensive, but enjoy jokes about politics. Once they know where the lines are drawn, they can refrain from saying ''funny'' things they know will offend the other person. Because humor is such a personal matter, the occasional mistake will still happen, but it should be rare.

DIALOGUE FOUR

F: ''When you act the way you do, <u>you</u> make me feel like some kind of second-class <u>citizen</u>! It's dis<u>gusting</u>!''

M: ''I don't know what you're talking about.''

F: ''You do too! You know perfectly well!''

M: ''I don't. I don't have any <u>idea</u> what you're talking about!''

F: ''How can you stand there and SAY that to me?! You DO know! DON'T TELL me you don't know!''

M: ''Okay, I won't tell you—but I STILL don't know!''

This exchange is going nowhere. It's totally counterproductive, and is the linguistic equivalent of an unskilled fistfight. He may have done something that justifies her anger and her complaint, and he may know what it was, or she may have imagined the whole thing; there's no way to tell. And instead of airing her grievance, they are arguing about whether or not he knows what that grievance *is*!

Let's assume that she has come home from work and found such a mess in the kitchen—from snacks he made for himself earlier—that she can't start cooking dinner until she either spends fifteen minutes cleaning it up herself or goes through the process of getting him to clean it up. Let's assume that this has happened several times before and that she has already told him how much she objects to it. That would account for the emotional content of her opening line in Dialogue Four. She could then use the following three-part message:

F: "When you leave a mess in the kitchen after work, I feel really angry, because I can't start cooking dinner until it's cleaned up."

Notice that she doesn't say "because only children make messes and just walk off and leave them" or "because it's bad enough having to come home and make dinner without having your messes to deal with." Telling him off is not the point; the point is to get him to stop messing up the kitchen.

DIALOGUE FIVE

M: "I'm <u>sick</u> of the way you waste money! We both work hard earning it, but <u>you</u> work even harder <u>spending</u> it!"

F: "I'm no more extravagant than <u>you</u> are!"

M: "Oh, yeah? How about that <u>dress</u> you bought yesterday? <u>You</u> don't need that dress!"

F: "I suppose <u>you</u> needed those two new <u>shirts</u> I saw in your closet!"

M: "I only have five shirts! You must have <u>fifty</u> dresses!"

F: "I do <u>not</u> have fifty dresses! That's ridiculous! And—"

And so on. He will bring up her purchases for attack and defend his own; she will bring up his for attack and defend hers; and nothing at all will be accomplished. I suggest a rewrite. With *facts*.

M: "When you spend sixty-five dollars on a new dress, I feel angry, because it brings our bank balance down to two hundred dollars and we can't put any money in savings this month."

Now she might say a number of things, including these three:

F: "That's all right. I don't mind skipping the savings once in a while."

F: "That's all right. We can put a double payment in savings next month."

F: "I'm sorry; I didn't realize the account was that low."

Now they can discuss the fact that regular savings matter more to him than they do to her, or the fact that she feels she had a legitimate reason to buy the dress that justifies skipping the savings, or the fact that she wrote a check without checking the bank balance to see if she could afford it, or the fact that he complained about her purchase of the dress without first asking her why she bought it and listening to her explanation. This means arguing, sure. But it's a vast improvement over arguing about which one of them is the more extravagant person.

DIALOGUE SIX

M: "Whew, what a day! It's crazy out there!"
F: "I know. Me, too."
M: "Really? What did you do, break a fingernail?"

Nothing available for punctuation will tell us what tone of voice he's using for that line. There are three likely possibilities: tender, humorous, and vicious.

M: (Tenderly.) "Really? What did you do, break a fingernail?"
F: "It was rough around here, honey—I'm serious."
M: "I'm sorry. I was patronizing you again."
F: "Yes, you were. It doesn't help."

M: (Humorously.) "Really? What did you do, break a fingernail?"
F: "No. No broken fingernails. A pickup truck sideswiped me on the way to work and totaled my car."

M: "Oh, my god. . . . I don't know what to say."

F: "Try this: 'Are you all right?' "

M: (Viciously.) "Really? What did you do, break a fingernail?"

F: "You're a pig, you know that?"

None of these variations could be considered pleasant conversation. It would be far better to just eliminate gratuitous sarcasm like "What did you do, break a fingernail?" from your language inventory.

DIALOGUE SEVEN

M: "How could you forget my birthday again??!"

F: "I didn't forget."

M: "You didn't?"

F: "No. I've just been so busy I didn't have time to buy you anything, that's all."

M: [SILENCE]

F: "Did I say something wrong?"

Once in a hundred years it might be true for someone to say "I was so busy I didn't have time to buy you a present." The rest of the time, it's not that the person didn't *have* time but that he or she didn't *take* time. Anyone today can pick up the phone or fire up the fax machine and have a gift sent; the amount of time required is insignificant. And this man could use that to construct a justified three-part message, like this:

F: "Did I say something wrong?"

M: "When you say you didn't have time to buy me a birthday present, I feel hurt, because sending a gift today takes five minutes, maybe six."

(If she is wise, she will answer his complaint like this: "But it takes much longer to find something so special that I'm willing to send it to you. I'd rather be late with your gift—even if it makes you mad—than send something that isn't that special.")

We learn the "I didn't have time to do it" line as children, and we tend to use it without thinking. If it's false, it adds insult to injury; better to admit that you forgot, and apologize. If it's true, it requires careful explanation to make that clear, as in "I've been too busy to get you anything. I've been working around the clock since the forest fire started, and we don't have either phones or fax machines on the fire line."

DIALOGUE EIGHT

F: "This is a joke—okay? With the body you've got, we won't need a beach umbrella!"

M: [SILENCE]

Openly labeling an utterance as one speech act when you intend something else entirely—"I'm apologizing, okay?" "All RIGHT, this is a PROMise!" "I'm only kidding, all right?"—doesn't qualify it as that speech act. It's always a mistake. Don't do it. I suggest that he answer this with a three-part message:

"When you insult me and claim that it's a joke, I feel hurt, because calling an insult a joke makes it even more insulting."

What if she tries to argue about the "because" part of the message, which is his opinion but not verifiable in the way that "because tomatoes die if you don't water them" is verifiable? For example, what if she says, "Oh, come on! If somebody says it's a joke, then it's a joke!"? Then he should say this:

"That may be true for you; it's not true for me. And now that you know that, I'm sure you won't do it again."

♦

CHAPTER 8

How Metaphors Filter Perception and Complicate Communication

"No way!" said John, flicking past the channel. "I'm not going to waste my time listening to that! Men and women speak different languages? That's ridiculous!"

"Maybe," Paula answered. "And maybe not. For example—there was that awful fight we had when Heather was here last week."

John turned his head to look at her face, and when he saw that she was serious he turned off the television set. "Honey," he said, "if it had just been the two of us here you would have understood what I was saying, and there wouldn't have been any fight."

"You're sure of that?"

"I'm positive."

"Tell me, then," said Paula. "Tell me what you would have told me if we'd been alone, without Heather here to complicate matters. I would really like to understand this business with Mary Clayton."

"All right. Here goes. From the first day Mary was in the office I wondered if we'd made a mistake hiring her. I did everything I could to help her along, but nothing helped. She's a serious problem for us. So, as soon as it was clear to me that things weren't going to get better, I set up a strategy to make her uncomfortable enough so that she'd resign. It's as simple as that."

"But that's—"

"Wait, honey; I know what you're going to say. I couldn't just fire her, Paula. She hasn't done anything to be fired for. She does her work and she does it well. If I fire her she'll sue us, and she'll win. I couldn't just talk it over with her—I've tried, and it's a waste of time. If those options had been open to me, I would have chosen them. They weren't, and I moved to Plan B because it was the only choice I had. Okay so far?"

"But that's not what you said when Heather was here!"

John stared at her, bewildered. "We're not talking about that!" he protested. "I'm explaining to you what my strategy with Mary is, and why I've had to use it. Why are you changing the subject and bringing up that business with Heather again?"

"Because you lied to us, John, that's why."

"I did what?"

"You lied to us! You tried to convince us that you were a poor innocent oaf constantly being dragged into messes by Mary Clayton. Always having to smooth things over after she'd messed them up and upset everybody else in the office. Remember? And now you're saying that almost from Day One you've been working against her as a deliberate, calculated strategy!"

"Paula," John said slowly, "I think you've got it wrong. It's not easy to remember every word that was said, because I was so busy trying to figure out what was going on. But it seems to me that I said the same things then that I'm saying now. I tried to keep it light because I didn't want to bore Heather or you with every little detail—and I was sorry it got so intense before it was over. But I wasn't lying."

"John," Paula insisted, "it's obvious that half the things we fought over, bad as they sounded then, didn't happen the way you described them at all. On top of that, what you're doing with Mary is only possible if you lie to her all the time, every time it fits into your master plan! And you expect me not to disagree with you? YOU must be out of your MIND!"

John picked up the remote control again and flicked the set on, running through the channels, his face grim.

"What are you doing?" Paula demanded. "I thought we agreed to talk about this!"

"I'm getting that program back again," he said coldly. "The one about how men and women speak different languages. I've decided they're right after all. Maybe I can learn something."

◆

What's Going On Here?

John's Point of View

As John perceives it, Paula's behavior is incomprehensible. He considers her intelligent and sophisticated. He expects her to appreciate his attempts to be courteous to his sister-in-law, to keep the conversation light, and to avoid controversy over things Heather wouldn't have understood without a lot of added detail. He realizes that his tactics failed that night, but he doesn't believe it was entirely his fault, and he's learned his lesson: He will never talk even the most casual kind of business around Heather again.

That Paula could still be angry about the fight, which is over and done with and was ridiculous in the first place, baffles him. It's baffling that she would interrupt their serious discussion, when he was taking her fully into his confidence and explaining something she said she was eager to understand, to argue again about the evening with Heather. But what he *really* minds are Paula's accusations. Calling him a liar! He considers that totally unjustified and unfair. Nothing he said that night would have done anyone any harm if the two women hadn't overreacted as they did, in his opinion; certainly nothing he said counted as a *lie*. As for saying that his strategy to convince Mary Clayton to move on is lying—that's the sort of naive nonsense he'd expect to hear from a child. John thinks, for the many-thousandth time, that he will never understand women. He seriously wonders if he has overestimated Paula's ability to understand business, or her basic common sense. That saddens him. How can a woman as intelligent as Paula be so totally confused?

Paula's Point of View

Paula is *shocked*. Shocked that John would have deliberately set up a campaign of behavior intended to maneuver a woman in his employ into quitting her job. Shocked that he would carry on a deception over a period of months like that. Shocked that he sees nothing wrong with his behavior. Shocked that he doesn't hesitate to involve her and Heather in his silly games. She finds his behavior disgraceful. And for him to sit there and insist that he hasn't *lied*! At the same time that he's bragging about an entire *campaign* of lies to Mary Clayton! It defies human comprehension.

She thinks, for the many-thousandth time, that it is impossible to understand men. And it saddens her. How can a man as intelligent as John be so totally irrational?

◆

This is a serious communication breakdown, and will be hard to repair. It will be obvious to you that a major factor here is the question of how to define a *lie*. Both Mary and John agree that lying is wrong. For Mary, as for most AME-speaking women, a lie is a false statement made deliberately. For John, however, as for most AME-speaking men, a false statement is a lie only if it carries an additional semantic feature: [+HARMFUL]. But this well-known semantic difference doesn't seem to provide an adequate explanation. Because it's clear that John believes it's *okay* to deceive Mary Clayton repeatedly—even at the cost of harm to her—if it's for the sake of his company.

Something more than just a definitional difference is at the heart of this tangled situation, something larger in scope. The scenario is a classic example of the way language can fail when people are communicating from within the semantic framework of different *metaphors* and are unaware that that's happening. Let's look at this phenomenon more closely, and consider some possible ways to deal with it effectively.

Technique #7
Metaphor Analysis and Semantic Modulation

The word *metaphor* as commonly used refers to a language pattern with the form "X is Y," as in "Time is money." There is a similar but somewhat weaker pattern called a *simile*, as in "Time is like money," and there are others. The terms are correct, but narrow. In this book we will be using "metaphor" in the broader sense that it has in linguistic science: to refer to any use of language for the purpose of comparing two different things on the basis of the characteristics that they share.

Metaphor is the most powerful device available to us for changing people's *attitudes* quickly, effectively, and lastingly. Let me give you one very clear and simple example from my personal experience.

I've always been annoyed when people I was visiting left their television set on constantly, even when nobody was watching it and we were all presumably involved in other things. I found this insulting. I came to unflattering conclusions about the people involved. To me, their behavior made no sense. Why leave the set on if nobody's interested in watching it? On the other hand, if people *are* interested in watching, why pretend to be interested in talking to *me*?

And then I read a statement by Camille Paglia in the March 1991 issue of *Harper's*: For her generation, she said, *the television set is the flickering fire on the hearth*. That metaphor changed everything for me— instantly. It made the incomprehensible transparent; I now understand why the television set is left on. I am no longer insulted by it, or annoyed at the people who leave it on. I no longer think they're being rude to me or are only pretending to be interested in my company. I wouldn't expect them to put out the fire in their fireplace during my visit or be insulted if they didn't; why should they turn off their television?

Only metaphors have the power to bring about this kind of change so quickly and so completely. You can bring about drastic changes at the point of a gun (or checkbook), but they will be temporary changes. You can turn attitudes around by the patient application of persuasion over years and years, but that is an excruciatingly slow process. Metaphors are much more high tech for the purpose. They are the closest thing in language to the *hologram*; it takes only a small piece of a metaphor to evoke the whole. When someone says to you, "Hey . . . your boss just slithered in the door!" You don't have to hear the words "Your boss is a snake" to understand the metaphor; you understand it from your knowledge of the presuppositions of the word "slither" and from the context.

When a single metaphor permeates an entire culture, it serves as a *unifying* metaphor, and it will let you do substantial amounts of linguistic work almost effortlessly. You need only say "Wagons, ho!" and your AME-speaking listeners will retrieve from their own memories the entire semantic map of the Old West, complete with cowboys, dance-hall girls with hearts of gold, Good Old Doc, covered wagons, and all the rest. You know that not every detail of the metaphor will be identical for everyone present, but you can be sure the parts that matter will be enough alike to make the metaphor do the work you want it to do.

The United States lags behind Japan in the science and technology of robotics, with serious effects for the United States economy. There are various reasons for this difference; one of the major ones is a metaphor. In the twelfth century, Japan had big wooden dolls that served tea, called *karakuri*; the Japanese metaphor is something like "a robot is a friendly and useful doll." The American metaphor is quite different, with its roots in terrifying movies and other media, and we can summarize it roughly as "A robot is a dangerous metal monster." It's also safe to say that the Japanese robot—the doll—can be feminine (and thus nonthreatening and easily controlled), while the American one is unquestionably either neuter or *male*. The fact that it's not logical to assign gender to machines is irrelevant in the realm of metaphor. (See Michael Colpitts, "Inside the Robot Kingdom," in *BCS TECH*, November 1991, pp. 1–3.)

Metaphors as Perceptual Filters

Earlier in this book I said that we have no way to know what "reality" is actually like; we don't know how much of what we consider real is "out there" and how much is the creation of human perceptions. The models of reality that human beings put together and live by are made up primarily of metaphors; the models themselves are and can only be metaphors. Within any culture, people tend to structure their behavior around that culture's unifying metaphors to such an extent that their perceptions are filtered through the metaphors and shaped by them in predictable ways. That is, they are largely predictable *if you know which metaphor is being used*. When human beings interact in groups, we find at least three communication situations relative to metaphor:

1. "We all speak the same language here."

Everyone involved in the group effort is using the *same* metaphor as a perceptual filter. Things go smoothly; vast amounts of time and energy are saved. People may disagree, but nobody's behavior is *baffling* to the others.

2. "We all speak the same language here, except for Rami."

There are people in the group who are functioning with a different metaphor as perceptual filter than the majority, and everyone involved is *aware* of that and alert to the potential communication problems. For example, suppose nine people on your project team are native New Yorkers, but the tenth member has spent his entire life previously in Pakistan. In such a situation, people know they will need to provide extra information for the Pakistani colleague to help him match his model of reality to the one everyone else is relating to. This may slow things down, and it may be a nuisance from time to time, but it's manageable.

3. "We all speak the same language here, but some of us are <u>nuts</u>."

This is the situation that's dangerous: when it is *assumed* that everyone in the group is functioning from within a single metaphor, and it's not true. In this situation, communication problems aren't anticipated. And when nobody can make any sense of Tracy's behavior, everybody assumes Tracy is incompetent, or deliberately uncooperative, or irrational, or worse. No one gives Tracy the extra information that could clear up the confusion, because *it's taken for granted that Tracy already has it.* Now you have real problems, and they can be devastating.

Let's examine a typical example of the third situation; it will help us sort out the events in Scenario Eight.

The World as Football Game versus the World as Schoolroom

The most common metaphor mismatch for AME speakers in my experience is the one in which some of the members of a group have The Football Game (or one of the other major team sports, such as basketball or baseball) as their unifying metaphor and other members have The Traditional Schoolroom as theirs. This situation typically breaks down by gender, with the males filtering their behavior through the world of football and the women filtering theirs through the world of the schoolroom. When the clash is not by gender—for example, when one man in a group has the schoolroom metaphor and all the rest have football—matters are even worse, but this is unusual.

In a football game it's okay to behave as if you have the ball when you don't have it, or vice versa. It's okay to behave as if you're going to run one direction when you fully intend to run the other. It's okay to set up deceptions in which two or three of the players work together to mislead the other team. None of this is called "lying" or "cheating" or "breaking a promise." The better a player is at doing these things, the greater the player's value to the team. In the traditional schoolroom, however, even the smallest deviation from the truth is called a *lie* and will get you into trouble. In a schoolroom, the effort that's rewarded is individual effort; working with other people, except in very narrow and rigidly controlled situations, is called *cheating*, and is severely punished.

In a football game, you try one play and if it doesn't work you try another. No big deal. If a strategy doesn't go well, you change strategies; if you can devise a better play, or a more effective strategy, that's rewarded. You always play as well as you possibly can, but you know what to expect: You win some, you lose some, and it's that way for everybody. There will always be another play, another game, another season. In the traditional schoolroom, on the other hand, as long as you work hard on your own, follow all the rules to the letter, and do your very best, you can be sure you'll be rewarded. That's how good grades are earned, that's how prizes are won and how you get to be on the honor roll. Innovation is not welcome. After all, if you're allowed to do something, everybody else might want to do it too, and that might lead to the forbidden condition of disorder. And failure? Failure is *disgrace*. Disaster! Nobody says, "Oh, well, I failed fifth grade; no big deal. There'll always be another grade."

The rules in these two metaphors—these two models of reality— are drastically different. The behaviors they encourage and reward are diametrically opposed. The Schoolroom person uses the words "lying," "cheating," and "unfair," and so does the Football Game person—but the meanings attached are not the same. Many of the things most admired in football are considered simply *wrong* in the schoolroom. Not just in the sense of error, but *morally* wrong.

When one person uses the Schoolroom metaphor as perceptual filter in a group where everyone else is using the Football metaphor, major misunderstandings are almost guaranteed. To have one person in a couple filtering everything through the Football metaphor while the other filters perceptions through the Schoolroom metaphor is a recipe for communication failure. Especially when, as is usually the case, no one realizes that this is what's really going on. (For example, as with John and Paula Gellis in Scenario Nine, both of whom have almost decided, with some sadness, that the other has gone over the edge.)

Metaphor Analysis

Just being aware that the metaphor mismatch problem exists as a possible source of conflict *helps*. This is not empty reassurance; it's genuinely practical and valid. Once you are aware that any conflict may have metaphor mismatch behind it, the data coming in to your sensory systems for processing will be the same, but your reactions *to* the data will be different. You'll make allowances, as you would when interacting with someone from another culture. You will be prepared to provide missing information when needed, and to request and accept missing information when the gap is on your side. You'll be less likely to blame disagreements and confusions on other people's supposed negative characteristics. When you are part of a group or a couple and someone else's behavior seems incomprehensible to you, you'll know that it's time to apply Miller's Law. Time to ask yourself: *For that person's messages to be true, what else would have to be true? What metaphor would have to be filtering his (or her) perceptions of the world?*

Many, if not most, women in the AME culture have never played football; women who *do* play don't play often. Even women who watch football regularly and with pleasure rarely have any deep understanding of the complex strategies used in the game. This makes it difficult for women to use the Football metaphor as men do. But *all* men in the culture have been part of the traditional schoolroom at some point in their lives. Furthermore, they were part of it for years at a time, and they know it well. The schoolroom, unlike the football game, is an experience stored in detail in the memories of both genders, and it provides a foundation from which both can work toward better communication.

The man who discovers that a woman is outraged by behavior he considers absolutely normal can stop and ask himself: "What would happen to me if I behaved this way in a schoolroom? What would the teacher think? What would the other pupils think? What would my behavior be called?" He can do this easily, because he's had extensive experience in the Schoolroom reality model and he knows its rules. When the answers to his questions turn out to be crucial to resolving conflict, he can explain—in the same way that he would, without hesitation and without leaping to conclusions, explain the rules of football to someone who was trying to play and obviously didn't know how. If the Schoolroom metaphor turns out not to be the basis for her reaction, he has at least eliminated that possibility as a source of confusion. (There are other possible metaphors she might be using and toward which he could turn his investigations, such as The Happy Family, The Proud Ship Sailing, The Old West, or The Old South.) This is a start, and it's many yards closer to touchdown than "Women are impossible to understand; I give up."

The woman who finds a man's behavior incomprehensible can use her awareness of potential metaphor clash to do repairs. She can ask herself, "If he did that in a football game, how would I react to it? What would it mean in that context?" If a limited experience of the game makes it impossible for her to answer that on her own, she can ask him for clarification. She can say, "I don't understand what you did; I need some help. Is this like something that happens in football? If that's it, would you explain it, please?" The man may tell her no, it's more like something that happens in baseball, or tennis, or chess, or even in military combat—

that's fine. That will identify the metaphor that's causing the trouble. They can then use language to investigate the meaning differences and clarify matters in both directions.

Usually it's the woman who uses the Schoolroom metaphor and the man who has Football or another sport as perceptual filter—but not always. When it's the other way around, both people involved need to be particularly careful to do the metaphor analysis without mixing in stereotypes about gender. For a man to perceive a situation as if it were a schoolroom is not "feminine"; for a woman to perceive it as if it were a football game is not "masculine." Unless this is kept in mind, the stereotypes will introduce additional misunderstandings.

It may occur to you that a general solution in metaphor mismatch would be for one person to change metaphors, so that the mismatch— and the differing perceptions of reality—would be eliminated. That's true in theory, but not in practice. Most of the time it won't be possible for an adult who has always been a Schoolroom person to simply switch to being a Football person, or vice versa. Whether that can happen depends on at least the following factors, for each individual:

- How long the metaphor has served as a perceptual filter.
- How many areas of the individual's life it's applied to.
- How deep an emotional investment there is in the metaphor as "right" and "natural" and "the way things are *supposed* to be."
- How well the metaphor *works* in particular situations.
- How much pressure there is to accept the metaphor and maintain it— from the culture, from the family, from peers, etc.
- How deeply change (of any kind) is disapproved of or feared.

However, let me repeat: being aware of the situation is often more than enough to bring about dramatic improvement. I am never going to become a person for whom a television set is a fire on the hearth; that change isn't possible for me. But it's not necessary. Knowing that the metaphor is behind the behavior is sufficient to eliminate the potential for conflict.

Semantic Modulation

Semantic modulation is a process for getting from one side of a metaphor to another. The tools used are already familiar to you: they are *semantic features* and *reality statements*. To make the process itself clear, let's go through a simple case that's also familiar to you now—my misunderstanding when my hosts left their television sets on. Let's suppose that, instead of muddling along until I fell over Paglia's metaphor by chance, I had actively used semantic modulation to try to clear up that problem.

Step One: I would have begun by applying Miller's Law (see Chapter 2) and giving my hosts some credit. The message they were transmitting could be summarized as "In spite of the fact that this television set is flickering and humming all the time in the background, we are glad you're here and we're enjoying your company." Instead of reacting to the baffling message by concluding that something had to be wrong with *them* (and deciding it was rudeness or deception), I would have kept an open mind. The television set had to represent something—in their model of reality—that made it appropriate and consistent with their message; I just needed to find out what it was. I now had one half of the metaphor:

✦   A TELEVISION SET IS . . . [X].?

Step Two: I would have listed all the characteristics of the television set that seemed to define it in the situation, including at least:

• a flickering light
• a soft, constant, varying background noise
• a central location in the house, where people gather and interact with one another

Remember that, for metaphors, only the characteristics the two items have *in common* matter. Many characteristics of fires—they give off heat, they can burn you, they make you uncomfortable in the summertime—would not have been relevant in this context. Other things about television sets—they're in a case, they can be bought on the installment plan, they present comedies and music—would not have been relevant. I would probably have listed all of these things, nevertheless, as I was working on my analysis.

Step Three: Finally, I would have asked myself what *else* had the characteristics on my list, might be valued by my hosts, and would be consistent with their claim of hospitality. I should then have been able to get to the other side of my metaphor and complete it:

✦   A TELEVISION SET IS A FLICKERING FIRE ON THE HEARTH.

And with my metaphor complete, I would have realized that there was one more shared feature: The television image and sound are framed by the border of the television screen in the same way the hearthfire is framed by the fireplace.

You can use this process that we've just gone through step by step whenever you're baffled by someone's behavior in your personal life or in the workplace. If it had been my husband who insisted on leaving the television set on while he and I were trying to talk, I would have been even more annoyed than I was when others did it. And it would have been even more important to find out why he did it, so that I didn't conclude that he was being rude to me or was only pretending to be interested in talking to me.

Identify the behavior that is distressing you. Assume that an explanation exists for it that's not composed of negative judgments about the other person. Set up the problem as the left side of the metaphor, like this:

- Taking showers at two o'clock in the morning is . . . [X]?
- Refusing to have two credit cards is . . . [X]?
- Putting catsup on almost all foods is . . . [X]?
- Eating Sunday dinner with his/her family every week is . . . [X]?

Then continue through the steps, as in the television set example, and complete the metaphor.

(Those of you who are familiar with the *Gentle Art* series will be aware of a more complex form of semantic modulation—not discussed in this book—that involves moving from one completed metaphor to another. For details, see Elgin 1990 or 1991.)

Another Look at Scenario Eight

We can now straighten out the communication tangles that were demonstrated in Scenario Eight. It will be clear to you now that they revolved around two separate *interacting* linguistic differences that are typically associated with differences of gender:

- The female definition of "lying" does not require the [+ HARMFUL] semantic feature in the male definition.
- The metaphor mismatch between John and Paula, where Paula's

choice—The Traditional Schoolroom—is in conflict with John's choice—The Football Game.

Either of these differences can lead to conflict; to have both going on at once makes things very difficult.

Although John and Paula agree that he was making false statements and giving false impressions to Mary Clayton, only Paula understands that as lying. From John's point of view, he not only wasn't harming Mary, he was helping her out of a situation guaranteed to make her unhappy; therefore, he was not lying.

In addition, even if John could be convinced that he's doing Mary harm with his campaign of deception, he still wouldn't agree that he was doing anything wrong—because he's following the rules of the *game*. What matters in the Football metaphor is not the welfare of any single individual but the welfare of the *team*. If an individual must be sacrificed to accomplish that, even by systematic deception, it's nothing personal and it's not a moral issue; it's just *the way the game is played*. Within the context of John's metaphor his behavior (which would be wicked in a schoolroom) is entirely moral and acceptable. The one thing in question is his skill: He would be the first to agree that he should have been able to find a better strategy—more effective, less cumbersome, and above all *faster*—for getting rid of Mary.

If Paula understands that John's deceptive behavior toward Mary is, as he perceives it, like pretending to have the football when you know perfectly well that somebody else has it, her reaction will be different. She's no more likely to approve of what John's doing than she was before, but there will be a drastic difference in her perception of *him*. To see him as mistaken is one thing; to see him as wicked, and proud of it, is quite another. Paula will still disapprove of John's behavior, but she will no longer see him as either immoral or irrational. Similarly, John will still disagree with Paula's ideas about what he should do to get Mary Clayton out of his office. But if he understands that her perceptions are being filtered through the metaphor of the Schoolroom, he will no longer feel that she's too illogical or too uninformed to understand business.

This is a major improvement for both Paula and John. And their experience in this instance can be applied each time they find themselves in one of these "men and women speak different languages" controversies.

Discovering metaphor mismatches won't solve every communication problem between men and women. It won't guarantee that we all live happily ever after. But it can be extraordinarily helpful. I've seen it lead to seemingly miraculous results for a number of my clients, over the years.

Dialogues for Analysis

DIALOGUE ONE

M: "Well, what did you think? Are they going to buy it?"

F: "Probably. But only because you lied."

M: "When?"

F: "When you told them we were sure we had the book club sales sewed up. That's not <u>true</u>."

M: "Okay, it's not true. I agree with you. But it wasn't a lie. Not in <u>that</u> situation."

F: "That's ridiculous! It doesn't make any sense at all! A lie is a lie!"

M: "Do me a favor, will you? When the big boys are playing, <u>you</u> stay off the <u>field</u>."

These two people are not going to agree, no matter how long they continue to trade lines back and forth. Nothing but bad feeling is going to result from lines like his final one, which is an obvious effort to make her feel like a rebuked child. If this is an isolated incident between two people who normally don't interact, it will be quickly forgotten. But if they have to go on working together routinely, there'll be many more disagreements like this one, creating an atmosphere of tension and strain.

Let's assume that this is an ongoing association. In that case the best outcome would be something like Dialogue Two below.

DIALOGUE TWO

F: "No—I'm not willing to stay off the field. But let's set that aside for now. I'm sure you only said it because it's been a long, hard afternoon."

M: "That's right; I'm not ordinarily that crude."

F: "However, we have to work together on this project, and on a lot of other projects, and this issue—this business of what is and what isn't lying—is going to keep coming up. I think we would be very wise to sit down and thrash this out, so that we know what to expect from each other."

This resolution is what is known as "agreeing to disagree." Neither one expects to be able to convince the other that his or her definition of a lie is the correct one. He isn't taking back his warning that she doesn't know how to play the game and should stay where she can't get hurt or do harm; she isn't going to accept that judgment or agree to abide by it. But she is saying that since they must work together they need to learn one another's positions thoroughly enough to avoid getting in each other's way. They have to work out the *details* of the agreement to disagree. For example:

* He needs to know how far from her definition of truth he can go without having to be afraid that she'll challenge him in public.

* She needs to know whether she can trust him not to put her into situations in which she feels that she is being implicated in what she perceives as his lies.

If he is wise, he will agree to this negotiation process. And if he is wise, he'll begin with a metaphor, like this:

M: "Suppose you had a young daughter who was without question homely, and who was probably never going to be attractive. Suppose she came to you on her way to some school function and said, 'I look ugly, don't I?' Would you say, 'Yes, you do, dear, but don't worry about it'?"

F: "Of course not."

M: "Exactly. You'd say something like 'You look very nice, dear,' even though you know it's not true. Which shows that you and I both agree that there are situations in which a false statement is the right statement."

With that common ground established, they can go on to determine precisely how the lines are drawn and how they will be observed. Notice that they are both Leveling throughout; when this is possible, it always saves much time and energy.

DIALOGUE THREE

F: "Are you upset about something? You look pretty grim."

M: "I am grim. It's this job. Every day, the same hill to climb, and every day it's steeper."

F: "Oh, you're just tired. You'll feel different about it tomorrow, once you've had a good night's sleep. What kind of dressing do you want on this salad?"

He has answered her first question clearly, and he's handed her a perfect metaphor:

"My job is a steep hill I have to keep climbing, every day."

Her response does three unwise things simultaneously:

- It trivializes his distress.
- It cuts off the possibility of *discussing* his problem.
- It punishes him for being open with her, making it unlikely that he'll answer her honestly in the future.

Suggestion for Her: You may have thought it would be better for him not to dwell on his negative feelings, and you may have intended your remark about only needing a good night's sleep as comfort. Both are mistakes. Instead of cutting him off, investigate the metaphor he offered you. Ask him what happens when he gets to the *top* of the hill, or what it's like going down the other side. Don't change the subject; the salad will wait.

Suggestion for Him: You need to make it absolutely clear to her that her response isn't appropriate and that you're not willing to accept it. Her intentions were probably good, but it's important to make her understand that you don't want to be soothed and babied and hushed. Level with her, and don't mince words. Say with neutral intonation: "That response is not appropriate, and I'm not willing to accept it. You asked me what was wrong and I answered you truthfully; if you're not willing to follow through, it would be much better not to ask."

DIALOGUE FOUR

M: "Why do you say we can't go to the mountains for the weekend? I don't understand."

F: "We can't afford it, that's why."

M: "I still don't understand. There's more than enough money in the account."

F: "Honey, we're much too heavily in debt to spend money on a fancy vacation."

M: "But we've never missed a payment on anything, and we've never been late with one—heck, we're usually early!"

F: "What does that have to do with it?"

The phrase "in debt" has a variety of definitions. Because money is known to be one of the major sources of friction between couples, it's important for both parties to be using the *same* definition of the phrase. In this dialogue we have a woman for whom being "in debt" means owing money that must be repaid, and a man for whom being "in debt" means not being able to keep the payments on your debts up to date. Her reality statement is "Debtors are people who owe others money"; his is "Debtors are people who haven't paid their bills on time." People tend to assume that key words and phrases have only one definition because their own seems to them to be the only possible choice—and they find themselves in interactions like Dialogue Four.

One of the pair in this dialogue should call a halt and ask the other: "When you say that somebody is 'in debt,' what does that mean for you?" And then they should discuss their definitions reasonably, without making judgmental remarks. Without "But that's not what it means! I can't believe you said that!" and "No rational adult would define it that way!" and "No wonder people think you're nuts!"

DIALOGUE FIVE

F: "How could you possibly have told her that you were going to marry her?"

M: "If I hadn't, she wouldn't have gone to the Bahamas with me."

F: "But you had no intention of marrying her!"

M: "Like I said . . . I had to say that, or she would have turned me down."

F: "But look, you had to know she was going to be badly hurt. Doesn't that mean anything to you at all?"

M: "Sure. If there'd been some other way to get her to go, I would much rather not have lied to her. But I didn't have any choice."

Once in a while, you're going to encounter a situation like this. This is a man who believes what he's saying. Pushed to the wall, he will eventually claim that his behavior was the fault of the woman he took to the Bahamas, because she didn't simply agree to go in the first place. He will claim that she forced him to lie, and he will mean that. Nothing you could say to him is likely to make him see things any differently; that's a task for an expert, and not an easy one. The best move for the woman in Dialogue Five is to bring the conversation to a close and avoid this man in the future. A good closing line for her is this one:

F: "I don't understand you at all, and I don't want to; there's no point in continuing this conversation."

To which he will probably answer, "Whatever you say," and go on about his business.

But let's suppose she can't avoid him, because he is her brother, or her boss, or something similar. In that case she must decide whether to try to make things *better* or just to try to make them more neutral by keeping her conversations with him to a minimum and always on neutral subjects. If she decides she'd like to work toward genuine improvement in the communication between them, and if she can get him to cooperate with her in that effort, her best first move is to use semantic modulation to find out what metaphor(s) he uses in his romantic relationships.

CHAPTER 9

◆

Using the Language
Traffic Rules

Scenario Nine

"I <u>know</u> it's hard for you to understand!" Mary told them. "You
really don't have to keep telling me that!"

"Jobs don't grow on trees, you know," her father said,
frowning. "Throwing away a good job like you had, just because
you got your feelings hurt—"

"Dad, that's not fair! You sound like my boss, you know
that? <u>He</u> called me a prima <u>donna</u>! And he said—"

"Mary, darling," her mother broke in, "should I get new
slipcovers for this couch, or am I just imagining that it looks
bad? What do <u>you</u> think?"

"Susan," Gary Jones said sharply, "Mary's trying to talk
about something important here! <u>Never mind</u> your slipcovers!"

"Well, she didn't <u>want</u> to talk about it, you know. <u>You</u> were
the one who insisted—"

"Mom," said Mary, "let's just get it over with! I would
really like to make you and Dad understand that this was <u>not</u>
simply a matter of my 'getting my feelings hurt'! It was much
more than that!"

"But, honey, don't you think—"

"I don't follow you, Mary Anne," her father said, cutting
Susan off. "I'm trying to be fair here. I've listened to everything
you had to say, and I don't hear anything you couldn't have
handled. You just had to make it <u>clear</u> to those guys that you
expected them to treat you like a <u>lady</u>, and that would have been
all there was <u>to</u> it! Why did you have to get all dramatic and

quit? You say I sound like your boss—well, you sound like one of those feminists!''

Mary sighed. ''I'm not going to get suckered into that discussion again, Dad,'' she said wearily. ''I'm too tired, I'm too worried, and I know it's a dead end. Let's just drop it, okay?''

''No, it's not okay. Tell me again. What exactly did these men say that made you get up on your high horse—''

''What I think,'' said Susan, ''is that we ought to go out on the porch and take advantage of this pretty weather! It won't last, you know—they said last night on the news that we were in for thunderstorms by noon. And—''

''MOTHer!''

Susan stopped, startled.

''Both of you ought to be ashamed!'' Mary said furiously. ''I come here for a few hours to get a break from all the hassle! And then Dad insists on arguing about why I quit my job—which I did not want to talk about, and I told you so!—and then he keeps interrupting me and bullying me, and you keep interrupting us both with stuff that's clear off the subject, and the two of you argue with each other and ignore me . . . I'm sorry I came!!''

Gary and Susan stared at her as if she'd lost her mind, hurt written on their faces, and Mary gave up, shaking her head sadly. She sat down on the couch and spoke to the living room wall. ''Oh, damn!'' she said. ''WHY does it always have to be like this?''

———————————— ◆ ————————————

What's Going On Here?

Gary's Point of View

As Gary sees it, the story Mary's telling makes no sense. He doesn't understand why she left her good job. He doesn't understand why the incidents she's complaining about were such a big deal to her. He doesn't understand why he doesn't understand; surely, he thinks, he must have missed something the first time she told them about her problems, something that he'll pick up if she repeats it for him. He particularly does not understand why she's accusing him of not caring. If he didn't care about her, would he be wasting his time with all this foolish talk that never goes anywhere? He has other things to do with his time, if he didn't care, and

Mary should have sense enough to realize that! He loves his daughter with all his heart, and he wants nothing more than to help her when she needs help—but *first* he has to be able to put the details together into something roughly like a coherent narrative.

Susan's Point of View

Susan wants to help, very much. She thinks she does understand what Mary's trying to say, although she feels that her daughter has probably overreacted. She thinks she understands what Gary is trying to say as well, and she understands that his problem is that he can't follow Mary's story. She knows how proud he is of Mary, and how upset he must be when he finds himself unable to take her side in this situation. She would have liked, more than anything else, to distract *both* of them from this miserable subject and get them talking about something more pleasant. Susan keeps trying, unsuccessfully, to accomplish that goal.

Mary's Point of View

As Mary perceives it, she is already as near the end of her rope as she could be and still function; there's no need for her parents to make things worse. She's had to give up a job she badly wanted to keep, because she couldn't have maintained her self-respect if she'd stayed. She's going to have to look for another job, and that will be hard to do with her confidence so badly shaken. She's worried about what kind of reference John Gillis will give her. What she needs now is sympathy and support—and to be *listened* to, instead of being interrupted every dozen words, and fussed at. It seems to her that her parents, of all people, ought to be willing to do that for her!

◆

This is a sorry state of affairs, and unfortunately it's a typical one. These people love each other and genuinely want to be helpful, but they're not communicating. And as Mary says, it's *always* this way.

Like many families, this one has a set of language habits that make useful communication almost impossible, even when intentions are good, and they don't know how to make it better. They aren't unpleasant people. The situation isn't hopeless. For example, things would improve for them if they applied the techniques and strategies discussed in previous chapters of this book. But they would have difficulty doing that until after they had dealt with their most basic problem: *their constant violations of the traffic rules of language.*

The Metaphor of Language as Traffic

There is no clearer metaphor for American Mainstream English language interactions—and none more appropriate—than this one:

✦   LANGUAGE IS TRAFFIC.

Communication isn't handing packages of meaning back and forth, and it's not a business transaction in which messages are the product. The traffic metaphor is more useful because everybody who has to get around in traffic can apply it to communication and use it instantly and effectively—provided they're aware that the metaphor exists and are willing to make the effort. It's not easy to break the communication habits of a lifetime.

Road Traffic Rules/Talk Traffic Rules

Let's take a look at a few examples of the application of the metaphor.

Road Traffic Rules	Talk Traffic Rules
You have to have a car to drive, or you can't go anywhere.	You have to have a topic to talk about, and a language with which to do the talking.
Don't cut out in front of other people; don't cut them off.	Don't interrupt the person who has the floor and don't barge into other people's conversations.
When you come to an intersection, slow down, signal your intentions, and yield to the person who has the right of way.	When it's somebody else's turn to talk, slow down, stop talking, and make it clear that you're ready to hand over the turn to that person.
Stay in your own lane and make it possible for other people to stay in theirs.	Don't change the subject.
Never stop in the middle of an intersection.	Don't block communication by delivering monologues; take *turns*.

We could continue, but it's not necessary; you know this model of reality well, and you'll have no difficulty extending the metaphor. We can summarize, using the word "conversation" as a cover term for language interactions in general:

✦   If conversation—like traffic—is to flow smoothly, so that people can reach their communication goals, everybody has to cooperate and follow the rules.

Regulating Language Traffic

This is all obvious—so obvious that you may wonder why it needs pointing out. However, consider the facts about language behavior versus driving behavior; it's equally obvious that not everyone has noticed the parallels. People who would never think of stopping their cars in the middle of an intersection sit and talk endlessly, monopolizing the floor so that nobody else can get in a word. People who would never cut in front of another driver go right ahead and cut off the words of other speakers, as if nobody else had any right to the conversational space. People who are law-abiding drivers at all times simply ignore the language traffic rules. Why? The parallels are so clear; why aren't good drivers also good conversationalists? In almost every case, the answer is that they're unaware of the facts.

Because people can't immediately see the results of language traffic violations, they don't realize that there's a connection between their language behavior and the negative consequences—for themselves as well as for others—that only appear later.

Hostile language can kill you as surely as hostile driving can. The most serious risk factor for heart disease is chronic exposure to hostile language interactions. Hostile language hurts and frustrates and confuses people. It makes blood pressures soar and hearts pound and stomachs churn. It causes ulcers and strokes and migraines and depression. It makes people so flustered that they have dangerous accidents, in their homes and workplaces and in their cars. It can drive people to physical violence. All this is well known. The problem is that—unlike what happens when you run head-on into a speeding car in the wrong lane—the damage usually takes place slowly, over time, and the wounds aren't readily visible. It's easy to see that violating the rules on the road is dangerous; it's much harder to see the dangers when the space being shared is *linguistic* space.

Gender Differences: Who's the Better Driver?

No specific gender difference has been proved to exist for the language traffic violations of AME speakers. Research has produced the usual conflicting results. One stereotype is that women do most of the talking and most of the interrupting; another is that men never support the topics women introduce into conversation, while women always support those introduced by men. When you try to test such ideas, however, you find that things are not that clear-cut. Always, it *depends. It depends on the people involved and the situations in which they find themselves; it depends on where they are at the time and what they're doing.* You can line up the stereotypes in a row and test them one by one, repeatedly; the results will almost never be tidy. In most cases, the only reliable conclusion will be that *certain trends and tendencies* exist. And this is exactly what you would expect to find if you consider the problem from within the Language Is Traffic metaphor.

When you're driving, you expect other people to follow the rules—but if a gigantic truck wants your lane, you get out of the way. At an intersection, you expect to be allowed to go through when it's your turn—but you don't argue with a bulldozer. You follow the speed limit and you think others should—but when you see a new sports car coming up behind you at top speed, you move *over, fast.* There are trends and tendencies, but what drivers *do* varies with the circumstances.

Power Plays in Traffic

The issue is sometimes POWER. For some drivers their vehicles are tools for demonstrating their dominance of the road and of the world. If they can manage to get vehicles big enough or fast enough to make it possible for them to break the rules, they'll break them. Similarly, there are people who use *language* to demonstrate their power over others, and if they can get away with it they'll break the rules, too. This is true for both men and women. On the road, such people tend to believe that they're immune to traffic accidents; in conversation, they're equally unaware that they're in any danger from their language behavior. Even if they suspect a connection between language and the problems of others, they're confident that such things could never happen to them.

And the trends and tendencies? Men are usually bigger and stronger, which means they can often drown other people out; women are more likely to start crying, a different kind of power play that nevertheless brings conversation to a halt. Women are perhaps a little more polite in public; men are probably more concerned about moving things along as quickly as possible. But for both genders, there are situations in which it's the other way around. People have a variety of ways of creating, and preventing, conversational gridlock. This behavior is tied not to gender but to the power relations in the particular interaction. The number and range of variables this introduces *guarantees* confusion in research results.

Traffic flow can't be managed by moralizing. Nobody would tell a speeder at the wheel of a big truck that he or she *should* follow the traffic rules and expect that to take care of the problem. Instead, we make it clear to such drivers that although they may get away with their behavior temporarily, they will *eventually* be caught by a cop and lose their license to drive the truck. It may take a while, we tell them, but in the end, you'll get caught and lose your license. It is therefore in *your own best interest* to follow the rules. Most of the time, this works. If that weren't true, nobody with only an ordinary car to drive would dare get out on the road with the trucks and the fancy sports cars.

Similarly, you can't persuade people to stop interrupting other speakers and monopolizing the floor and changing subjects and talking about things that are boring or offensive by telling them what they *should* do. That's useless. What they need to know is that it is in their own interest— it is good for *them*, in the long run—to follow the traffic rules of language. They need to understand that although they may be able to rule the linguistic road for a long time, *eventually* their lawless language behavior will bring them down, if only because nobody wants them around. Remember: Research has proved that people who are disliked and lonely have far more health problems than people with a strong social network. There is no surer way to become a disliked and lonely person than to be a chronic violator of the language traffic rules.

When the Problem Is Not Power Plays, but Ignorance

One more difference between road traffic and talk traffic must be pointed out here. Kids grow up seeing not just the way their parents drive, but also the driving habits of all the other people on the road. In the unusual case of their breaking traffic rules because they've seen their parents do it and don't realize it's not allowed, they'll get caught—quickly enough, because they're so inexperienced, to make it impossible for them to go on breaking rules out of *ignorance*.

With language traffic, it's different. Many kids grow up in homes where the only models they have for language are parents who ignore the rules, and television shows where the person with the meanest mouth gets all the applause. They may very well grow up with road hog language habits just because they don't know there's any other way to get around in the conversational space—and they may go on to raise families that carry on the tradition. There are no State Language Patrols to interfere with this process, which can go on for generations.

This common problem is a primary reason for the communication breakdown in Scenario Nine. It could be that Gary and Susan are interested only in demonstrating to Mary that they're more powerful than she is, but it's unlikely. It's unlikely that Mary is trying to achieve dominance. It's far more likely that their behavior is the result of either ignorance of the traffic rules or ignorance of their importance, rather than a deliberate intention to break them. What Mary and Susan and Gary need is a model—a pattern for the perfect conversation—that they can follow, and an awareness that it is to *their* advantage to do so.

Technique #8
Managing Language Traffic
The Perfect Conversation

Let's assume that the participants in this perfect conversation are a woman named Helene, a man named Mario, and a man named Tom, all speakers of American Mainstream English. Let's assume that they intend to keep the messages moving so that everyone reaches his or her conversational goals, and that they know how that's done. Let's assume that Helene speaks first (it could be any one of the three). The pattern for their interaction would look like this:

1. Helene introduces a topic that is neither deathly dull nor grossly offensive, and she talks about it for no more than three sentences. While she's doing that, Tom and Mario listen, which includes paying attention to nonverbal signals.

2. As Helene reaches the end of her turn, Tom signals that he wants to talk next, by making eye contact with her. Helene brings her own turn to a close by slowing down, ending her sentence, and pausing; then she hands the turn to Tom by giving him her full attention or speaking to him directly.

3. Tom takes up Helene's topic and supports it, for no more than three sentences, while the others listen. Then, since Mario has not yet said

anything, Tom makes eye contact with him to indicate that he's willing to give him the turn. If Mario doesn't accept the turn, he gives it back to Helene.

4. This process goes on until everyone has had a chance to say a few sentences on the topic introduced at the beginning—or has been offered the chance and has declined it.

5. Someone introduces a new topic and the sequence is repeated; or the conversation ends.

6. Emergency Option: If there is a genuinely urgent reason to deviate from the pattern, the person who does so apologizes and explains.

This is the perfect—the *idealized*—AME conversation. Most conversations won't be this flawless. One person will talk a little longer than the others; one person will take two turns in a row instead of letting the third person have a turn. There will be variations: Someone will say only one sentence instead of three, or five sentences instead of three. As is true for road traffic, the more people there are involved, the more variation there will be and the more each participant will have to adjust to the needs of others. But this basic pattern holds:

✦ One person talks about something other people are willing to talk about, for a brief period of time, while others give their attention to what is being said; and then another person is given a turn to respond on the same subject in the same fashion, until everyone's had a fair opportunity to use the conversational space and the conversation either ends, or shifts to a different subject.

When the interaction is not a conversation—when it's a job interview, or a meeting between a banker and a loan applicant, or a medical interview, or a cross-examination in a court of law—the rules are different. However, they are all derived from this basic pattern for conversation.

You would be astonished at how many educated and intelligent adults are unaware that this is how conversations are supposed to go. Furthermore, although they're aware that people don't enjoy talking with them, they are quite sure they know why. Among my clients, the explanations offered are essentially predictable. It's because they are of a particular ethnic group, they tell me. It's because they're overweight by current fashion standards. It's because their nose is too big or their ears are too small or they're too tall or too short. It's because they can't afford to "power dress." It's because they have an accent. Although a client will sometimes *begin* our association by saying "I don't know why people avoid talking with me," once trust is established between us, the suspected reason appears. Almost always, it's like one of those I just listed. But when I've had the opportunity to observe the client's language behavior I discover that the problem, nine times out of ten, is none of these things. Rather, it is *a persistent violation—sometimes deliberate, often innocent—of the language traffic rules.*

This is hard for the people involved to believe. It's too simple; it's too basic; it doesn't cost enough; you don't even have to fill out a form. They don't want to accept the idea that something so *elementary* is the source of their problems. It usually is, however. There are physical conditions that can interfere with effective communication even when all the rules are followed. A severe and readily visible physical handicap can do that; a failure to bathe regularly can do it; drunkenness or illness can. But under ordinary circumstances, most people are avoided by others because they are language traffic violators. Fortunately, unlike many serious difficulties we face in our daily lives, this one can be *fixed*.

The Four Basic Conversation Skills

You need only four skills in order to carry on satisfactory conversations in which all the traffic rules are observed:

1. Introduction of appropriate topics
2. Support of topics introduced by others
3. Management of turns
4. Handling the occasional emergency

None of these skills has much to do with gender, physical appearance, accent, or the other factors typically put forward as "the reason I don't have many conversations." Let's consider them briefly, one at a time.

1. Introduction of Appropriate Topics

There are two kinds of inappropriate topics: those that are boring, and those that are offensive. In addition, there is the problem of the person who has only *one* topic, and who—no matter what others are talking about—will do everything possible to switch the conversation to it.

Adults do know what topics are boring to others. People will say to me, "Sure, I know it's boring, but she's my wife. She's supposed to listen to me talk, whether it's boring or not!" Or "He's my husband" or

"They <u>work</u> for me" or "They're my <u>friends</u>"—and so they're supposed to put up with all the boring topics. Sometimes people tell me, "It's not boring to <u>me</u>; there's no reason why it should bore anybody else." Or they claim that "only somebody who's stupid" (or some other negative phrase) would find their topic boring. They tell me that they have to choose the topic because what *other* people want to talk about is boring.

Don't introduce boring topics. It not only guarantees unsatisfactory conversations, it's also bad for you personally. When you see your listeners' eyes glaze over, change the subject or let someone else talk. Forcing other people to listen to talk that bores them is a *power* play, nothing more, and people who insist on it will find themselves lonely and ignored as soon as they are no longer in a position of dominance.

As is true for talk that's boring, adults do know which topics are offensive, and should avoid them. Don't introduce topics that other people find repulsive. You may consider the gory details of a surgery, or a play-by-play account of a bloody tragedy, fascinating. But it's unlikely that other people will agree with you. The only people who will be interested in hearing about such things are people who have a repulsive topic of their own that they intend to introduce as soon as they get the floor. Unless you can be certain these are the only people you'll need to associate with, such topics have no place in your conversation.

2. Support of Others' Topics

This one is easy, and it comes naturally. When someone introduces a topic, don't change the subject. Listen—really listen—to the topic on the floor, and make an encouraging noise now and then. Comment on the topic, or ask a question about it. If nothing else occurs to you, just say "That's interesting. Go on." Being a good listener is one of the most admired conversational skills.

In their essay titled "Conversational Relevance in Multiple-Goal Settings" (Conversational Coherence: Form, Structure, and Strategy (Sage Publications, 1983) pp. 116–135), Karen Tracy and John P. Moran propose that there are three ways to support a partner's topics. Suppose that your partner has opened a conversation by saying, "I just don't think this town <u>needs</u> another airport." Here's an example of a supporting response of each of their three kinds, in what I consider to be their order of desirability.

- **Continuing the topic introduced.** "You may be right. It would mean a lot more traffic and a lot more noise."
- **Linking the topic to a new one.** "You're right; it would be just one

more bureaucratic mess. Did you notice that they've switched the one-way streets <u>again</u>?''

—or—

''I know what you mean. I feel the same way about the plan to keep switching the direction of the one-way streets every couple of months.''

- **Closing the topic and then introducing a new one.** ''You may be right; I don't really know. I do know that the very idea of a new airport distresses me. Would you be willing to talk about something more pleasant? Like the new Arts Building, for example. I saw it yesterday for the first time, and. . . .''

Any one of these methods will do; choose among them on the basis of the situation you find yourself in. And remember that you can always substitute an attentive facial expression and an occasional ''Mmhmm.''

3. Management of Turns

This includes getting the turn, keeping the turn, passing the turn to someone else, accepting the turn from someone else, and refusing the turn; in other words, changing lanes and getting safely through the intersections.

The basics for this skill can be taken directly from what you know about traffic on the road. The only difference that matters is that in conversation you don't have automatic and unambiguous turn signals. For AME the signals that matter most are these:

- Making eye contact with the person you plan to give the turn to (and avoiding eye contact with the speaker if you don't want to talk);
- Coming to a full and unmistakable *stop* when you're through with your turn (and avoiding lengthy pauses at all other times); and
- Using clear language to clarify matters when necessary, as in ''Bill, did you have something you wanted to say about this?''

You need to be able to give these signals, and you need to be able to observe them and act on them when they come at you from other people. Getting good at this is like learning to drive well: You have to pay attention to what you're doing, and you have to practice.

4. Handling the Occasional Emergency

There will be times when you'll need to violate a rule and it can't be helped. In such situations, you say things like these.

- "I'm sorry to interrupt you—we have to leave now, and the last bus goes in five minutes."
- "Forgive me for interrupting—I haven't seen that movie, and if you go on and tell the ending, you'll ruin it for me."
- "I'm sorry—I need a doctor. Immediately."
- "It's not my turn to talk; I know that. I apologize. The reason I'm talking now is that I have to leave."
- "I'm sorry, I didn't hear your first few words and I'm not following you. Could you fill me in, please?"
- "I'm sorry. You obviously misunderstood me. I suggest that you stop right now, before we have a serious problem on our hands."

The temptation to decide that all of this is too simplistic to bother with should be resisted. No one, of either gender, will ever avoid you because you *follow* the rules for the four basic skills of conversation.

Listening

The ability to *listen* is crucial to managing language traffic. You can't support topics introduced by others unless you listen to what they say. You can't keep track of the conversational turns if you aren't listening. If you don't listen to the responses others make to your speech, you won't be able to monitor their reactions to *your* topics. Without competent listening skills, conversation—or any other language interaction—cannot take place.

Because it's so critical to communication, we can be grateful that listening is a mental process that takes place automatically *as long as people don't interfere with it*. All of the items on the list below—none of which is unique to either gender—interfere with the listening process and make it difficult or impossible.

- Sitting on the edge of your chair watching for an opportunity to break into the interaction and take the floor.
- Thinking about something entirely unrelated to the conversation you're part of.

- Thinking about how badly the speaker is putting things and what you would say in the speaker's place.

- Deciding in advance that the speaker couldn't possibly have anything to say that's worth hearing.

- Rehearsing what you're going to say when you get the turn.

- Doing something that requires substantial amounts of your attention, such as reading or writing . . . or staring out the window at something taking place outside.

People who feel that you don't listen to them when they talk will quickly decide to avoid talking to you and will instead make an effort to talk to others whose behavior is less insulting. This is as true for the two people in a couple as it is for anyone else. When one partner begins complaining that the other "never <u>listens</u> to me!" trouble is inevitable.

Learning to Listen

If your listening skills are weak, you have a perfect "teaching machine" available for strengthening them: your television set. Turn on a program composed primarily of talk—*real* talk. The interactions in most situation comedies, game shows, soap operas, and sports programs aren't suitable. Neither are programs such as "Crossfire," which are primarily demonstrations of how to violate as many language traffic rules as possible. Find a televised speech or sermon or lecture or discussion. Your public television channel has plenty of useful material. Public affairs programs like the "McNeil-Lehrer News Hour," "Wall Street Week," and "Washington Week in Review" are excellent. Because "Washington Week in Review" comes so close to following the "ideal conversation" pattern on pages 168–169, I routinely assign it to my clients as homework. C-Span, which covers Congress, is another good source.

It doesn't matter if you find some or all of these programs boring. You become a better runner when the courses you run challenge you; the same principle holds for becoming a good listener. Turn on the program, sit down, and really listen. Give the speaker your complete attention, *as if* every word mattered to you personally. Each time your attention wanders away from the speaker, bring it back—no matter how many times it happens. This is listening *practice*, and is the only way to master the skill. Unlike live human beings, televised speakers can be turned off at your convenience and their feelings can never be hurt; their speech is your best training source.

Your goal is the ability to listen attentively and easily for ten uninterrupted minutes. No one speaker in a conversation (or any other language interaction, as opposed to a *performance*) has the right to expect your full attention for any longer than that.

Good listeners are highly valued, so much so that many people in the AME culture are willing to pay large fees to professional listeners like therapists and counselors. And good listeners get a valuable fringe benefit: Research has proved that attentive listening is actually good for your health. (See Lynch 1985 for details.) When you are really listening, your blood pressure goes down, your heartbeat moderates, and your body shows the healthful changes associated with relaxation.

Now let's go back to Scenario Nine and analyze it in the context of the information about language traffic management, so that it will be clear why everything went so badly for the speakers involved.

Another Look at Scenario Nine

Almost every line in this scenario shows one or more violations of the language traffic rules. If you analyze the scenario for traffic rather than content, this is what you get:

1. Gary insists on a topic that neither Mary nor Susan wants to talk about (Mary's resignation from her job), *knowing full well that they both find it objectionable*.

2. Mary interrupts Gary.

3. Susan interrupts Mary, with an abrupt switch to a totally unrelated topic.

4. Gary grabs the turn that Susan had offered to Mary and changes the subject back again.

5. Mary interrupts Susan's attempt to defend herself.

6. Gary interrupts Susan's attempt to answer Mary, and in addition introduces yet another topic (feminism) that he knows both women will be unwilling to support.

7. Mary refuses to support Gary's topic.

8. Susan interrupts Gary's attempt to force Mary to support his original topic and again tries to change the subject drastically and abruptly.

9. Mary interrupts Susan and terminates the conversation for all three by verbal force.

This is the domestic version of the confrontational talk shows on television, and it is literally toxic. Everyone involved will come out of an interaction like this feeling miserable and frustrated; often they will feel physically sick. Nothing will destroy a relationship faster than chronic participation in non-conversations like the one shown in Scenario Nine. The remedy is simple: observation of the language traffic rules.

Dialogues for Analysis

DIALOGUE ONE

F: "I heard something on the news this morning that I almost couldn't believe."

M: "Is this low-fat milk?"

F: "Does it taste like low-fat milk?"

M: "If it did, would I be asking?"

The traffic patterns here will be obvious to you. She introduces a topic and expects a response, but instead of supporting her topic he asks an entirely unrelated question. She then abandons her topic for his, but not willingly. The number of unusual emphatic stresses on her words clearly signals her anger about doing so. His reply, which has no extra stresses, continues his topic—and demonstrates that he wasn't listening. He didn't *hear* her anger.

Suggestion for Her: Don't abandon your topic in a situation like this one. His question is not the linguistic equivalent of a huge truck roaring up behind you—don't get out of the way. Answer his "Is this low-fat milk?" with "No, it's regular milk. Now, as I said before, I heard something almost unbelievable on the radio this morning." This may not work. He may ignore you again and continue talking about the milk. Don't let that deter you. It's important for you to establish the fact that you're not going to be run over in this way, even if it takes multiple tries and requires considerable effort on your part. For example . . .

M: "Is this low-fat milk?"

F: "No, it's regular milk. Now, as I said before, I heard something almost unbelievable on the news this morning."

M: "You know I'm not supposed to drink regular milk. Why didn't you get low-fat?"

F: "Tell you what—I'm willing to negotiate. First we will settle the issue of the milk. Then we will talk about what I heard on the news this morning. Fair enough?''

M: "Did you say something about the news?''

F: "I did, and I plan to say it again. But first, the milk. I got regular milk because they were <u>out</u> of low-fat milk.''

M: "Oh . . . okay.''

F: "Now. When I was listening to the news this morning. . . .''

Suggestion for Him: The problem here is that you're not listening to her. You didn't hear the topic she introduced and you didn't hear the anger in her voice when she answered you. It's all right (and won't cause anger) to do this when you face a crisis, but not otherwise. If you already know how to listen, listen to *her*; if you don't know how, follow the instructions in this chapter for using the television set to improve your listening skills. You can still find out about the milk. Just wait until after you've supported her topic and it's your turn to introduce one of your own choice.

DIALOGUE TWO

M: "One thing I really like about eating in the hotel restaurant is that—''

F: "Hey, I think these flowers are <u>real</u>!''

M: "Well, that goes with eating in a hotel restaurant instead of a fast food place.''

F: "Did you want fast food? I thought you said you wanted to eat at the hotel.''

M: "I <u>did</u>. I <u>do</u>!''

F: "Are you mad about something?''

He introduces a topic; instead of supporting it, she introduces a different one. But it's clear that she wasn't just deliberately ignoring him or changing the subject. She wasn't listening and didn't hear what he said; as a result, she misunderstands his next utterance and—not surprisingly—this leads to conflict. Here's a rewrite.

M: "One thing I really like about eating in the hotel restaurant is that—''

F: "Hey, I think these flowers are <u>real</u>!''

M: "Exactly. When you eat in the hotel restaurant, you get real flowers instead of fake ones. And as I started to say, something I really like about eating here is. . . ."

DIALOGUE THREE

F1: "Have you seen anything in the paper about the plan for the new elementary school?"

F2: "No . . . and I don't understand why! You would think that with thirty kids in every class they'd be <u>doing</u> something. How are the kids supposed to learn anything?"

M: "I can tell you what's happening."

F1: "They have room in the paper, you notice, for everything else. Everybody's wedding. All the sports. The <u>astrology</u> column. But when it comes to the schools—"

M: (Talking over the top of her words.)"I <u>said</u>, I know what they're doing! I can fill you in."

F1: "—they don't seem to care about keeping people informed."

F2: "I know what you mean. It makes me furious."

Here we have two people so deeply engaged in talking to one another that the third person in the interaction becomes invisible and inaudible. The two women not only aren't offering this man his fair share of the conversation, they are treating him as if he weren't there at all. This behavior is inexcusable. In such a situation, the move is his, and it would be understandable if he just got up and left. Suppose, however, that he values his relationship with one or both of the women and is willing to work to maintain it. In that case, he should Level, as in this continuation of the dialogue.

F2: "I know what you mean. It makes me furious."

M: "All right, that's <u>enough</u>."

F1: (Startled.)"What?"

F2: "What do you mean, 'that's enough'?"

M: "I mean, that's enough of you two talking to each other as if I weren't here. I know what's going on with the new school and I know why it hasn't been in the paper. I'll be glad to tell you about it. I'm just waiting for an empty space to come by in this conversation."

It's important for him to say this in Leveler Mode. His goal is to state the facts neutrally and insist that the women follow the language traffic rules, not to complain that he's being mistreated (Blamer Mode) or to plead for better treatment (Placater Mode).

DIALOGUE FOUR

F: "Jennifer had her baby this morning, honey."

M: "She did? That's great. Boy or girl?"

F: "It was a little boy."

M: "Terrific. Tell her I said congratulations."

F: "She had an awful time. First her water broke at the mall, can you believe it? And then by the time she got to the hospital her contractions—"

M: "Did the plumber call you today?"

He has interrupted and changed the subject, but it's not because he wasn't listening. It's because he doesn't want to sit through a detailed account of Jennifer's labor and delivery, because he either thinks the topic is boring or finds it offensive. Ideally, he would tolerate it a little longer for courtesy's sake (as a woman might tolerate a blow-by-blow account of a hockey game she found equally undesirable as a topic of conversation), but he's not willing to do that. However, his line about the plumber is the linguistic equivalent of cutting off another car at an intersection. It's better for him to come right out with the fact that he objects to the topic and to explain why.

If He Thinks the Topic Is Boring:

M: "Wait—stop, please. I like babies. I'm glad Jennifer's baby arrived safely. But in my opinion a blow-by-blow account of the arrival <u>process</u> is about as interesting as root canal work. I'm not willing to be that bored. Let's talk about where to put your new rosebush, instead."

If He Finds the Topic Offensive:

M: "Wait—stop, please. My stomach just is not strong enough to handle that subject. Let's talk about where to put your new rosebush, instead."

Neither of these rewrites is particularly courteous, but both follow the traffic rules. They interrupt, certainly, but—unlike "Did the plumber call you today?''—they refer to the topic on the floor and close it with an explanation. And he goes out of his way to offer her a new topic that she might have chosen, which *is* courteous.

There's no such thing as a close relationship between two human beings in which neither partner is ever rude. Even someone who is unfailingly and scrupulously polite to strangers and casual acquaintances will sometimes lack the strength or the patience to maintain that record in a private relationship. In such a situation, less damage is done if people are rude *by the rules*.

DIALOGUE FIVE

M: "Boy, it sure is hot today, isn't it?"

F: "It sure is."

M: "Do you remember it ever being this hot in June before?"

F: "No."

M: "It's too hot to <u>do</u> anything."

F: "Yes, it is."

M: "Well, maybe it'll rain and that will cool things down."

F: "Mmhmm."

Sometimes this sort of talk isn't intended as conversation. Sometimes, especially in long-standing relationships, it's just a kind of mutual acknowledgment of one another's company, with no need for much semantic content. In that case Dialogue Five will serve the purpose. But suppose that's not what's happening here. Suppose this is a dialogue between two people who would *like* to have a conversation. The problem then is that conversation can't begin until a topic is established, and neither of these people seems capable of doing that. He keeps bringing up the weather, but seems unable to switch to another subject when the topic fails; she is apparently unwilling or unable either to support his topic or introduce one she'd like better. I suggest two rewrites, one in which he takes the initiative and one in which she does.

M: "Boy, it sure is hot today, isn't it?"

F: "It sure is."

M: "Do you remember it ever being this hot in June before?"

F: "No."

M: "It makes you wonder. . . . Maybe they're right about global warming and the greenhouse effect."

F: "Do you really think so? Don't you think they're jumping to conclusions? They base the whole thing on computer models, you know. And every time any little thing goes wrong in this world, somebody blames it on 'computer error'!"

M: "That's true, but. . . ."

M: "Boy, it sure is hot today, isn't it?"

F: "It sure is."

M: "Do you remember it ever being this hot in June before?"

F: "No. But it's been a heck of a lot hotter in July and August. The heat just got here earlier this year, I think. And it's probably good for the gardens. Which reminds me—did you ever find out what was eating your strawberries?"

M: "I sure did. You're not going to believe this, but. . . ."

DIALOGUE SIX

M: "Look at those kids, will you? They're really having a good time!"

F: "Like my bosses' kids. <u>They</u> always have a good time, too. On <u>her</u> salary, that's easy. Did I tell you about the time she. . . ."

It makes no difference what topic he introduces. She will always find a way to convert it to the only topic she has any interest in: the boss she despises. Unless she stops being such a Janey-One-Note, she is going to be very lonely and much avoided. It would be a good idea for him to explain that to her and try to help her change.

DIALOGUE SEVEN

F: "We've got to talk this out, and that's all there is to it. I'm not going to let you avoid it this time."

M: "We've <u>already</u> talked it out! We've talked it to <u>death</u>! And I'm not going to talk about it any <u>longer</u>!"

F: "<u>Listen</u> to me: <u>You</u> have to do more of the housework, or <u>I</u> am going to have to quit my job! I <u>mean</u> that!"

M: "You've said that fifty <u>times</u>! I <u>hear</u> you! Now let it <u>drop</u>, <u>please</u>! There's nothing to be gained by going over and over and OVER it!"

F: "But you still don't understand what I'm <u>say</u>ing! You're saying you'll do more, but you're just saying it to shut me <u>up</u>! That's not <u>good</u> enough. I'm not the Wicked Witch of the West, I'm just asking you to be <u>fair</u>!!"

M: "I will be. I promise. Now please, let it go. I can't talk about it any more."

F: "NO! Let's get it SETTLED, for once! I'm SICK of you starting arguments and then running out on me in the MIDDLE! And don't you DARE just walk out on me this time!"

Most men are physically bigger and stronger than most women, in the sense that they can lift heavier loads and are better suited for rough contact sports. But one area in which research makes it clear that they are *weaker* is in verbal confrontations. A number of studies of men and women involved in verbal fights have demonstrated that men suffer more severe physical effects—rapid heartbeat, rising blood pressure, churning stomach, and the like—than women do. The woman in Dialogue Six needs to understand that this man's urgent pleas for an end to the argument are probably not based on a deliberate strategy of starting arguments and then abandoning them in midstream. It's far more likely that they're based on the alarming physical symptoms he's feeling. Arguing like this *literally* makes him sick. No matter who's right or wrong about the issue in question, it's counterproductive to go on.

I'm not suggesting that she should drop her efforts to convince him to do his share of the housework, or that he should be allowed to simply refuse to negotiate that with her. I'm saying that nothing will be accomplished by forcing him to go on with the argument when he can't handle the physiological consequences. He won't be able to either listen or talk, and that makes negotiation impossible. She needs to let it go for now and find a way to communicate with him about it that doesn't produce such distracting effects.

In such situations, one of her best strategies is to write him a letter or record a tape. He can then read (or listen to) her message without having her present, which will reduce the tension. Afterward, he may be both willing and able to discuss the problem thoroughly and join her in finding a solution; if not, he should answer by letter or tape, and the exchange can continue until the matter is settled. Couples often forget that face-to-face talking isn't the only method they have for communication on high-anxiety topics.

CHAPTER 10

◆

Patterns of Verbal Abuse and Verbal Violence

Their food had arrived and it was at last possible to talk without being interrupted. John set down his wineglass and began. "I've been thinking," he said. "It's been a month. It seemed to me that it might be a good idea for us to talk this over one more time."

"Why?"

"Because," he said, "you are very good at what you do, Mary. You won't be easy to replace. I'd like to discuss the possibility that you might reconsider and come back to View Inc. On a trial basis, of course. I'm sorry about the way things turned out; how about giving it another try?"

Mary put her hand over the top of her glass as he reached to refill it. "No thank you," she said. "No more wine, please. What do you mean, you're 'sorry'?"

He raised his eyebrows, but he answered her with grave courtesy.

"I mean that I'm sorry you found the situation unpleasant. I'm sorry unkind words were exchanged."

Mary sat silently, watching him eat, and he waited.

"Well?" he asked finally.

"I'd like some time to think it over," she told him.

He had been charm itself until then, but now his mouth and his eyes narrowed, and he leaned toward her. "Then you can forget it!" he said.

"It's <u>not</u> an unreasonable request!" she snapped.

"You don't think so?" He leaned closer, and his words came

hard and fast. "First you turn my office into a soap opera, with
everybody walking on eggs for fear of hurting Your Majesty's
royal feelings! Then you quit on me in the middle of a dozen
projects where you have a critical role! Without a moment's
thought about what that might mean for the people who have to
find some way to go ON when you abandon ship! They have
bills to pay TOO, you know! But that doesn't MATTER to you,
DOES it? YOU don't even CARE! I make the stupid mistake of
thinking, well, hey, maybe we could work something out . . .
and YOU need time to think it OVer! YOU have one hell of a
NERVE, Mary!"

He'd kept his voice low in the crowded restaurant, and Mary
was glad of that, but in some ways the soft menace of his words
was worse than if he'd been shouting them. And it was true;
leaving the way she had, she'd left a lot of people in a bind.

"You're wrong!" she said bitterly. "It's not FAIR to accuse
me of not caring! Even YOU should realize that I only left
because I felt I HAD to! You could at least TRY to understand!"

"Clayton," he said, "I've gone a lot further than halfway
here. I told you I was sorry, and I am. It was all stupid; I'm
sorry it happened. But let me tell you: If you REALLY wanted
to get ahead in your field, you'd stop behaving like a CHILD!
What's the MATTER with you? What kind of a fairy tale world
do you WANT? It's not perfect? So it's not PERFect! You're not
the ONLY person who ever noticed that, you know!"

Mary stared at her plate, trying to think what to say to him if
he ever stopped his flood of angry words.

"Have you found a job yet?" he demanded.

"No."

"You do realize that View Inc. is the top company in your
field? You realize how hard it's going to be to explain to another
company why you want to move DOWN? You want to end up
flipping hamburgers somewhere? GROW UP, Mary!"

Mary swallowed hard. He was right, of course. She hadn't
been able to explain it to him, and he'd been there. She hadn't
been able to explain it to her parents, who loved her. Jobs were
hard to find, and employers could pick and choose. How was she
going to explain it to a prospective boss?

"I'm going to say this one more time," John said coldly,
"and then I'm through. I'm offering you your job back. Same
salary. Same deal. On a trial basis. Six months, Mary. If it

doesn't work out, then we call it quits for good. That's my best offer, and it's final. Take it or leave it. YES, or NO?''

And Mary heard herself say yes. In a voice she hardly recognized as her own.

◆

What's Going On Here?

John's Point of View

As John perceives it, he has forgiven Mary for a host of failings and has generously agreed to let bygones be bygones. He was not so foolish as to expect gratitude from her, but he *did* expect a prompt, if chilly, acceptance of his offer. It annoys him that this meeting over lunch turned into a fight—he wonders whether Paula would still have pressured him to make the offer if she'd been present and had a chance to observe Mary's behavior. On the other hand, he doesn't take fights like this one seriously; for him they are essentially sport. On the whole, he's satisfied with the results of his move. Having Mary gone has meant less stress at the office in some ways, but it's been extremely inconvenient in others, especially on the new project she'd put together almost entirely on her own just before she quit. He's prepared to wait and see, and he hopes that his past experience with Mary—plus a month of wearisome discussions of the situation with Paula—will make it possible for him to head off any future hassles. If not . . . well, he's made it clear that the job is being offered on a trial basis only. Putting an end to it this time will be simple and straightforward.

Mary's Point of View

As Mary perceives it, she has once again allowed John to maneuver her into a position where she couldn't defend herself or justify her actions. She wishes she'd been able to stay cool and calm when he started laying guilt trips on her. She wishes she hadn't let her nervousness over not having a job yet weaken her resolve so much. She wishes she had stuck to her guns and *forced* John to understand that she knows the difference between "I'm sorry you didn't think everything was perfect" and "I'm sorry for what I did wrong," and that she resents the phony apology. She hopes she hasn't made a serious error in agreeing to work for John again. And she hopes that her past experience with the men at View Inc.—plus the cooling-off period that everyone has had during her absence—will make it possible for her to avoid a repetition of the incidents that forced her to leave a job she liked so much.

---------------------◆---------------------

One of the things men and women in the United States spend a lot of time—too much time—doing is *fighting*. Both genders are in agreement about that. Both agree that there's too much violence between the genders, both physical and verbal; both would like to see it stop. And both are forever finding themselves involved in interactions like the one in Scenario Ten, even when all parties present started out determined to maintain a pleasant language environment.

The scenario presents a classic interaction between a skilled verbal abuser and a chronic verbal victim. It's a typical episode in an ugly game *that nobody can play without a partner*, and it comes straight from the American Mainstream English grammar of verbal violence. We'll look at it in some detail, and then go on to a proven method for dealing with such episodes.

The Verbal Attack Patterns (VAPs) of English

In some languages, hostility and anger are expressed by adding a special word to a sentence; in others, extra pieces are added to words to carry the negative messages. (Haden 1987) In English the words are not what matters. What makes a given sequence of English a hostile one, or turns it into a verbal attack, is its *intonation*: the tune the words are set to. As you know, making intonation clear with only punctuation as a tool is difficult. The set of examples below should help with the task.

1. "Why do you eat so much junk food?"
    NEUTRAL; the questioner is genuinely interested in knowing the answer.

2. "Why do you eat so much junk food?"
    INTENSE; the questioner is concerned, or surprised, or distressed.

3. "WHY do you eat so much junk food?"
    ANGRY; the questioner is opposed.

4. "WHY do you eat SO MUCH JUNK food?!"
    ANGRIER; VERBAL ATTACK. The questioner couldn't care *less* what the victim eats, or why.

The only way to be absolutely sure of intonation, of course, is to *be* there—to hear the words spoken, in a real-world context. But the rough approximations above will serve our needs for the moment.

The only difference in *form* between the neutral question (#1) and the corresponding verbal attack (#4) is in their intonation. The major difference in terms of *function* is that the verbal attacker *has no interest in the answer to the question.* Verbal attackers, of either gender, are interested only in the fight.

Native speakers of English learn its verbal attack patterns (VAPs, for short) the same way they learn the rest of the patterns of their language, as infants and toddlers observing the language others use in their hearing. By the time they're old enough for kindergarten they have the most common VAPs well under control, and they use them freely—and with amazing success—against adults. For adults these patterns are as internalized as the patterns for asking questions or giving commands. They're part of daily life, and their presence in the language environment is taken as a given.

Here are a dozen example VAPs (with some common variations), chosen because they're the kind of things men and women say to each other when anger takes over. There are others; but the total set is undoubtedly small, and the principles for dealing with all of them are the same. Look at the examples—which you'll find immediately familiar—and then we'll return to the discussion.

1. "If you REALLY loved me, YOU wouldn't waste MONEY the way you do!!"
   (And "If you really LOVED me, YOU wouldn't . . ." or "A person who really LOVED another person wouldn't . . .")

2. "If you really LOVED me, YOU wouldn't WANT to smoke!"
   (And variations as for #1. Also common: "If you really LOVED me, YOU wouldn't WANT me to be miserable!"/"If you REALLY loved me, YOU'D want me to be HAPpy!")

3. "WHY do you ALWAYS try to make me look STUPid?!"
   (And "WHY don't you ever try to make ME look good?")

4. "EVEN a WOMan ought to have brains enough to change a TIRE!"/ "EVen a MAN ought to be able to balance a CHECKbook!"
   (And the all-purpose "EVen YOU . . .")

5. "You could at LEAST CALL me when you're going to be late!"
   (And "The LEAST you could do is CALL me . . .")

6. "DON'T you even CARE if you're BREAKing my HEART?"
(And "DON'T you even CARE IF YOU'RE BREAKING MY
HEART?")

7. "HOW COULD you tell my mother an awful thing like that!"
(And "HOW could you SAY/DO such a terrible thing?!'')

8. "EVERYbody underSTANDS why you can't do your SHARE around
here, you know!"

9. "EVen if you DO lose your job, I'LL still love you!"

10. "YOU'RE not the ONly person in the world who hates HOUSEwork,
you know!"

11. "You KNOW I'd never try to tell you what to DO, dear, but YOU'D
have to be out of your MIND to take that job!"

12. "SOME people would really be FURious if you spoke to them the
way you're speaking to ME!"

Technique #9
Recognizing and Responding to the Verbal Attack Patterns of English

All VAPs have two parts. One is the open attack called the *bait*, which
is the part intended to get your attention by hurting and/or angering you.
The other part is the *presupposed* attack, which is better hidden and less
likely to attract your immediate notice. (There may be more than one of
each.) For example:

> "If you REALLY loved me, YOU wouldn't YELL at me all the
> time!"

OPEN ATTACK (BAIT): You yell at me all the time.

PRESUPPOSED ATTACK: You don't really love me.

In some of the VAPs, as in this one, the two parts are clearly separated;
in others, they are tangled together.

The VAPs are *action chains*: sequences of behavior with a rigid and
ordered set of steps which, if interrupted, cannot be completed.

Step One: The attacker throws the VAP at the victim.

Step Two: The victim takes the bait and responds to it directly and emotionally.

Step Three: There is a volley of attack and counterattack until one of the people involved gives up.

These patterns are part of your grammar; you've been hearing them and using them all your life. You will recognize them by three predictable characteristics:

- By their melody—all those extra strong stresses on words and parts of words, which signal anger and hostility;
- By the fact that the person using them isn't interested in getting a neutral response; if the VAP is shaped like a question, for instance, the attacker isn't interested in the answer;
- By the presence of the two kinds of verbal abuse included—one open attack, and one attack (or more) hidden in a presupposition.

You recognize the VAPs *automatically*. The question is, how do you *respond* to them?

How to Respond Effectively to VAPs

The rules for responding to VAPs are very simple:

- ✦ **RULE ONE:**   Ignore the bait.
- ✦ **RULE TWO:**   Respond directly to a presupposition.
- ✦ **RULE THREE:**   Whatever else you do, transmit the message, "Don't bother trying that with me; I won't play that stupid game."

If the victim interrupts the action chain—by ignoring the bait, no matter how outrageously tempting it may be, and responding to a presupposition instead—the attack *cannot be completed*. Compare Dialogues A and B below.

A: The Victim Takes the Bait and Runs with It
Tracy: "If you really LOVED me, YOU wouldn't CHEAT on your DIET all the time!"

Brooke: "What do you MEAN? I do NOT cheat on my diet!"

Tracy: "Oh, YEAH? What about that DOUGHnut I saw you eating this morning? I suppose THAT's on your diet!"

Brooke: "WHY are you ALWAYS SPYING on me?"

Tracy: "If you'd eat what you're SUPPOSED to eat, I wouldn't HAVE to spy on you!"

(And so on, till somebody surrenders.)

B: The Victim Follows the Rules for Responding to VAPs (and Stops Being a Victim)

Tracy: "If you really LOVED me, YOU wouldn't CHEAT on your DIET all the time!"

Brooke: "When did you start thinking I don't love you?"

In Dialogue B, the potential victim has ignored the crack about cheating on a diet and has responded directly to the presupposed "You don't really love me." This isn't what the attacker was expecting; it isn't what the attacker had planned; it interrupts the action chain and makes it impossible to continue with it.

Sometimes the foiled attacker's next line will be bewildered silence, which is much better than the fight that was intended. If the attacker has always been able to count on this victim to play the game before, the attack will often be repeated: "Wait a minute—you didn't hear what I said! I said, if you really LOVED me, YOU wouldn't cheat on your DIET all the time!" (To which the victim should say once again, "When did you start thinking I don't love you?") Sometimes the attacker will respond with "When you forgot my birthday yesterday, that's when!"—which makes it clear that the anger wasn't about a diet at all, and brings the real reason into the open where it can be discussed. All of these outcomes are a tremendous improvement over Dialogue A.

But there's also this possibility.

Y: "When did you start thinking I don't love you?"

X: "When I saw you cheating on your DIET again, THAT'S when! WHY do you keep DOing that?"

When that happens, the intended victim's proper move is something I call the Boring Baroque Response. One of the presuppositions of "WHY do you keep DOing that?'' is the one that goes with all questions: ''You have an item of information, and I am asking you to share it with me.'' In the case of this VAP, the victim knows the request for the information is a phony, but it's there to be taken advantage of all the same. The proper move is a Boring Baroque Response like this one:

> ''I think I do it because of something that happened when I was a little kid, frankly. We were living in Detroit at the time . . . at least, I <u>think</u> it was Detroit. No, wait a minute! It must have been Indianapolis, because I remember that was the year it was so <u>hot</u>. Anyway, we were living in Indianapolis, and my Aunt Evelyn came to see us, and . . .''

Are you bored yet?

This kind of response, *with neutral intonation only*, delivers the ''I won't play that stupid game'' message superbly well. (Said sarcastically, or with the multiple-stress melody of verbal violence, it's nothing but another counterattack.) It says ''Ask a phony question; get a phony answer.'' It says ''Playing the VAP Game with me will be <u>no</u> fun. It will be <u>awful</u>!''

When you need to use a Boring Baroque in response to a statement rather than a question, just begin with something like this: ''Hearing you say that reminds me of something that happened to me when I was just a little kid. . . .''

VAPs have just one purpose: to demonstrate the attacker's power to get and keep the victim's attention, which provides the attacker with pleasure. You may have been thinking that people who would let rude remarks get past them without challenge and switch to my recommended responses instead are suckers—that they're letting the attacker ''get away with it.'' WRONG. What constitutes ''letting them get away with it'' is taking the bait and providing the verbal abuser with a handy victim for carrying out the action chain.

Think about it. Put yourself into this situation. Pretend for a moment that *you* are the one being accused of cheating on your diet. You had a plan for the way you wanted to spend the next fifteen minutes; there were things you intended to do with that time. But your attacker has *other* plans for you. Your attacker needs the emotional fix that goes with getting your attention, watching you get all upset and angry, tying up your time and your energy, and proving that he (or she) can push your buttons and pull your strings.

When you take the bait and go along with that agenda, that's letting the attacker get away with it. Every time you do it, you're *rewarding the attacker for verbally abusing you and training the attacker to be an ever better verbal abuser. That*, not ignoring some foolish abusive remark, is letting the attacker get away with it.

Sadly, there are many adults in our society—from every sort of background—who are unaware that any mechanism for dealing with disagreement exists except the VAPs. They grew up in homes where that was how disagreement was handled, whether it was over the color of somebody's nail polish or the morality of going to war. Homes where every disagreement, no matter how minor, had to be settled in such a way that there was a clear winner and a clear loser. If the VAPs are where you *start*, the only direction you can go is straight down. If the VAPs don't settle the conflict, what comes next is the open exchange of flat-out insults and epithets and obscenities—the linguistic equivalent of punches and kicks, and sometimes their accompaniment.

Sane adults don't walk up to other people and knock them down, out of the blue; first, there is angry *talk*. (And for couples in abusive relationships, this is the point at which there's a chance to deal with the problem—while the anger is still being expressed verbally and before it escalates to physical violence.)

Saving Face

The popular conception AME-speaking individuals have of the problem of "face" is that it's associated only with other cultures, such as the Japanese. Americans are used to hearing that you must be careful not to make a Japanese person lose face. The truth is that losing face is just as grave a matter for Mainstream Americans as it is for the Japanese or any of the other ethnic groups discussed in this regard. It's another of those situations where you have to compare the damage from hitting a speeding truck head-on with the damage from living for fifteen years over a toxic waste deposit. The two kinds of damage are equally severe; the two situations are equally dangerous. But one happens much more openly and swiftly and dramatically (and, because it is more easily recognized, gets the victim more sympathy). Mainstream America is not a culture where adults commit suicide over a loss of face, although teenagers may. That doesn't mean that losing face is trivial for AME adults, only that they handle it better than teenagers do.

It's common for people in my seminars and consulting practice to insist that it's *okay* for every disagreement to be handled by VAPs and to end with a clear winner and a clear loser. Because "That's the American way! It's a jungle out there! Everybody's out for Number One! Only wimps negotiate! You have to get them before they get you!''

There are two very serious problems with the idea that VAPping is good clean sport. First: You can't "get" anybody else without getting yourself at the same time. Exposure to chronic hostile language is as dangerous to *you* as it is to your opponent. That's not winning. Second: When your opponent in one of these encounters gives up first, leaving you the alleged winner, it solves nothing. *Especially* if, as is usually the case, the victim has lost face.

Unless you happen to have as your victim somebody who is at the absolute bottom of the pecking order, the hostility and anger stirred up by the interaction will just be passed on to somebody else. If you're a nurse and you manage to make a verbally abusive physician look stupid in a VAP session, the doctor will just go down the hall and take it out on the patients. The manager VAPped by a vice president will go take it out on the clerical staff or the salespeople. VAP your spouse and "win," and it will be your kids who bear the brunt, or your neighbor's kids, or the mail carrier. All you do when you hostility-wrestle someone to the floor is pass the hostility along to someone your opponent outranks. All you do is spread more toxic waste around your language environment and make it ever more hostile and dangerous. And then you have to live in the resulting mess.

When you use the *Gentle Art* responses to VAPs, loss of face is kept to the barest of minimums. The attacker has been denied the game, that's true; the attack has failed. But there is no *open* challenge. There is no public, or private, scene. Both people involved can walk away with their dignity intact. *The Gentle Art of Verbal Self-Defense* is an exact analog of the classic physical martial arts; there is no loss of honor on either side. There's always the hazard that the attacker may be frustrated enough to go looking for another victim, of course. Much of the time that can be prevented, however, because the *Gentle Art* responses will defuse the hostility sufficiently to make a rational discussion possible. And when it *can't* be prevented, the attacker will at least approach the next potential victim in a less furious state.

The final section in this chapter, as in all the others, will be a set of dialogues in which communication between men and women is going badly, followed by brief analysis and suggestions for repair. In this chapter, each dialogue will illustrate an attempt by one person to use a VAP against someone of the opposite sex, so that you will have an opportunity to observe cross-gender exchanges using the patterns shown on pages 187–188. You'll find details on each of the patterns, with suggested responses and discussion, in that section.

Another Look at Scenario Ten

John Gellis begins his verbal abuse after Mary asks for time to consider his job offer and replies angrily to his "Then you can for_get_ it!" response. He switches abruptly from his previous courteous speech to Blamer Mode, accusing her of having disrupted his office and his business in various ways, including total indifference to the needs of her colleagues. As is common in an extended sequence of abusive language by a skilled verbal abuser, he works around the basic VAPs like a jazz musician weaving notes around a basic melody. Notice:

John: "They have bills to pay TOO, you know! But that doesn't MATTER to you, DOES it? YOU don't even CARE!"

This is just a skilled variation on "DON'T you even CARE if your COLLEAGUES can't pay their BILLS?" Mary's move should have been a calm and neutral response: "Of course I care about the others at View, Inc.; their welfare was and is important to me." Instead, she takes the bait, provides the emotional response he's expecting, and then counterattacks, using two VAPs one right after the other. "Even YOU should realize that I only left because I felt I HAD to!" she says. And "You could at least TRY to understand!"

John continues with the action chain he started, and his reply includes another VAP: "If you REALLY wanted to get ahead in your field, you'd stop behaving like a CHILD!" And Mary, already feeling insecure and incompetent because of her family's disapproval and her failure to find another position, backs down without presenting him with any sort of effective challenge.

One of the most important things to recognize in this scenario is that *while Mary is taking the interaction absolutely seriously, John is only playing games.* The offenses he accuses her of are very grave indeed; if he *meant* his accusations, he certainly wouldn't be offering her her job back. He doesn't mean the things he's saying. He is choosing them because they are things that he believes—correctly—can be counted on to distress and intimidate Mary. Suppose she had been able to maintain her composure and defend herself. Her proper move would then have been to answer the sequence ending with "YOU have one hell of a NERVE, Mary!" like this:

In Leveler Mode:
    "John, you're wasting my time and yours. You don't mean the accusations you're making. You aren't so incompetent at business

that you'd rehire someone guilty of that list of crimes. I suggest that you stop playing games so we can discuss your offer.''

In Computer Mode:

''No competent businessperson would rehire an employee guilty of that list of accusations; a discussion framed that way is only game-playing, and a complete waste of time.''

This would have put the ball back in John's court and made it clear to him that Mary was aware of his strategy and had no intention of participating.

Finally, it's worth noting that although John could and would insist after this interaction that he had apologized to Mary—four times!—that would be false. Here are his lines.

''I'm sorry about the way things turned out.''

''I'm sorry you found the situation unpleasant.''

''I'm sorry unkind words were exchanged.''

''It was all stupid; I'm sorry it happened.''

That is, from a lofty stance that nowhere contains the words ''I'm sorry for what I did'' or ''I'm sorry for the way I treated you,'' he says he is *sorry about the events in question.* These are not apologies but statements of regret, like ''I'm sorry it rained.'' When you say you're sorry it rained, you don't mean that you consider the rain your fault in any way, and you're not apologizing. Mary recognized this, but she was too involved in the verbal victim role to defend herself against it.

Dialogues for Analysis

DIALOGUE ONE

F: ''If you REALLY cared about the success of this business, you wouldn't be so ARROgant with our CLIents!''

M: ''Oh, come on! You're being ridiculous! I'm no more arrogant than anybody else is!''

F: ''Oh? How about yesterday afternoon, when you told George and Helen Anderson that the only reason they weren't willing to close the deal was—''

M: ''WAIT a minute! That's NOT a typical situation!''

F: "For YOU, it is!"

M: "Hey, MOST people aren't neuROTIC, you know! MOST people reSENT being treated like CHILdren, which is the way YOU operate!"

(*The bait in the opening sentence is "you're arrogant with our clients"; the presupposed attack is "you don't really care about the success of this business."*)

The intended victim takes the bait, responding to it immediately and directly with an angry defense ("I'm no more arrogant than anybody else is!") and a counterattack ("You're being ridiculous!"). This is exactly what the attacker wants; it provides her with the opportunity to begin running through her list of alleged evidence for the claim that this man is arrogant with clients. For as long as he's willing to participate, she will bring up one incident after another to be argued about. Eventually one or the other of these people will back down and bring the exchange to a close; its length is limited only by the motivation and endurance of the attacker and victim. Let's try a rewrite.

F: "If you REALLY cared about the success of this business, you wouldn't be so ARROgant with our CLIEnts!"

M: "When did you start thinking I don't care about the success of this business?"

F: [Pause] "Well . . . you don't seem to care. When I showed you the figures from last quarter, you didn't even blink. And they gave me cold chills!"

M: "Let's talk about those figures for a minute; I don't think they're nearly as bad as they seem at first glance."

You see how this works. By ignoring the bait and responding directly and neutrally to the presupposition, he has short-circuited the action chain of abuse, defused the attack, and shifted the subject from his alleged arrogance to a discussion of numbers. *All without in any way sacrificing his own dignity or escalating the hostility*. If he wants to return at some point to her claim that he's arrogant with clients, he can do so—on his own terms. The attack has failed.

DIALOGUE TWO

M: "If you REALLY cared anything about me and the kids, YOU wouldn't WANT to neglect us and go back to work!"

F: "That's a STUPID thing to say! It's not TRUE that I'd neglect you if I started working again! How can you SAY such a thing?"

M: "All right! YOU tell ME, then, who's going to take the kids to school when it's RAINing?"

F: "It won't hurt the kids to walk to school in the rain! For heaven's SAKES!"

M: "It WON'T, huh? That's easy for YOU to say—YOU'LL be in a nice, comfortable, dry CAR!"

F: "Well, so will YOU!!"

M: "Sure! But I'LL be feeling BAD about it, okay? And who, I'd like to know, is going to stay home when the kids are SICK? Or maybe you don't CALL it neglect to leave a sick child home alone!"

(*The bait in the opening sentence is "you want to neglect us" and "for you to go back to work would be to neglect us"; the presupposed attack is "you don't care anything about me and the kids." In addition, there is a presupposition signaled by "you wouldn't WANT" that we can summarize as "People can control their desires by willpower alone if they're just willing to do so."*)

He will go on with this, raising one example of her alleged neglect after another, until one of them gives up. Because the AME culture has for so long held women almost totally responsible for the routine care of children, the chances are that it will be the mother who yields; the load of guilt laid on her as the argument continues will be heavy.

She can respond with a when-question: "When did you start thinking I don't care about you and the kids?" "When did you start thinking . . ." is always preferable to "Why do you think . . ." or "What makes you think . . .," for three reasons: It's more neutral; it can't be mistaken for the beginning of a "WHY do you . . ." attack; and it has a good chance of getting a response that is a specific incident rather than a generality. Or she can respond to the same presupposition with a statement, as in the rewrite below.

M: "If you REALLY cared anything about me and the kids, YOU wouldn't WANT to neglect us and go back to work!"

F: "Of course I care about you and the kids. You mean more to me than anything else in the world."

M: "It's hard for me to believe that. You know what it would be like with you working. The kids would suffer, and so would I."

F: "Maybe you're right; maybe you're worrying unnecessarily. Let's talk about it. Tell me what worries you most, for starters."

M: "Well, for example, who's going to stay home with the kids when they're sick?"

Now they can discuss the various problems associated with her return to work. A new fight may begin at some point, because the issues involved are emotional ones, but *this* fight has been avoided.

There were two relevant presuppositions in this attack: the one about the mother's indifference to her family and the one about willpower being enough to control desires. In this particular dialogue it wouldn't be appropriate for her to respond to the latter presupposition, but sometimes that's the best move. Dialogue Three is an example of this alternative.

DIALOGUE THREE

F: "If you REALLY loved me, YOU wouldn't WANT to smoke!"

M: "The idea that people can control their desires by willpower alone is a genuinely interesting concept."

Of *course* his response sounds contrived; of course she'll know what he's up to. That's quite all right. For him to say openly "Don't try that with me—I won't play" would be confrontational and would cause her to lose face. His Computer Mode response to the presupposition delivers exactly the same message, but it leaves her a graceful exit, and it terminates this attack. She can start a new attack, or she can change the subject and discuss the philosophical issue he has raised about willpower—but she can't go on as she had planned.

Notice that the bait in this attack depends almost entirely on its *cultural* context, and on the fact that it appears inside a VAP. On the surface, it's composed only of "you smoke," which is not in itself anything negative. But the AME speaker or listener knows that associated with "you smoke" is a set of negatives about the danger smoking poses to health, the dangers of passive smoking to the health of nonsmokers, the expense of smoking, and so on. And the pattern is so powerful that it overrides even the absence of rational context. As in "If you REALLY loved me, YOU wouldn't WANT to win a Nobel Prize!"

DIALOGUE FOUR

F: "WHY do you always contraDICT me in front of your FAMily? I never know where to LOOK or what to SAY, and you KNOW it!"

M: "I do NOT always contradict you in front of my family!"

F: "You DO! Every time your parents or your sister are around, you knock yourself OUT to make me look stupid!"

M: "That's ABSURD! Give me ONE example!"

F: "YESterday! Remember yesterday? Yesterday afterNOON, for example, when I said we were going to New Mexico for our vacation, and YOU IMMEDIATELY said that we hadn't definitely decided yet! And then—"

M: "Look, I ONly contradict you when you're WRONG! It's not MY fault that being around my family turns off your BRAIN, you know!"

(*The bait in the opening sentence is "you always contradict me in front of your family." The presupposed attack is signaled by the heavily stressed "WHY." Like "why" in neutral questions, it presupposes "You know the answer to this question and I am asking you to share that information with me." In addition, however, it presupposes that no matter what the answer is, the attacker declares* in advance *that it's unacceptable and inadequate.*)

There are two possible explanations for what's happening here. One is that this woman is verbally abusive, that her claims have no real justification, and that she's making them only to pick a fight. In that case, *she* is at fault, and his most appropriate response—instead of falling into the trap as shown above—is a classic Boring Baroque defense. Like this:

M: "I think it's probably because of something that happened to me when I was a little kid and we used to go over to my Uncle Nelson's house for barbecues on Sunday afternoons. I never wanted to go because there were always so many arguments, and—No! Wait a minute. It wasn't Uncle Nelson's house where that went on. It must have been at my grandmother's place, because. . . ." (Et cetera)

The other explanation is that she's right about the man's behavior— he really *does* always contradict her in front of his family. This distresses her and she has every right to ask him to stop doing it. Unfortunately, she abandons the moral high ground when the method she chooses for making her request is a verbal attack, because the resulting fight guarantees that her valid complaint will get lost in the verbal debris.

It would be nice to think that he would recognize that she is right, that he would realize that she's using a VAP not because she is a verbal abuser but because she's so upset that she's not thinking clearly, and that he would bring the entire episode to a positive close. Not by defending himself, since he is in fact in the wrong, but by Leveling. If that happened, she would make her accusation and he would respond as follows:

"You're absolutely right. I keep doing that, and I'm sorry. I'll try to do better."

This is always an alternative way to short-circuit a VAP and avoid an otherwise inevitable fight. When it's appropriate, it cannot be improved upon. The problem is that people often feel that responding in this way is ruled out because it constitutes "losing the argument" and they believe they are obligated to win—even when they're wrong and even when it means pain for someone else. Unless they are able to recognize (a) that no loss of face occurs when you admit to a fault honestly and without toadying and (b) that "winning" an argument of this kind is a false victory, they will consistently reject this option.

There's one more way to deal with a "WHY" attack, and that is to make the "always/never" false right then and there, on the spot, as in Dialogue Five.

DIALOGUE FIVE

F: "WHY do you ALways do just what YOU want to do? WHY don't you ever think about what might make ME happy?"

M: "Okay. Tell you what. Why don't we go see your sister this weekend?"

Now this can go two ways. Either—

F: "That's a great idea! I'd really like to do that."

M: "Good enough."

—or—

F: "That's an awful idea! I really don't want to do that!"

M: "No problem . . . you don't have to. We'll do something else."

In either case, he has demonstrated that "you always do only what you want to do/never consider what I want to do" is false, and the attack has failed. It's critical in using this strategy to offer something you're willing and able to follow through on if it's accepted, and willing to do without if it's turned down. The point is not the content of the offer or what happens to it, but the demonstration that the "always/never" accusation cannot be maintained.

DIALOGUE SIX

M: "You could at LEAST CALL me when you're going to be late! EVen a WOMan should have brains enough to use a PAY phone!"

F: "Oh, REALly! Listen, SOME women would walk OUT on you for a crack like that!"

M: "WHY do you always do that? Couldn't we have just ONE RATIONAL ADULT DISCUSSION without you threatening to go home to MOTHER?"

F: "YOU call THIS a rational disCUSSION?"

Here we have four VAPs in the space of only four utterances. The baits are flying about, both participants are grabbing them and running with them, and almost no communication is taking place except the mutual emotional metamessage: "I'M FURIOUS WITH YOU!" This couple is fluent in the language of verbal violence and appears to be evenly matched. And some of their VAPs cannot be tidily divided into bait and presupposition the way the "If you REALLY . . ." attack can. Because this dialogue is so complex, let's begin by looking at simpler examples of the patterns used.

1. "You could at LEAST make the BED!"
   (*Tangled bait and presupposition. The combined message is "I have such a low regard for you that I wouldn't think of asking you to do anything but the absolute trivial minimum; you could prove to me that you're a human being by doing that minimum."*)

2. "EVen a MAN could answer THAT!"
   (*Tangled bait and presupposition. The combined message is that men are inferior and the question is stupefyingly easy; the attacker considers one or both presuppositions sufficiently infuriating to the victim that the act of* saying *them will serve as bait.*)

3. "SOME women would be ANGry if their husbands were always late!"
   (*Bait: "You're always late." Presuppositions: "There are women who would be angry if their husbands were always late" and "You should be very grateful that you're lucky enough not to have to deal with one of* those *women instead of me."*)

4. "WHY do you always yell?"
(Bait: "You always yell. Always. Without exception." Presupposition: "I'm asking for your answer to this question, but I'm telling you in advance that it's not good enough.")

Now let's return to the analysis. After any of the attacks in Dialogue Six, the potential victim could have ignored the bait, responded to a presupposition, and transmitted the "I won't play that stupid game" message. Here are a few examples.

M: "You could at LEAST CALL me when you're going to be late! EVen a WOMan should have brains enough to use a PAY phone!"

F: "The idea that women are somehow inferior is something you hear once in awhile, but I'm astonished to hear it from <u>you</u>."

M: "Okay. I'm sorry. But I've been worried sick. Why didn't you call me?"

She has ignored the bait about not having decency enough even to do the bare minimum and call this man; she has ignored the bait represented by his *making* the sexist remark about women being too stupid to use a device as simple as a pay phone. She has chosen to respond directly to the presupposition of "EVen a WOMan . . .," which is that women are inferior, second-rate, etc. And she has gently pointed out that she doesn't think he's the sort of man who uses language in this way and is surprised to find him doing it.

F: "Listen, SOME women would walk OUT on you for a crack like that!"

M: "You're absolutely right."

Whenever a VAPper offers you an attack containing a vacuous presupposition you can simply agree with, do so. She's undoubtedly right that there are women who, having heard his remark, would walk out; he's quite safe agreeing with that and ignoring the bait about what he said being so terrible that walking out would be justified, as well as the part about how lucky he is to have *her* around. This sort of neutral statement of agreement—"You're right" or "I couldn't agree with you more" or "You bet!"—is also the proper response to VAPs like "YOU'RE not the ONly person with PROBlems, you know!"

M: "WHY do you always do that? Couldn't we have just ONE RATIONAL ADULT DISCUSSION without you threatening to go home to MOTHER?"

F: "I have an idea. Let's stop yelling, let's start over, and let's try having a rational adult discussion."

She has ignored the accusation that she *always* threatens to leave when he tries to discuss things with her. She has ignored the additional bait—that she's so immature that if she *did* walk out she'd run straight to her mother. And she has proved the presupposition false by offering to participate in a rational adult discussion on the spot.

DIALOGUE SEVEN

F: "DON'T you even CARE if my HEART is BREAKING?"
M: "No. No, I don't."

I'm quite serious. If she is in great distress and wants to talk to him about it, there is a way to do that: by Leveling. Like this:

> "I'm desperately unhappy, and it seems to me that you're not troubled by that at all, which makes it worse. I'd like to talk to you about it."

Not as good, but acceptable, would be a neutral question without all the extra stresses: "My heart is breaking; do you care?" And his response (unless it would be a lie) should be, "Of course I care," followed by encouragement to talk, and attentive listening.

The attack in the dialogue above mingles the bait and the abusive presupposition. The presupposition is "Any decent human being would be upset about my breaking heart." The bait is "You're not a decent human being." Only the most desperate and extreme situations can justify using the "DON'T you EVen CARE . . ." pattern, even *without* the multiple stresses on words and parts of words that mark it as a VAP. It says, "You're loathsome; you're beneath contempt; you're not even human." It's unfortunate that many people use it almost casually. If she is a chronic verbal abuser and this is a typical example of her language behavior, his response is fully justified. If she is an ordinarily nonabusive woman who has suffered some serious injury that is distorting her behavior, that's different, and I suggest this rewrite.

F: "DON'T you even CARE if my HEART is BREAKING?"

M: "I don't believe that's what you wanted to say to me; it doesn't sound like you. Could you try again?"

F: "I'm absolutely <u>miserable</u>!"

M: "I can see that. Tell me what's wrong."

DIALOGUE EIGHT

M: "EVERYbody underSTANDS why you can't get ALONG with anybody, you know!"

F: "What do you MEAN, I can't get along with anybody? I have PLENTY of friends!"

M: "Oh, yeah? NAME one!"

F: "Carolyn is my friend."

M: "She's your cousin; that doesn't COUNT. I bet you can't name anybody ELSE!"

(*Bait: "You can't get along with anybody." Presupposition: "You have something wrong with you, something that's obvious to everybody, that makes it impossible for you to get along with people."*)

Attackers use this pattern for the usual reasons: to demonstrate power over the victim and to get an emotional "fix" of attention. But they have one of two additional agendas. They may suspect that the victim has some secret that worries him or her terribly, and they use the VAP as a fishing expedition to manipulate the victim into telling that secret (as well as for the usual reasons). Or they already know what the secret is, but they enjoy behaving as if they don't and watching their victim's efforts to hide it. No one should allow themselves to be suckered by this unsavory VAP; I suggest a Boring Baroque response, like this.

M: "EVerybody underSTANDS why you can't get ALONG with anybody, you know!"

F: "Hearing you say that reminds me of something I read in the paper the other day. It was Wednesday, I think . . . no, maybe it <u>wasn't</u> Wednesday, because I remember that it had just started to rain and I was wondering whether I should wait for it to stop or go on to the office. It must have been Friday, because. . . ." (And so on)

CHAPTER 11

❖

The Problem of Sexual Harassment

It was obvious to Bill that Mary was tense and nervous on her first day back, and he could understand that; he wouldn't have enjoyed finding himself in her situation. Determined to let her know that she was welcome, he went to her office just before lunch.

"Welcome back, Mary," he said warmly. "It's great to have you here again—we've <u>missed</u> you. You look terrific this morning!"

She smiled at him and said thank you, but it was a very pinched-looking smile and her words were not much more than a mumble. *Poor kid*, he thought, *she's worried sick!* And he leaned across her desk and patted her shoulder.

What happened next stunned him. She stiffened as if he'd pinched her, and said "<u>You</u> just keep your <u>hands</u> to yourSELF!"

Bill stepped back swiftly and raised both hands high, palms out and fingers spread, at shoulder level. "<u>Well</u>," he snarled, "excuse <u>me</u>! I was JUST LEAVing!"

Mary watched him whirl on his heel and head out the door; he was so angry he was very nearly trailing smoke. She understood why, and she didn't blame him; in his place, she would have been angry too. Her words had been more reflex than anything else, but there was no way Bill could be expected to know that, and she'd offended him badly. She sat at her desk, her lower lip caught tightly in her teeth, her hands clenched in nervous fists, and wished she <u>were</u> working at a fast food place. As she probably would be! Bill was almost certainly headed for John's office to tell their boss what a serious mistake it had been to hire her back.

◆

What's Going On Here?

Bill's Point of View

Bill has the very best of intentions. He genuinely likes Mary and is sincerely glad to see her back. His only purpose was to let her know that and reassure her about the situation. As he perceives it, a woman has to have a very small and dirty mind to turn a few pleasant words and a friendly pat on the shoulder from a colleague into a sexual overture. He finds himself wondering: Has he misjudged Mary all along? Is he perhaps making a mistake when he openly supports her? Is she as paranoid as John has sometimes claimed? He knows what John would say to him on the subject, and for the first time he thinks that maybe he could learn something from the older man about how to deal with women in the workplace. He won't risk any supportive words or gestures with Mary again; not after the way she turned on him this time.

Mary's Point of View

The instant Mary snapped at Bill about touching her, she knew she'd made a mistake and that he was only trying to be friendly. She lashed out at him because she was tense and uneasy about how the men at View Inc. were going to react to her return, and because the many strained male/female encounters she'd had during the preceding year had made her hypersensitive about the problem. And because he had preceded the touch with yet another compliment on her appearance, which is how the episode leading to her resignation *started*. She's sorry to have hurt Bill and would like nothing more than to take back her harsh reaction. But she knows no safe way to do it.

Suppose she's wrong, and Bill *was* trying something. Then her apology will be perceived as encouragement, and if she complains later he'll be able to report truthfully that she gave him reason to believe she had no objections to being touched. An apology would also give him a chance to play the old game of "What? Me make a pass at you? You think you're hot stuff, don't you, honey?"

On the other hand, if she's correct that he meant nothing sexual, her apology will still sound like a woman knuckling under—and it will give Bill a perfect opportunity to lecture her about her behavior. In *either* case, the last thing she wants to do is appear to support the idea that it's okay for a man to touch a woman whenever it strikes his fancy! It seems to her that she has no choice; all she can do is behave as if it never happened, rely on Bill to realize that first-day-back nerves caused her to react as she did, and try to make up for it in the future.

◆

This is an unfortunate communication breakdown, and one that demonstrates the way the sexual harassment issue has become a major barrier between men and women in their efforts to get along together in this world. This is a gender gap that badly needs bridging; in this chapter, we'll discuss it in detail.

What IS Sexual Harassment?

The EEOC defined sexual harassment as "unwelcome sexual advances, requests for sexual favors and other verbal or physical contact of a sexual nature" that are connected to decisions about employment or that create an intimidating, hostile or offensive work environment. (Ronni Sandroff, "Sexual Harassment in the Fortune 500," *Working Woman*, December 1988)

And now my definition is this: If it *offends*, then it's sexual harassment. (Captain Bill Thomas, quoted in *In the Men's House* [Poseidon, 1986], C. Barkalow's book about her experience as one of the first women students at West Point)

Everyone in the AME culture will agree that it's sexual harassment when an employee is told by a superior that unless they have sex the employee will be fired or otherwise penalized. When that happens, the employee should make an immediate, formal complaint, and the complaint should be followed up in accordance with the law. That's clear, although it's less simple than it may sound. The problem of proving that the complaint is true remains, as does the problem of being *afraid* to complain; the possibility of false complaints made for revenge or other personal reasons is a troublesome factor.

Everyone understands that sexual harassment is taking place when— without invitation—a man fondles a woman's breasts or buttocks, or a woman touches a man's crotch. That's not at issue; but it's *also* not simple. If no one witnesses the alleged behavior, exactly the same problems arise as when the advance is in words rather than physical acts, and there's always the possibility that the person accused will insist that there *was* an invitation. However, this kind of Neanderthal behavior is so unacceptable in public that few people past adolescence are brutish enough to engage in it at the workplace; it's a small part of the problem.

In cases like those just described, although the legal problems of proof and evidence are substantial, society agrees that the person who truthfully complains of such incidents is *justified* in complaining. Even people who feel that a woman "was asking for it" because of the way she dressed or moved or behaved (a charge almost never made about a man) will agree that the sexual overture should have been in the form of a *request* rather than threats or grabs.

The disagreement isn't over these clear-cut cases. It's over words and acts that some people perceive as having sexual implications and thus constituting harassment, while other people insist that this is nonsense and paranoia. In this, as in many other areas of our lives, the perceptions may or may not be false, but the consequences are unquestionably real. The issue has become so troublesome that, like day-care workers terrified even to hold a child's hand, men and women have literally become *afraid* to be friendly to one another in the workplace.

Closely related problems are found in private life, where we are now forced to deal with "date rape" and "marital rape" issues. Again, disagreements rarely occur over unambiguous use of brute force, or threats of brute force, to obtain sex; it's unusual for anyone to claim that such behavior is acceptable. Disagreements occur over the perception of sexual intentions when one person involved insists that none were intended and the other insists that they were. And over the definition of the word "rape"—when one person perceives what happened as rape and the other does not, and where the gender difference in defining the word "violence" makes communication extraordinarily difficult. Most of us will remember boxer Mike Tyson, accused in 1992 of having raped a woman, insisting that he hadn't *hurt* her—because he did not break her nose or her ribs or leave her obviously bruised and bleeding. His behavior did not qualify for *his* definition of "violence."

Oh, What a Tangled Web We Weave

Within the context of the sexual harassment issue, the abuses don't stop at the offering of unwanted sexual attention; many other possibilities for doing harm exist. Here are just a few examples.

- A man might make a sexual overture when he actually has no interest in the woman, to trick her into making a complaint that he could meet with an outraged denial.

- A woman might make a sexual overture to a man to trick him into a response that she could then claim he made without invitation.

- A man might make a sexual overture to someone he considered so unattractive that no one could be sexually interested in her—feeling that it would be safe because no one would believe her if she complained, or to trick her into a response that he could then talk about and use to make her an object of ridicule.

- A woman might make sexual overtures to a man as a deliberate campaign of harassment, and dare him to complain, knowing that he would find it too humiliating to do so and would not expect to be believed.

- A woman might pretend to be willing to accept a man's overtures only because she was afraid not to do so, and might then make a complaint and *deny* that she had accepted.

- A man might pretend sexual interest to trick a woman into responding so that he could tell her it was only a joke and humiliate her.

All of these things have been reported in the literature of sexual harassment; they're part of a seemingly endless list of variations. Some—for example, the idea that a man might feel he could safely harass a woman he didn't consider beautiful—may strike you as improbable. Improbable or not, they happen. Consider the case of the Alabama trial in which a judge dismissed Katherine Young's charges of sexual harassment by stating that Young didn't use makeup or color her hair, and that the accused supervisor's wife was more attractive than Young was! When similar behaviors involving homosexual individuals are included, the list becomes even more extensive and more complicated.

What must be remembered in every case, *from the point of view of self-defense*, is that no matter what the motive for the behavior is, all variations on the basic "Hey, good-lookin', how about it?" scenario have one thing in common: DECEPTION. In any interaction where a perception of sexual harassment could arise, what everyone involved needs to know is whether the other person(s) can be *trusted*.

Body Language and Sexual Harassment

Anyone can learn to spot deception, because it is betrayed by body language, including the intonation of the human voice. When the words people say are in conflict with their true feelings, their bodies will always betray them. Their reasons for wanting to deceive will require further investigation, but the fact that deception is *intended* will be betrayed—and that is the information the potential victim really needs. This is as true for perception of sexual overtures where none exist as it is for someone facing unwanted sexual advances. The only exceptions to the rule about body language betraying the intention to deceive are brilliant actors and conscienceless sociopaths or psychopaths, neither of whom are encountered often. The basic principle to rely on is this metamessage:

✦   ANY MISMATCH IS A WARNING SIGN.

If the words being said and the body language that goes with them are in conflict, that's mismatch. If the usual body language of the speaker deviates from its normal characteristics—if the pitch of the voice goes higher than the pitch normally used by that individual, for example, or the rate of eye-blinking becomes faster or slower than usual—that's mismatch. If the words and the gestures convey courtesy and consideration, but the tone of voice is aggressive and hostile, that's mismatch. When mismatch is detected, recognize that *something* is going on that requires your attention: Come to full alert and be on your guard.

It's easy for men to claim that although a woman was saying the word "no" they were certain that she meant "yes" and acted only on that certainty (or for a woman to make that claim about her actions toward a man). But that excuse is useful only in an atmosphere of public ignorance about body language. It is to the sexually abusive man's personal advantage, of course, *not* to pay attention, or to pretend he cannot understand, but men who are paying attention to the nonverbal signals women give them will rarely be confused. Men can tell the difference between a woman who is saying "no" and is literally pulling her body away as far as she can get, and a woman who is saying "no" and at the same time *offering* her body. They can also tell the difference between a woman who is saying "yes" with both words and body, and one who is saying "yes" out of fear or a desire not to offend, but is doing so with a rigid, reluctant body.

Most AME-speaking men have a grammar rule for paying attention: Watch the person's *face*. It was a man who wrote the song lyric about a woman whose lips were telling him "no, no" while she had "yes, yes" in her eyes. In a potentially sexual situation, this male rule won't do; looking at the woman's face and eyes isn't sufficient. Men must look at the whole body—and not just its erogenous zones, either—for the message to stop or to proceed. And what about people of either gender who insist that this communication strategy may be possible for others but that they personally are *incapable* of learning to read body language accurately? If what they say is true, then they will have to follow these two rules:

- Arbitrarily accept every spoken "no" as meaning precisely that— "No"—and nothing more.
- Accept a spoken "yes" only after carefully making certain that it is sincerely meant.

It goes without saying that women who need to know whether a man's advances are genuine, whether a man's seeming advances are only friendliness, or whether a man is misunderstanding *their* behavior, must rely not on words but on body language. They must observe the entire body, listening especially to the voice. Because most women don't follow the "To pay attention, watch the face" rule, this will be easier for them than it is for men.

One point that has to be repeated here (and that applies to *all* language sequences of English) is that *the words themselves are the least important part of the communication*. For someone to say an off-color word or phrase or sentence tells you nothing useful; at most, it tells you that this is a person who is not being *careful*. It is the intonation with which the off-color items are said, and the rest of the accompanying body language, that carry the essential message.

One man will say "That's a pretty dress" so suggestively that every word in the sentence might as well be one of the classic "four-letter" ones; another can say "Nice tits" as inoffensively as if he had said "Yankee Doodle." The women around him may object to his saying "tits" either to them or in their hearing, and are free to tell him so, but they are fully able to distinguish between these two varieties of language.

In 1991 we had an astonishing example of the need for public awareness of the facts about nonverbal communication. In the hearings regarding Anita Hill's charges that Clarence Thomas had sexually harassed her—held in a room filled with sophisticated adults with academic de-grees—everyone present behaved as if intonation did not even *exist* in English, much less carry meaning! The focus was entirely on *words*. Whether Clarence Thomas said the words "pubic hair" to Anita Hill or not means very little. The question is, if he did say them, what *tune* did he set those words to? (We'll come back to the Hill/Thomas hearings later in this chapter.)

What to Do About It—Basic Guidelines

The guidelines below are intended to help you prevent sexual harassment problems in typical workplace situations and in business and professional environments. They are also recommended for social situations that are business-related. They don't include procedures for making formal com-plaints after a sexual harassment incident has already occurred; those procedures will vary from place to place, according to company policy and applicable legal constraints.

Basic Guidelines for Men

Let's begin by assuming that you have no intention of sexually harassing women in your workplace, or of being *perceived* by them as doing so. Let's also assume that you'd like to be able to have friendly relationships with those women. In that case, I suggest the following:

1. Use all the *Gentle Art* techniques described in this book, to build trust and rapport between you and the women you talk with. So that if they're not sure about your meaning, or you're not sure about theirs, both of you will feel *safe* asking for an explanation. So that if they're puzzled about your intentions, they will be willing to give you the benefit of the doubt. And so that they won't feel any necessity to communicate with you other than honestly.

2. Pay attention—very close attention—to the body language of women as you talk with them. Listen carefully to what they say and how they say it. Drop the rule about looking only at the face, if it's part of your grammar. Some common signs that listeners who are speakers of AME are feeling uneasy with you include:

- Clenching the fists, or opening and closing the hands repeatedly; or attempting to hide the hands from sight.
- A trembling voice; or hands (or any other part of the body) that are obviously trembling or shaking.

- Eyelids blinking more rapidly than you know they would in casual conversation.
- Refusal to make eye contact with you, even when you make an obvious effort to initiate it.
- Biting the lips; or holding the lower lip with the teeth.
- Pale or flushed skin; or a forehead or hands that are damp with perspiration not explained by heat in the environment.
- Voice pitch that changes significantly from the pitch you know they maintain in casual conversation.

When you observe these signs of stress—unless you can be absolutely certain you know their cause, and it has nothing at all to do with you—back off.

3. If you ask a woman in your workplace to go out with you, say a few preliminary sentences first, so she doesn't feel leaped at. If she says no, say "I'm sorry to hear you say no. It is all right if I ask you again another time?" If she says no, it's not all right, don't ask her why—and don't ask her out again. Strategies that are appropriate for singles bars are going to be perceived as harassment by most women in a work situation.

4. Don't compliment a woman on her physical appearance, her clothing, or her hairdo. This doesn't mean it's morally wrong to offer such compliments, or that women aren't often very happy to hear them. It's simply common sense. This is an area where people's perceptions of what is appropriate differ drastically and opportunities for misunderstanding are abundant—it's like playing ball in a minefield. If you want to compliment a woman at work, compliment her *on* her work. Say, "I enjoyed your talk" or "I thought you made an excellent point in that meeting" or "I wish I could make a hamburger as well as you do" or "I was impressed with the way you handled that sale" or just "You do good work."

5. Don't use obscenities or sexual vocabulary around the women you work with. Don't tell dirty jokes around them. Don't tell them about your sexual problems or experiences. Don't brag about your sexual abilities. Period.

6. Don't *tease* women. I'm not talking about sexual teasing, but the sort of teasing little boys do toward little girls. Adult women don't think it's funny, and it's one of the quickest ways to destroy trust and start trouble. It will make it very hard for you to use "I was only kidding" as an excuse when you really *need* it as an excuse.

7. When it's clear to you that you've offended a woman, even when you're certain the offense is an error of perceptions on her part, apologize

at once. Say, "I think I've offended you. I had no intention of doing so, and I'm sorry."

8. When a woman tries to explain to you *why* something you said or did—or someone else said or did—is offensive, make an effort to listen and understand. *For her to make the effort to explain* is a compliment.

9. Keep your hands to yourself.

10. Read the section for women, below.

You may be afraid that following these guidelines will turn you into a wimp; the very idea of following them may be offensive to *you*. Many men feel that observing such rules makes a pleasant work environment impossible, and that they interfere with business performance. They may be right. But until mutual trust between men and women at work can be reestablished, these guidelines are necessary, and as long as you follow them you are unlikely to find yourself facing sexual harassment charges.

Basic Guidelines for Women

Let's assume you'd like to maintain friendly relations with the men at your workplace, that you have no intention of sexually harassing them, and that you have no desire to have them terrified that you will interpret their every word as an attempted pass. Then I suggest the following:

1. Follow the guidelines for men listed above, making the necessary changes of "woman" to "man," "she" to "he," and vice versa. They are appropriate for both sexes.

2. When something a man says to you (or says in your hearing) offends you, but does not seem *intended* to offend, tell him about it. But don't tell him in front of other people if it can be avoided. (Unless you feel unsafe alone with him, in which case you should take one other person with you as witness when you talk to him.) Tell him how you feel about what he said—*without trying to raise his consciousness, educate him, or improve his morals*. It's important to remember that your goal here is to change his behavior—consciousness-raising is a separate task. You can't do both at once. Just say, "When you say [X], it offends me. Please don't do it again." If he wants to discuss it with you—and his body language tells you that he really does want to discuss it, as opposed to wanting to fight with you or escalate the sexual language—make an effort to do that. People resent having to censor their behavior on someone else's orders; if the order makes sense to them, the resentment will be less.

3. When you must refuse a man's courteous request to go out with him, or to be otherwise personally involved with him, do it as clearly and as politely as possible—and *without making him lose face*. Shaming a man is foolish. Shaming will make him determined to get your agreement no matter how long it takes, just to prove that you can't say no to him. Shaming will make him hostile and angry; he'll take that out on you at the first opportunity, or he'll take it out on someone else, or both. Don't contaminate your language environment unnecessarily.

4. Telling a man you don't want him to say "tits" around you—or whatever—is all right. Tell him the words offend you; tell him that they distract you from your work; tell him that they're likely to cause you to misunderstand him and misjudge him at other times. But remember that there's nothing wrong with any word, in itself. Words aren't dirty; words aren't insulting; words aren't hurtful. It is the human voice saying them, and the body language being used with them, that makes them dirty or insulting or hurtful. If it's clear to you that the man who said the words didn't intend them to offend, give him credit for that.

5. When a man clearly *does* intend to offend you with his words or behavior, object *immediately*. Be firm and be brief; just say "That's offensive to me. I know I can count on you not to do it/say it again." And then change the subject, firmly and immediately.

Sexual Harassment and Touch Dominance

You will remember that in Chapter 6 I briefly discussed the problem of *touch dominance* (sometimes referred to as tactile or kinesthetic dominance). The touch dominant person finds the senses of sight and hearing less useful for processing information than the sense of touch, and relies on touch whenever possible. This is a handicap in the "Keep your hands to yourself!" AME culture, and it can be a complicating factor in determining whether or not a particular situation constitutes sexual harassment.

Remember that the touch dominant person's preferred vocabulary tends to be perceived as inelegant by eye and ear people. Remember that the touch dominant person tends to spend a lifetime being "in trouble" with other AME speakers and to experience frequent rejection that may be very difficult to understand. Add to that the obvious fact that a touch dominant person, in situations of tensions and stress that lock him or her into Touch Mode, is more likely than the sight or hearing dominant to resort to touching as a means of communication—or to be painfully aware of both the need to communicate by touch and the AME rules against doing so. The sum of these difficulties, for all but the most fortunate, is a barrier to effective communication.

No one should be able to make unwanted sexual overtures to another person and then say, "Hey, I can't help it—I'm touch dominant!" I'm not suggesting that. What I *am* suggesting is that it would be worthwhile, when you feel that such overtures are being made, to stop for just a moment and ask yourself whether it's possible that the seeming offensiveness is the result of touch dominance. If the individual is one whom you *know* to be touch dominant—perhaps because of a constant complaint of "I don't understand things unless I can get in there with both hands and just <u>do</u> it!"—perhaps he or she is genuinely innocent. *Even when the behavior or language would otherwise be, without question, inappropriate.* This is worth keeping in mind, not as an excuse but as an explanation. The offending behavior is no less objectionable, but the reasons behind it have nothing to do with sexual advances.

The most effective way to manage an interaction where a touch dominant person is relying more heavily on touching than is comfortable for you is simply to switch to Touch Mode language yourself, if possible. This will reduce the tension that may be triggering the problem, and the behavior you find disturbing should then decrease.

Two Case Studies—Anita Hill and Frances Conley

In 1991, two sexual harassment cases broke the traditional silence on the subject and went very public indeed. One, Anita Hill's charges against Supreme Court nominee Clarence Thomas, put the accuser's face on the cover of the October 21st issue of *Time*, whose cover story reported that the hearings in the case had "transfixed a nation." The other, Frances Conley's charges against male colleagues at Stanford Medical School, would in any other year have been the top story on the issue. Even with the Hill/Thomas Senate hearings to draw attention away from her case, Conley was interviewed at length on National Public Radio, the story was featured in newspapers and magazines nationwide, and it was the cover story in the October 1991 issue of *MD*. The two cases had striking similarities, but there were even more striking differences.

The Case of Frances Conley

When Frances Conley announced that she was resigning her position as a tenured full-time professor of neurosurgery at Stanford after twenty-three years on its faculty, she said that she was tired of being called "honey" by her male colleagues, tired of their inviting her to their beds, tired of having them fondle her legs under the table at meetings, tired of having her dissenting positions in university and hospital business attributed to her menstrual cycle, tired of what she described as an incessant campaign of sexism that permeated every part of her professional life. She had put up with it all those years; she did not hesitate to say that going along with it was crucial to achieving her status as one of the top three women in neurosurgery.

The behavior of the men Conley worked with wasn't anything she couldn't handle, and it certainly didn't hold her back in her career. The incident that provoked her resignation was Stanford's intention to promote Dr. Gerald Silverberg—a man she described as one of the worst offenders—to the chairmanship of her department, where he would determine policy. But behind that was her realization that if she didn't speak out she *herself* was part of the problem. In her position as role model for women in medicine, her silence about the harassment supported and perpetuated it. She resigned her post, sent letters to the newspapers explaining why, and, according to *MD*, "set off a firestorm of reaction." As a result, Stanford appointed both a faculty senate committee on sexual harassment and a task force on discrimination, instituted new procedures for dealing with sexual harassment, and put Silverberg's chairmanship on hold. After which Frances Conley withdrew her resignation and returned to her post.

At no time was any serious effort made to dispute either the validity of Conley's charges or the need to take steps to change the situation, although *MD* noted that "Among some men, the subject is viewed privately as a joke."

The Case of Anita Hill

When Anita Hill went before a United States Senate committee to present her case, she claimed that Clarence Thomas (now a Supreme Court Justice) had sexually harassed her when he was her boss in Washington in the early 1980s. According to Hill, Thomas had pressured her to date him, had talked to her in the most graphic and lurid terms—at the office—about pornographic movies, about sexual practices, and about his own sexual habits and abilities. The Senators questioned her in great detail; they also questioned Clarence Thomas, who denied all Hill's charges passionately and furiously. The entire proceeding was carried out on television, in prime time, before the astonished eyes of the American public.

Hill was not treated gently by her questioners. In her article for the winter 1992 issue of *The American Prospect* ("Race, Gender, and the Supreme Court"), Deborah A. Stone described what happened to her this way: "Hill was verbally battered by older white men who asked her in a hundred ways why she hadn't behaved as they would have in such a situation." The Senate decided to confirm Clarence Thomas for the Supreme Court, demonstrating in a very final manner that they did not believe Hill's testimony. And Hill was subjected to every kind of abuse during and after the hearing, not only from the usual crackpots but also by the most respectable of the media. The March 1992 issue of *The American Spectator* carried an article by David Brock ("The Real Anita Hill") attacking her with a viciousness that would have been appropriate toward a convicted serial murderer. Professor Hill, like Frances Conley, has gone back to living her life and making occasional speaking appearances before groups sympathetic to women's causes.

What Went Wrong?

Here we have two women professionals holding substantial academic posts who brought public accusations of sexual harassment against one or more male professionals. Both had been quiet about the problem for many years and had broken their silence reluctantly; both went public because of the nomination of a man—a man they accused of sexual harassment—to a position of power and prominence. Both were interviewed by the media and were the subject of intense public scrutiny. Both have been congratulated for bringing the subject of sexual harassment out of the cobwebs and making Americans aware of the issue as never before. But in the American Mainstream English culture, obsessed as it is with winning and losing, it has to be said that there is a single unmistakable difference: Frances Conley won—Anita Hill lost. Why?

The facile answer—racism—won't wash here. Hill is black, but so is Thomas. And Hill is not an inner-city high school dropout living as a single mother on welfare. The real answer is that Frances Conley was never asked to step out of the real world and take a role in a morality play, while Hill apparently did not realize that that was what she had agreed to do. In the June 1, 1992, issue of *Time*, Lance Morrow described the hearings as "one of those vivid, strange electronic moral pagents . . . that are becoming a new American art form. This is national theater. . . ." He is absolutely on target. But Anita Hill was under the impression that she was in the real world.

In the morality play the Senate had cast her in, the only role Hill could play that would have let her win was Decent Woman Done Wrong; there is no morality play role for Decent Law Professor Done Wrong. Asked by the Senators to repeat the lewd words she claimed Thomas had said to her, Hill—like any competent lawyer and university professor—calmly complied and repeated them. But the audience knows that no Decent Woman will appear in public and say "pubic hair" or "Long Dong Silver." There is a major difference between a decent woman, who might say anything she pleases, and Decent Woman, who must follow a script written by the culture. Much if not most of Hill's audience concluded that even if Hill was telling the truth, a woman who could say all those scandalous things so serenely, in front of millions of people, could not possibly have suffered any damage when she heard somebody *else* say them.

Clarence Thomas knew better, or was better advised. Playing the role of Decent *Man* done wrong, he adamantly refused to use *any* sexual words or phrases, he forbade the Senate to ask him *any* questions about sexual matters, and he prevailed.

When Hill was asked to say the offending words, her proper move was to look the questioner right in the eye and say firmly, "No, I will not repeat to you the things Clarence Thomas said to me!" And when the Senator objected—"But, my dear Professor Hill, unless you tell us what he is alleged to have said we cannot get to the bottom of this dreadful matter!"—she should have said, "That is your problem, Senator, not mine," and left the ball in his court.

Unfortunately, Hill behaved according to the rules of language that apply to a confident and successful woman professional. And that was the *wrong script*. That is: It was the wrong script if her strategy was to be perceived as a woman who had been intimidated by Clarence Thomas, rather than as a woman who cannot be intimidated by senators. The hearings were a *performance*, staged and ritualized from beginning to end. Either nobody told Anita Hill that, or she refused to believe it.

There were three clues signaling the distance between reality and the Hill/Thomas hearings:

- There was the fact, already mentioned, that the entire procedure focused on the specific *words*, rather than on how the words were said. Every male in Congress has said those *words*, or words very like them, himself; the words were not the real issue.
- There was the theatrical setting in which it all took place, and the lofty public language, utterly different from the language of daily life, used by the participants.
- And there was the extraordinary fantasy factor introduced by the unanimous pretense—even from Hill and Thomas!—that they both had always been governed by the rules of American Mainstream English even when they were alone together.

Orlando Patterson noticed the third clue, and turned it against Anita Hill. Writing in *The New York Times*, he claimed that the sort of talk Hill was attributing to Thomas was perfectly normal African-American courtship talk and that Anita Hill knew that. He claimed that she was the one behaving immorally, when she failed to translate the talk in question into sentences appropriate to the courtship talk of privileged whites. Most tellingly, he stated flatly *that this meant that if Clarence Thomas was lying, he was fully justified in doing so.*

Technique #10
Using Metaphors as a Basis for Choosing Roles

I am no more able to say what the facts are in the Hill/Thomas case than any other member of the general public, nor would it be appropriate for me to state my opinions on that subject here. In many sexual harassment disputes, as in this one, there are no witnesses and no hard evidence. Observers can only choose between the word of the accuser and the word of the accused, and people will not always agree as to which one is telling the truth. I *can* say, however, that Anita Hill's *communication strategy* almost guaranteed that she would lose, no matter what the facts were. The error wasn't in her choice of words or body language; rather, she chose the wrong *role*.

Communication strategy is learned by most AME-speaking men— but not most AME-speaking women—early in life, usually within a context such as the Football Metaphor. In noncasual communication situations, men *automatically* ask themselves "What position am I playing?" and then watch for the appropriate signals. They learn that there are two kinds of strategic error:

- Choosing the wrong role in the interaction. (As when you decide that you're the quarterback and proceed by the rules for quarterbacks, when you *should* be playing the fullback position.)
- Choosing the right role, but failing to follow its rules. (As when you *should* be quarterback and you choose that position, but you proceed by the rules for fullbacks.)

Professor Hill made the first error. She chose the role of Distinguished Law School Professor, and she followed the rules of that role superbly well. The problem—in the Morality Play metaphor that everyone else with any power in the situation was using—is that the role that would have given her a chance to be believed was not Distinguished Law School Professor but Decent Woman Wronged. Clarence Thomas did not make that error; like most successful men, he had been thoroughly trained in communication strategy.

Until this gender difference is changed, until little girls and young women are provided with the same information about strategic use of language as little boys and young men, women's alleged "verbal advantage" will continue to be useful to them primarily in certain specialized environments: most notably that of the Traditional Schoolroom.

A detailed presentation of communication strategy is beyond the scope of this book. But I can briefly introduce one strategic technique here that is useful to *both* genders, building on the foundation provided by the *Gentle Art* techniques in previous chapters and focusing on the question of *how to choose the proper role*. The steps to be followed are these:

Step One: Identify the metaphor being used by those in control of the interaction. (The Football Game; The Old West; The Noble Battle; The Traditional Schoolroom; The Proud Ship Sailing.)

Step Two: Identify the roles that the metaphor contains. (Quarterback; Cowboy; Dance-hall Girl; General; Private; Ship's Captain.)

Step Three: Choose a role that isn't yet taken, that you're able to fill, and that you feel is most likely to be successful for you.

Step Four: Play that role, following *its* rules.

For example, suppose you find yourself involved in an interaction where you can identify the unifying metaphor as the Traditional Schoolroom and you don't have the power to change metaphors (or you have no reason to feel that a change would be useful or appropriate). Suppose someone else already has the role of Teacher. You can then choose from among three remaining roles—Student, Custodian, or Principal— according to your abilities and your needs. If you know the metaphor well, following the rules for that role will maximize your chances for effective and satisfactory communication in the interaction.

You cannot decide, even on the basis of the most admirable abstract principles, that you will choose the role of Quarterback or Cowboy instead and follow *those* rules. Not unless you're willing to try to function effectively in the face of almost certain communication breakdown.

And if you *don't* know the metaphor well? Then the proper strategy is to refuse to participate until it has been explained to you and you feel that you do understand it.

Now let's return to Scenario Eleven and look at it once more in its new context, before going on.

Another Look at Scenario Eleven

In the tense atmosphere prevailing in much of the workplace today between men and women, incidents like the one portrayed in this scenario are common. And very often, as here, although it can be truthfully said that everyone's intentions were good and almost nothing happened, such incidents lead to bad feeling and mistrust far out of proportion to their significance. Bill touched Mary only once, with a friendly and entirely nonsexual pat on the shoulder; Mary said only seven angry words, and she would have taken those back if she'd known how. Very minor matters! But the two of them will feel uncomfortable together from now on; their perceptions of one another and of one another's work will be distorted; and the consequences could be far from minor.

Either one could have set this right at the time; it's too late for that now. However, either one can accomplish some significant repair after the fact.

If Mary Makes the First Move:

Mary went to Bill's office, knocked softly on the doorframe and leaned inside. "Are you too busy to talk to me for a minute?" she asked.

"No," he said stiffly. "What is it?"

Mary went in and sat down. "I'm here to apologize," she

said. "You know how I feel about men who make passes at women in the office; I don't have to tell you that. But that's not what you were doing. You saw that I was nervous on my first day back and you were just letting me know that you were on my side. I'm sorry I repaid your kindness as I did."

"It was uncalled for."

"Yes, it was. But think about it—it proves what a good judge of other people's feelings you are. Because I would have to be very upset indeed to behave like that, and you know it."

He relaxed then, and smiled at her. It was not his old open smile, and she knew there were fences still to mend, but it was a genuine smile.

"Okay, Mary," he said. "I was in the wrong too, you know. I should have had sense enough to know it was no time for friendly pats, and I shouldn't have taken your reaction so seriously. Let's just pretend it never happened."

If Bill Makes the First Move:

Mary heard the knock on her office door and looked up to see Bill standing there, looking at her.

"Yes?" she said.

"May I come in, Mary?"

"Of course."

He sat down in the chair across from her. "I came back to tell you that I'm sorry I lost my temper," he said. "I'm not sorry I patted your shoulder. That was just friendship, and it would be hypocritical for me to pretend I see anything wrong with it. But I am sorry I didn't realize what a bad time this was for friendly pats; and I'm sorry I took your reaction so seriously."

Mary smiled at him. "It was my fault," she said, "not yours. I'm so nervous about coming back that I'm not really myself. Please accept my apologies—and my thanks for giving me a chance to explain."

"No problem," he said. "Let's just pretend it never happened."

Neither of these extensions of the scenario would be difficult to carry out. Neither requires either Bill or Mary to sacrifice principles or dignity. What's difficult for many people in similar circumstances is just these two things:

- Deciding that reestablishing a good relationship with a colleague (or spouse, partner, etc.) is more important than being "right."
- Being willing to be the first person to speak.

When those barriers can be crossed without compromising self-respect or losing face, they seem much smaller.

Dialogues for Analysis

DIALOGUE ONE

F: "Okay, let's start by looking at these figures."

M: "I have a better idea—let's start by looking at <u>your</u> figure!"

F: "That's not funny. Are you here to work, or not?"

M: "For <u>crying out loud</u>! I was just being <u>friendly</u>!"

F: "Take a look at column nine. That's where things don't seem to add up."

M: "What doesn't add up is a foxy lady like you wasting her time on a bunch of numbers! Let's do something more interesting."

He doesn't learn, does he?

This man has not used any sexual terms or made any explicit propositions or threats. He hasn't touched the woman. He may feel that his behavior is therefore in no way out of line and that she should not take offense. However, if the behavior were reversed, as in Dialogue Two, he might see things differently.

DIALOGUE TWO

M: "You see this column here, where the totals are so strange?"

F: "I can't see anything but <u>you</u>, when you're so <u>close</u>."

M: "Then I'll <u>move</u>." (He moves away from her.)

F: "Hey, I was only being <u>friendly</u>!"

M: "Like I was saying, the numbers in column nine just don't make any sense."

F: "What doesn't make any sense is a gorgeous hunk like you wasting his time on a bunch of numbers. Let's do something more interesting."

In both of these dialogues, one party has made a remark that is clearly a personal comment with a slight tinge of sexual suggestion. The other party has demonstrated, equally clearly, that the remark is unwelcome. At that point the appropriate move for the first speaker is to apologize and get down to business. Instead, in both dialogues the speaker answers defensively that he/she was only being friendly. And even when the offended speaker is willing to let it pass and go on with business, the harassment doesn't stop; the final line in each case is an overt pass.

The behavior of the harassing party might be appropriate in a social setting like a singles bar, where a major purpose for being present is to find someone to pair up with. But not in the workplace. The *first* personal comment could be an honest mistake, perhaps, based on misunderstood signals; there's no excuse for the second one.

DIALOGUE THREE

M: "I thought I'd let you know I'm in Room 615."

F: "Thank you; if I have any news after the meeting, I'll call you on the house phone."

M: "That won't be necessary . . . you just come on up. If you want to go on working for me."

F: "That's not funny!"

M: "It wasn't intended to be. I'll have the bed turned down and the champagne waiting."

This is the classic and unmistakable sexual harassment dialogue, left over from the days when women were expected to laugh at cartoons that showed the boss chasing the secretary around the desk. Unlike the cartoons, it hasn't disappeared; I hear half a dozen accounts like this from women every year, and occasionally I hear one from a man similarly harassed by a female boss. When the employee is in a position to risk the job, the right move is to immediately establish that he or she won't cooperate, like this:

M: "It wasn't intended to be. I'll have the bed turned down and the champagne waiting."

F: "Mr. Smith, I'm surprised. I thought better of you. But let's get this straight right now: There will never be any relationship between us except the business one. If you feel that the only choice available to you under those circumstances is to fire me, so be it. Now—I'm going to the meeting.''

It may not be this simple. She may have children to support, or elderly parents dependent on her. Jobs may be extremely hard to get, especially if this man refuses to give her a recommendation because she turned him down. She may be living from paycheck to paycheck, without funds to get by even for a short time. She may have to choose between her principles and feeding her kids. Her boss undoubtedly knows her situation, if that's the case, and he has counted on it to serve as leverage. It would be nice to think that all she has to do is file a formal complaint against him for sexual harassment and let justice take its course.

DIALOGUE FOUR

M1:   ''You should have seen the chick I took home with me last night!''

M2:   ''Yeah? Do I know her?''

M1:   (Chuckles.) ''In the biblical sense of the word, you mean? I don't think so.''

M2:   ''Well come on—tell me about it!''

F: ''Do me a favor: <u>don't</u> tell him about it! I'm not interested in hearing about it.''

M1:   ''That's all right. You don't have to listen. Now, the first thing this woman did, buddy, is. . . .''

If these men were called in because the woman made a complaint about their behavior, it's very likely that they would say what they said to her: that she didn't have to listen. That they weren't talking to her. That she should have minded her own business. That it takes all the pleasure out of working together to have her around. That it's like trying to work with your *mother*. And more of the same.

A variation on the dialogue above is the situation in which two or more men talk about a woman's physical appearance while she's present, being scrupulously careful to say only flattering things. Their defense is likely to be the same.

Women try different ways of dealing with such situations, all the way from joining in and trying to be ''one of the boys'' to quitting the job to escape from them. The only solution that is actually satisfactory is for the harassed person to do the hard work of creating in the harassers such a solid respect that they will voluntarily stop behaving this way. That's not fair; of course not. But all the other solutions are worse, or they are effective only temporarily. The best way I know to create that respect is to use the linguistic techniques presented in this book.

DIALOGUE FIVE

M1:   "You should have seen the woman I went out with last night!"

M2:   "Oh, yeah? Do I know her?"

M1:   "I don't think so . . . she's only lived here a couple of weeks. She's a knockout!"

M2:   "Well, come on—tell me about her."

F: "Do me a favor—<u>don't</u> tell him! I'm not interested in hearing that kind of talk."

M1:   "What do you mean? What 'kind of talk'?"

In this dialogue we have a woman who has leaped to premature conclusions. It's not inappropriate for a man to discuss his date of the previous evening with another man in front of her, and nothing in what was said indicates that the talk is going to turn sexual; for that matter, nothing indicates that she isn't included in the discussion. If she just misunderstood, she can repair the error like this:

F: "I'm sorry; I must have misunderstood. Go on . . . tell us about your friend."

DIALOGUE SIX

M: "Is it all right if I sit here?"

F: "Certainly. I'm almost through eating anyway."

M: "Don't hurry on my account."

F: "Of course not; I'm sure you wouldn't want to rush me."

M: (His voice changes from casual to sensual.) "Hey . . . you're absolutely right. The <u>last</u> thing I'd want to do is rush you, honey."

This is a common type of misunderstanding. She has tried to be polite and pleasant, but he has read more than that into her words and moved to accept what he obviously thinks is an invitation. Hundreds of old movies start with dialogues like this, and go on to portray love in a rose-covered cottage and everyone living happily ever after; in the real world, the consequences are likely to be less perfect. This is how absurd situations develop in which one party claims to have made a move only on the basis of clear encouragement, while the other insists that that interpretation is totally false. It's going to be difficult for the woman in this dialogue to extricate herself gracefully without causing the man to lose face; on the other hand, she couldn't have known that he would interpret her courteous remark as he did. The best outcome would be for them both to Level, like this:

M: "The <u>last</u> thing I'd want to do is rush you, honey."

F: "Sorry; wrong signal."

M: "Oh? <u>I'm</u> sorry! I thought you were coming on to me."

F: "No . . . just being polite."

M: "I apologize."

F: "That's all right; no harm done. Enjoy your lunch."

◆

CHAPTER 12

Breakdown Points—Time, Space, and Inner Space

───────── **Scenario Twelve** ─────────

"Frank," Mary said, "I am just about at the end of my rope! I keep wandering into one trap after another . . . I don't understand how these incidents start and I don't have any idea how to get out of them. What happened with Bill today totally ⸱ threw me—I don't know what I should have done. I've got to do something to straighten it all out. Maybe if I could just sit down and <u>talk</u> to the men about—"

"What?" Frank asked, looking up from the computer. "Are you talking to me?"

"Yes, I am," she said. "<u>You're</u> a man—you ought to be able to help me figure out how to <u>do</u> it."

"How to do what?"

"Like I said, I want to be able to talk to the men at work and explain to them, without sounding neurotic and without making anybody angry, why it is that—"

"<u>Wait</u> a minute!"

Frank swung around to face her, his hands still poised over the keyboard. "Am I imagining it or did you interrupt me just to start again with this same old flap at your office? The one about people telling you you're attractive and you not being able to tolerate that?"

Mary gasped. "<u>Frank!</u>"

"Well, is that what you're going on about, or isn't it? I'm <u>busy</u> here, Mary, and you can <u>see</u> that I am! Couldn't you at least wait until I took a break? You did see that I was working on accounts here, <u>right</u>?"

"Yes. I guess I did."

"Then why did you interrupt me for something so <u>ridiculous</u>?"

The fight that followed was one of the ugliest and bitterest disagreements Frank and Mary had ever had.

◆

What's Going On Here?

Mary's Point of View

As Mary perceives it, she needs to know whether she should be wary of Bill in the future; she needs to know whether her reaction to him was appropriate; she needs to know if there's some safe way to set matters right with him; and she needs to talk the incident over with someone she trusts. She needs advice on some way to *explain* to her male colleagues, once and for all, why these incidents keep happening and how they could be avoided. Because Frank is a man, she feels that he will be able to judge Bill's behavior more accurately than a woman could. She feels that if she discusses the basic concepts of sexist communication with Frank and gets his reaction and input, she should be able to find a way to do the same thing at the office without making everybody furious. And because Frank loves her, she feels that she should be able to count on him to take her concerns seriously and give her his full attention when she asks him for help. She wishes now that she had chosen a more opportune moment, but when he reacts as if she'd interrupted him to discuss her nail polish she is deeply hurt, and very angry.

Frank's Point of View

As Frank perceives it, Mary is forever spoiling their limited time together by launching intense discussions of situations in which she takes things too personally and too seriously. It seems to him that no matter how hard he tries, he always finds himself in the wrong in these discussions, and he works hard at *avoiding* them. It also seems to Frank that even when, as in this case, Mary can see that he's busy, she doesn't hesitate to interrupt him and demand that he involve himself in what he sees as her soap opera. He resents this, and does everything he can to discourage it.

Frank considers himself to be a man who is free of sexism. He has problems with other men in this regard—he either has to keep his mouth shut when he finds their behavior genuinely offensive, or he has to speak up and then listen to their remarks about what a wimp he is. To have to deal with these same issues at home seems to him to be unfair. If Mary is going to insist that she's the equal of any man—a position he's willing to back her in—then he thinks she should handle these personal hassles herself, without dragging him into them. That she started this particular episode when she could see that he was at his computer going over a screenful of figures is the straw that breaks the camel's back.

What to Do About It

Time and Space

Separating time and space—when and where—isn't really possible. They interact and are interdependent, one can never be found without the other, and the barriers between them exist by tradition only. Together they form the domain of *location*. April 15th at 3:30 P.M. is your location in time in exactly the same way that a bedroom at 102 10th Street, St. Louis, Missouri, is your location in space.

Every culture has as part of its grammar a set of rules for interacting with other people in terms of time and space. These rules specify at least the following four things:

- What is public spacetime and what is private, and how much of each a person is entitled to.
- What signals are to be used to set and to communicate the boundaries.
- How words and phrases such as "early/late/on time," "fast/slow," "far/near," and "empty/full/crowded" are defined.
- How these matters are to be talked about and what body language is to be used with the words.

There are dialects and idiolects for spacetime just as there are for every other aspect of human life.

Anthropologist Edward T. Hall is the recognized expert on the interaction between spacetime and human behavior, especially in terms of cross-cultural contact. We'll begin—doing our best to make the traditional artificial division—with a discussion of his useful concepts of *time* as they apply to male/female AME speakers.

Monochronic Time and Polychronic Time

Hall writes of monochronic time (M-time)—in which people do one thing at a time and finish it before they go on to do some other thing—as typical of American mainstream society. Monochronic time is the time system of business and high technology and bureaucracies and all the other activities of our society that demand rigid schedules and firm deadlines. He writes of polychronic time (P-time)—in which people do many things at once and feel no need to finish each one before starting something else—as typical of Arabic societies. But he also notes that in America it is for the most part only *men* who run on monochronic time. (Exceptions can be found among successful single women living alone and successful married women, without children, in two-career families.) This difference leads inevitably to problems of communication. So much so, he says in *The Dance of Life* (Anchor/Doubleday 1983), that:

> The time system of the dominant culture adds another source of trauma and alienation to the already overburdened psyches of many American women.

Most women are still responsible for the housework in the American home. Even when someone else does a part of it, they remain responsible for seeing that it is done, and anyone else doing it typically claims to have done it "for" them. Women are still responsible for the caregiving for children, elderly parents, pets, and anyone of any age who is sick or injured. Most women still do almost all of what I call "granny work"— that is, such things as remembering birthdays, sending out holiday cards, dealing with emotional hassles in the family, and the like. Men talk a better line today than in the past about believing that they ought to share this load, but even the most recent studies show that it's only talk; they actually do a *smaller* percentage of the work of the home today.

As a result, women are accustomed to doing fifteen things at once and to being constantly interrupted. They cook dinner while they help with the kids' homework while they clean the living room while they change the baby while they answer the phone while they keep an eye on the clothes in the dryer while they address the invitations to the dinner party . . . and so on. Not only that, they are expected to be able to move smoothly between the P-time system typical of the home and the M-time required of them in the workplace. This leads to one of the most painful sources of conflict between the genders, and one that tends to mystify everyone involved:

✦ For most AME women, the idea that people have to have a separate chunk of time set aside for each task, during which no one should interrupt them except in an emergency, is utterly foreign—especially within the spacetime of the home. And the idea that someone who is interrupted there cannot simply set aside the task, deal with the interruption, and then *return* to the task, strikes them as childish.

As long as the division of labor in the home continues to be as it is today, this gender difference will not go away. There are, however, some practical ways to avoid many of the usual cross-gender communication problems associated with it. The first one is the obvious measure of recognizing and remembering that the difference exists, which may go a considerable distance toward heading off and repairing misunderstandings. No one should find that controversial. The second measure I'm about to propose, however, is likely to provoke objections. Because, like housework, it throws the burden of responsibility on women yet again. Bear with me, please, while I explain.

Never mind whether, as the woman perceives it, what she sees the man doing meets her definition of "being busy" or of "doing something important." Her most efficient and sensible move when she wants to engage her male partner in noncasual communication is to follow this one rule:

✦ MAKE AN APPOINTMENT.

That is: Always say to the man, "I need to talk to you about something; I need some input from you. When will that be convenient for you?"

It's a ridiculous waste of resources to do this any other way. Not because it is "right" or "wrong," but because it's in the woman's own best interests. A woman who needs to talk to a man at length in the home has two choices. She can set up the block of time she needs formally by making an appointment, and know that she will be talking to a man who is reasonably attentive and nonhostile. Or she can waste her time breaking into the man's activities and arguing over whether she's justified in doing so, waste her emotional resources in the resulting fight, and try to fit the discussion she wanted into whatever is left over—with a man who is furious in advance and unwilling to participate. Making an appointment is far better strategy.

In addition, she must take the firm position that the man is to show her the same courtesy. It's unlikely that men can be persuaded not to interrupt her dinner preparations by demanding to know where their clean socks are; it's unlikely that women today can establish M-time in their homes across the board. But there's no reason why men who want to engage in serious conversation or discussion can't ask women when that would be convenient and negotiate a mutually satisfactory time. Because AME-speaking men spend so much of their lives running on M-time, it shouldn't be difficult to convince them of the reasonableness of this measure. When a man approaches a woman who is up to her elbows in dishes and says, "We've got to talk about this electric bill!," she should say, "Let me think for a minute and I'll tell you when I can fit that into my schedule." And she should then set a time they can both agree on and follow through on it. Women working outside the home, or working inside it in home businesses (the majority of which are run by women), have been able to adjust to the M-time requirements of that work. Men can learn to adjust to some M-time requirements in the domestic territory.

What Men Can Do to Help

As for men, my advice is that they give this strange state of affairs some thought and consider whether they could do anything to improve it. When women ask them for an appointment to discuss something, they should give it courteously, without any smart cracks and without prejudging the agenda for the discussion—and they should keep the appointment and take it seriously. When women ask them to adopt the same procedure, instead of insisting on the privilege of breaking into whatever the women are doing at will, they should agree and follow through.

Finally, men can resolve *never* to say this very stupid sentence: "If I ran my business the way you run this house, I'd go bankrupt." Whether it's a true statement or not is irrelevant. Homes aren't businesses; events there don't happen on rigid schedules; and the linear logic of M-time doesn't apply within their walls and yards.

Space and Time

Where space is concerned, most AME-speaking men and women share roughly the same rules. Hall carefully describes many cultural differences related to space—for example, speakers of Latino languages need less personal space while talking and thus want to sit or stand much closer *as* they talk than speakers of English do. This sort of difference doesn't apply with AME speakers, because the rules are shared by both genders. Men and women in the AME culture agree well enough on when a room is too full to add more things to it, when a door should be closed to signal a desire for private space, what is and isn't public space, when it's okay to move a piece of furniture, and so on. There are idiosyncratic differences, of course, but they are individual rather than tied to gender. The source of the problem is one that transcends gender, and has been well stated by Nancy M. Henley in *Body Politics* (Prentice Hall 1977):

> Though little aware of it we may be, our world is set up so that powerful humans own more territory, move through common areas and others' territory more freely, and take up more space with their bodies, possessions and symbols.

Because positions of power belong to men in our society more than to women, this means that management of space is more often controlled by men. Many studies have demonstrated that women are less likely to have a special room in the house for their use than men, who often have a "den" or a "study." Men are more likely to have a chair reserved for their special use, as well as to sit in the chair at the head of the table, than women are. In the workplace, men usually have larger offices, larger desks, and more expensive objects marking their territory. This is not because they are male, but because they are powerful; a woman who has equal power has equal control over space.

For the same reasons, and in the same way, men feel freer to *break* the rules regarding space than women do. Just as they feel freer to interrupt a woman's time, they feel freer to interrupt—to invade—her personal space. Men are more likely to crowd women or touch them unasked, more likely to approach them despite clear signals that they are requesting privacy, than the other way around. But it's important to realize that *they would feel free to behave the same way toward a man they considered weak.* This is not a difference of gender but a difference of power; it looks like a gender difference only because of the skew toward male power in AME society.

One thing both men and women can do to improve communication under these circumstances is to make an effort to reduce the *extra* confusion that's introduced into spacetime matters when their definitions of key words and phrases differ. They can use the *Gentle Art* techniques to discover whether they mean the same *thing* when they say that someone is "late" or that a room is "crowded" or that two chairs are "too far apart." They can use the technique of semantic analysis to find out whether such differences are further complicating this already complicated situation. And they can extend their investigation to potential differences in the definitions of key words not obviously from the spacetime vocabulary but frequent in the spacetime context. Let's consider one example of this kind that comes up frequently in the lives of couples.

Doing Things Together

As Deborah Tannen accurately points out in *You Just Don't Understand*, men feel that when two people are doing something *within the boundaries of what is defined as "the same place" and "the same time"* they are doing something *together*. For many women, this isn't enough; people are "doing something together" only if they are both doing the *same* thing. This (rather than a lack of appreciation of the importance of morning papers on the part of women) is why many men see nothing wrong with reading the newspaper during breakfast, while women would rather they didn't. For most men, although he is reading and she is not, they are still "doing something together."

The concepts of M-time and P-time complicate matters further. Consider the following dialogue:

M: "I wish you'd put down that knitting until we're through discussing this!"

F: "Why? You don't object if I knit while we're watching television . . . why do you care if I knit while we talk?"

M: "It's not the same <u>thing</u>! You ask the craziest questions!"

From the man's point of view, running as he does on M-time, serious talking is a single activity and one that—unlike eating—requires your conscious attention. (Eating doesn't appear to be defined by men as "doing something"; this is a definitional difference that would repay careful investigation.) M-time specifies that you do only one such thing at a time. To talk together, you have to both talk—and only talk.

When they were "doing something together" in the living room, on the other hand, his perception is that he was watching television while she knitted, and she was knitting while he watched television—each doing one thing, but not the same thing, and doing it "together." (For some men the analysis would be that he was watching television while she was keeping him company, because knitting, like eating, isn't "doing something.")

The couple in the dialogue aren't likely to explore this linguistic difference; they are far more likely to apply Miller's-Law-in-Reverse. He wonders what's the matter with *her* to make her ask such a crazy question; she wonders what's wrong with *him* that keeps him from understanding a simple English sentence.

This is one of the times when being aware of what's going on *will* help. Anyone who is aware of (a) the difference between M-time and P-time and (b) the way the two models of time are related to the two genders will be able to use *Gentle Art* techniques to anticipate and repair breakdowns of this kind.

Hazards in Inner Space

Inner space (more properly inner spacetime, of course) is the term used to refer to *mental* space: the cognitive space and time that exists inside the human mind and is now extensively used for techniques of visualization. When you imagine biting into a lemon and it makes your cheeks hurt, that's an *inner space lemon, but its effects are just as "real" as if it were a lemon you could hold in your hand*. If telepathy exists, it presumably exists in inner space. Scenario Twelve portrays an inner space problem that plagues many AME-speaking couples.

——— Scenario Twelve, Continued ———

(The day after the fight in Scenario Twelve.)

"Hi, honey," Frank said as he walked in the kitchen door. "I'm glad you're fixing that—it looks good."

"Thank you."

"How soon are we going to eat? I'm starved. . . . I had so many calls back-to-back this morning that I never did get a chance to go to lunch, and by the time I got through it was too late."

"Dinner will be ready in twenty minutes, Frank."

"Great! That gives me just time enough to take a shower. Or maybe I'll wait till after dinner for that. Maybe I'll go finish those accounts . . . or maybe I'll let that wait, too." Sighing, he pulled back a chair from the kitchen table and sat down.

He sat and talked to her about what he thought they ought to do about their car; she stood fixing dinner with her back to him, answering him in chilly monosyllables and curt phrases. "Yes, Frank." "No, Frank." "Whatever you say, Frank."

Until he noticed and demanded to know what was wrong.

"Nothing, Frank."

"Oh, come on! You can tell me—I live here!" he teased.

"All right," she said coldly. "I'll tell you. I waited all day for you to call and say we should go out to dinner tonight!"

He frowned . . . and then he nodded. "I get it," he said slowly. "Because of the fight we had last night."

"Precisely!"

"Well, I'd be happy to do that; it's a good idea! Why didn't you just <u>say</u> you wanted to go out to eat tonight?"

"If you really LOVED me," Mary said furiously, "you'd just KNOW! I wouldn't HAVE to ask!"

There was a long silence, while she peeled potatoes at lightning speed and he stared at her back. And then he spoke to her quietly—dangerously so. "You know, Mary," he said finally, "it doesn't surprise me that you keep getting into messes at work. It's impossible to please you, and it's impossible to have an adult conversation with you. The men you work with have my sympathy."

◆

What's Going On Here?

Frank's Point of View

Frank remembers the fight he and Mary had the night before, but so far as he's concerned it's over; he's ready to let bygones be bygones. All he expects Mary to do is what *he's* doing—going on as if nothing had happened, holding no grudges, not bringing up the hateful things that were said in anger. Behaving *normally*. The idea that she not only expected him to make a formal gesture of reconciliation, but expected him to know exactly what gesture she wanted, seems to him to be totally unreasonable. He cannot be expected to read her mind! This isn't the first time he's run into this problem with Mary, but he has never been able to figure out what the cues are that it's coming; it's always a surprise. It's one of the things he finds most infuriating and frustrating in their relationship; he's willing to go as far as he has to to make that unambiguously clear to her, so she'll cut it out. He's weary of fighting, and he'd like very much to have some peace for a change—but if a row is what it takes to get this point across to her, so be it! It would be worth it to him.

Mary's Point of View

Mary is truly bewildered by this sequence of events. As she perceives it, she's able to anticipate what Frank will want and need, not because she can read his mind but because she has made a diligent effort to learn from his behavior over their years as a couple. She doesn't believe that he could be so unaware of how distressed she was by their fight the night before—after all, in the course of the fight she told him repeatedly—that he would think it was okay to just come home and settle down to talk casually and expect her to accept that.

Mary knows that if she had asked Frank to take her out to dinner he would have agreed at once, and he would have enjoyed going. But to Mary, having to *ask* for something he should have known she wanted *without* being asked ruins it for her. Even if he immediately and willingly does what she asks, *she's had to take the subordinate role and say please, and he gets to be the one in control, the one who decides and grants her favors, as if she were a child.* It seems to her that he *does* know these things. It seems to her that he deliberately puts her in the position of having to ask or do without, as a power play, and she resents it bitterly. For him to hurt her like that—and then follow up the insult by siding with the men at her office in the most vicious possible way!—is incomprehensible to her. A man who loves a woman, she feels, could not and would not treat her like that.

◆

The Tender Telepathy Myth and How to Deal with It

The core of the communication breakdown in Scenario Twelve is an idea—"The Tender Telepathy Myth"—that causes endless trouble in people's lives. Women do pay very close attention to the behavior of those they live with, including their language behavior; one of the things women learn growing up in AME-speaking society is that they're expected to keep things clean and pleasant, and that applies to the emotional and linguistic environment as much as it does to the house and the laundry. Both men and women, during the courting phase of a relationship, observe the other person's behavior and try to internalize it well enough to be able to predict that person's every reaction. Women, and many men, continue to do this through the honeymoon phase, and both will do it in a crisis. But only for women is such observation a constant feature of everyday life after the courting and honeymoon phases are over.

Women don't succeed in the goal of knowing exactly how the man they live with will react to each and every thing, of course. If they did, presumably they'd never be baffled by the men's behavior and would never find themselves involved in unexpected arguments. Women are particularly bad at understanding men's motivations when everything is being filtered through a metaphor they don't share or, worse yet, don't suspect. Even in long-term relationships, men—like Frank, above—are often astonished at how badly their partner has misunderstood their intentions, their motives, and their actions.

Compared to the men, however, women do extraordinarily *well*. It's the difference between observing the data as closely as you can over a period of years and processing it with all possible efficiency, which is what most women do, and observing it only when something catches fire, which is what most men do. The result of this difference is the Tender Telepathy Myth: The idea women have that men give as much attention to learning to predict *their* behavior as women give to learning to predict the men's. To women who believe this it seems that men are only *pretending* not to know what the women want them to do in "couple" contexts. This lays potentially deadly mines in the language environment. (It's even worse for the *man* who believes the myth and must do so on blind faith; such men are so rare in the AME culture that we will continue to discuss the myth as a characteristic of women.)

Another concept from the work of Edward T. Hall is useful to us here. In his book *Beyond Culture* (Anchor Books 1977), he proposes that cultures are either "high-context" or "low-context" and that:

> People raised in high-context systems expect more of others than do the participants in low-context systems. When talking about something that they have on their minds, a high-context individual will expect his interlocuter to know what's bothering him, so that he doesn't have to be specific.

Hall's interest was in developing this concept as a mechanism for analyzing different national cultures. He says of the Japanese high-context culture, for example: "You are supposed to know, and they get quite upset when you don't." For anyone whose partner subscribes to the Tender Telepathy Myth, that sentence about the Japanese will strike a nerve. "*You are supposed to know*" means "*The information is presupposed.*" High-context women assume that every adult in a long-term, intimate relationship should be able to rely on information from the context in the same way and to the same degree that they do.

The Tender Telepathy Myth contains four propositions:

1. People who love you don't need to be told what you want or need; they just *know*.

2. Therefore, when you want something and you know they would be willing to do it—but they don't do it until you ask them to—that's a deliberate power play on their part.

3. Therefore, when they do what you want *after* being asked, it doesn't count.

4. Anyone who fits #2 and #3 doesn't really love you.

Suppose we apply Miller's Law to this set of propositions. We would get a result like this:

✦ The only kind of reality in which they could be truth rather than myth is one in which men, like women, automatically observe and process as much data about their partner's behavior as possible, with the goal of building a database for *predicting* that behavior.

Contrary to what soap operas and romance novels might lead us to believe, men in the AME culture do not routinely do this. They do it in crisis situations, but not under ordinary circumstances, and they must therefore operate in what is, comparatively speaking, an informational void. When women ask them "Well, what do *you* think I want you to do?" or "Well, what did you *suppose* I wanted you to do?," it's both futile and unfair; men don't know the answer to either question. In my opinion, men would be well advised to use the high-context information processing strategies in intimate relationships, as women do, but at the moment that's not happening.

What Women Can Do

The course women need to follow is like the strategy of making an appointment for a man's time: *Discard the myth, which only does harm, and ASK*. Mary should have called Frank or spoken to him before they left for work that morning and *told* him that she felt bad about the fight and would like to go out to dinner. Frank would then have said that was fine with him—thus avoiding the awful moment when, out of anger, he told her that the men who have to work with her have his sympathy.

Having to ask makes many women feel like children groveling to Daddy. This reaction is usually not to what their partner is doing, but to things *other* people have done. All the years of being a child and always having to say please, all the years in a society dominated by males with the power to say no in so many situations, are behind that reaction. Women must recognize that the man's behavior is based on ignorance— a genuine lack of information—rather than malice, and simply ASK FOR WHATEVER IT IS THAT THEY WANT. Notice: The word is *ask*, not beg or plead. This must be done in Leveler or Computer Mode rather than in Placater Mode. Here's an example of each:

Placating:
"Honey, I <u>know</u> you're probably going to get mad when I ask you this, but don't you think that after that terrible <u>fight</u> we had we ought to go out to <u>dinner</u>? I mean, doesn't it seem to <u>you</u> that that would be a good <u>idea</u>?"

Leveling:
"Honey, I feel too rotten about that awful fight we had last night to just sit down and go on as if nothing had happened. Let's go out for dinner and clear the air."

Computing:
"It's hard for people to have an ugly fight and then go on with their lives together as if nothing had happened. It's better to do something to clear the air—like going out to dinner."

What Men Can Do

Men who use the *Gentle Art* techniques will *automatically* find themselves less frequently involved in these inner space confrontations. All the techniques require close attention to the language behavior, both verbal and nonverbal, of the other person in the language interaction. This will improve the male informational database, and men *will* more often understand without having to be explicitly told.

In addition, men whose first inclination is to say "Why don't they just <u>ask</u>? Why do they make such a big <u>deal</u> out of something so simple?" should remember the metaprinciple: FALSE PERCEPTIONS HAVE REAL CONSEQUENCES. Men dislike having to go to men who outrank them and ask for things. They can use this metaphor as a basis for understanding. Women who perceive men's failure to offer what's wanted as deliberate dominance behavior—as a power play—feel the same way. The fact that the perception is false doesn't make the consequences any less real.

Technique #11

Using Presuppositions of Location in Time and Space to Reduce Hostility

When you respond to one of the English VAPs with "When did you start thinking that [X]?" you're taking advantage of the fact that "when" presupposes only "there was a time at which you started thinking that [X]" and asks only that the location in time be specified. Other words and phrases used to specify time and space have an equally convenient property for use in male/female communication: You can use them to *presuppose* something you want done, instead of having to openly request or order that it be done. For example:

> "While you're fixing that leaky faucet in the kitchen, will it bother you if I go ahead and make dinner?"

This question—because of the time word "while"—*presupposes* that the person it's addressed to will fix the leaky faucet. The strategy of using it is to avoid a dialogue like this one:

F: "I wish you'd fix that leaky faucet in the kitchen. Are you going to?"

M: "I don't know. Are you saying I have to do it right <u>now</u>?"

F: "No, that's not what I'm saying. But—"

M: "I'll get to it as soon as I can, then."

F: "What does that mean . . . 'as soon as you can'?"

M: "<u>You</u> speak English—what do you <u>think</u> it means?"

F: "Well, I don't see any reason why you can't go ahead and fix that faucet <u>today</u>! It's been leaking for <u>weeks</u>."

M: "Then it won't hurt anything if it leaks a little longer, <u>will</u> it?"

The presupposing strategy may not work. The man may respond to "While you're fixing that leaky faucet (etc.)" with "Are you saying I have to do it right <u>now</u>?" But he is far less likely to do so only for the single reason that *he resents being asked*. Notice: "Are you saying I have to do it right <u>now</u>?" presupposes that what was said was a command, not a question, and the extra stress on *now* signals annoyance. If the annoyance is because there really is a reason why the man needs to postpone fixing the faucet, that's one thing, and it can be explored and discussed. But if his annoyance is a kneejerk reaction to "being told what to do," even indirectly, he's likely to argue only because he's *annoyed*, and not because he can't or won't fix the faucet at that moment. Starting the question with "while" doesn't guarantee that the questioner will bypass that automatic negative reaction. But it substantially increases the chances of success, and it's skillful communication.

Other examples of the same strategy include:

"After you've finished fixing that faucet in the kitchen, I think I'll start dinner."

"I don't want to get in your way—I won't start dinner until you've finished fixing that faucet in the kitchen."

Like "while," "after" and "until" presuppose that the person spoken to will fix the faucet in the kitchen and they eliminate the need for either a request or a command.

It's also possible to add another piece to this strategy, as in these examples:

"While you're fixing that faucet in the kitchen, do you want me to stay out of the way or would you rather I went ahead and fixed dinner?"

"When you're through fixing that faucet in the kitchen, would you rather eat here or go get some pizza?"

Any adult native speaker of English will know what such questions mean and will understand what's happening; that's the reason therapists refer to this as offering an "illusion of choice." If the person offering has any power to compel the listener to do things, there *is* no real choice. But structuring the utterance this way avoids challenging the listener and reduces the possibility of loss of face. It reduces the pressure to react with a "You can't tell me what to do!" message. And offering the choice between two alternatives—even if the alternatives themselves are trivial—conveys this hostility-reducing metamessage: "I'm telling you what to do, that's true; but at the same time, I'm asking you to tell me what to do." This is a courtesy, just as saying "Would you fix the faucet in the kitchen?" instead of "Go fix the faucet in the kitchen!" is a courtesy.

Another Look at Scenario Twelve

It will be obvious to you that one language strategy needed in the scenario was a switch from Blaming to Leveling. When Frank realized that Mary had interrupted him to bring up her communication problems at the office, he should not have swung immediately into an attack. Instead, he should have said this:

> "Mary, I'll be glad to talk to you about the problem at the office; I know it's really worrying you. But I can't do it right now. Let me finish with these figures first."

And Mary should have agreed, let the matter drop for then, and—as soon as Frank was through with what he was doing—asked him when they could conveniently sit down and talk. She might also have approached him in the first place like this:

> "Frank, after you've finished with those figures, I need your input on a problem at the office; would you rather talk about it over dinner or wait until later this evening?"

When she says "after you've finished with those figures," she is presupposing that he will finish and that that will happen before he turns his attention to her problems at work. And she follows it up with a sequence of language that uses two useful strategies:

- She offers Frank an illusion of choice, with "would you rather talk about it over dinner or wait until later this evening?"
- She fits her request into the "I'd like to make an appointment" framework that Frank is accustomed to in his business life, as recommended in this chapter.

Dialogues for Analysis

DIALOGUE ONE

F: "I've asked you till I'm blue in the face: Will you PLEASE fix that faucet?! It's driving me _mad_!"

M: "Don't worry about it, honey. It'll only take me five minutes."

F: "Don't you DARE tell me that again!"

M: "Huh? Tell you _what_?"

F: "Don't TELL me that it'll only take five minutes!"

M: "But that is all the time it will take! What's the matter with you?"

Running as she does on polychronic time, this woman is used to being interrupted, leaving the task at hand to tend to the interruption, and going on from where she left off. She would never refuse to do that when what was asked of her was something easily done and requiring only a few minutes of her time. The idea that she has to keep asking him to fix this faucet when it's a quick and easy task annoys her—but for him to *stress* how quick and easy it is strikes her as incomprehensible.

Running as he does on monochronic time, this man is used to doing one thing until it's finished and then taking up something else. When he tells her that fixing the faucet will only take five minutes, his intention is to reassure her: This is something which, when he has an empty slot in his schedule to fit it into, he'll be able to do quickly. Furthermore, it's such a small task that he won't have to wait for a *large* chunk of time to come along. From his point of view he's already explained this to her before and he'll fix the faucet when his conditions are met. For her to keep asking about it annoys him—but for her to lash out at him when he offers friendly reassurance strikes him as incomprehensible.

These two people probably can't do much about their differing perceptions of time in the home. But there's no reason why they can't decrease the number of arguments that are based on ignorance that the difference *exists*.

One more factor is complicating this situation; it's shown in Dialogue Two.

DIALOGUE TWO

F: "I've asked you till I'm blue in the face, will you PLEASE fix that faucet?! It's driving me mad!"

M: "Don't worry about it, honey. It'll only take me five minutes."

F: "Don't you DARE tell me that again!"

M: "Huh? Tell you what?"

F: "Don't TELL me that it'll only take five minutes!"

M: "But that is all the time it will take! What's the matter with you?"

F: "Never mind what's the matter with me! I want to know why you won't stop right now and fix that faucet! This is the fifth time I've asked you! And every time, you tell me not to worry, it will only take five minutes! If it's such a trivial job, why don't you go ahead and DO it?!!''

M: "Because it's trivial, that's why! If it was something important, I'd stop what I was doing and fix it!''

Women in the AME culture learn early that when the interrupting task is minor *it takes less time to stop and do it than it does to stop and argue about doing it.* As demonstrated by Dialogues One and Two, such arguments can go on for quite a while and become very heated. Women base their decisions about agreeing to be interrupted on a variety of factors, of course, but this one—whether it's quicker to do it than to argue—is second only to whether there's an emergency involved. Whether the task is "important," in the male sense of that word, is almost irrelevant. It goes without saying that male and female judgments differ on what qualifies something as an important task.

One thing that makes a task "important" in an AME-speaking man's eyes is the fact that it's *on a schedule*, especially one that's written down somewhere. I therefore suggest the following opening line:

F: "Honey, that leaky faucet is really getting to me, and I need it fixed. Can you do it for me now or would you rather wait until this evening?''

She should do this with pencil and paper in hand. If he rejects both times offered, she should negotiate until he sets a time, and then write it down. To make doubly sure, she should then say, with neutral intonation, "Okay. Fixing the faucet is scheduled for Tuesday evening after dinner, before you go play golf. Thank you, dear.''

DIALOGUE THREE

M: "Did you take my suit to the cleaners today?''

F: "No, I didn't.''

M: "Why not?''

F: "I didn't have time—I'll try to get to it tomorrow.''

M: "I don't understand. How could you not have enough time?''

F: "I beg your pardon?''

M: "You don't have anything to do but look after the <u>house</u>! How could you not have time to take my <u>suit</u> to the cleaners?"

There should not be any men left alive today who are this ignorant about the running of a house. If she actually is married to one, she should take immediate steps, as in the ancient folktale, to turn the job over to him for a day or two so that he can learn what it's like. Alternatively, she can apply Miller's Law and proceed as follows:

M: "You don't have anything to do but look after the <u>house</u>! How could you not have time to take my <u>suit</u> to the cleaners?"

F: "Maybe you're right. Maybe I'm just not organizing what I do as well as I could."

M: "Exactly my point."

F: "In that case, I'll need your help. When would it be convenient for us to sit down and go over the list of everything I have to do and set up a more efficient schedule?"

The experience of working with her on a schedule—looking at the list of tasks she does, writing down the amount of time each task takes, and organizing the result—will put an end forever to his questions about how she could fail to have time for everything he wants. In the rare case when her problem really *is* poor organization, working out a schedule will be a valuable experience for her as well.

Finally, it's difficult to imagine a situation in which this man's remarks would be justified. He asks her, twice, how she could possibly not have enough time to run his errands; he tells her she has "nothing to do but look after the house." The things he says *presuppose* that her time is frittered away on trivialities, so that even taking his suit to the cleaners is more important than anything she might have needed to do. Only if he can be absolutely certain that she spends her entire day lolling by the pool do his remarks make any sense; if she is a woman who works outside the home in *addition* to running the house, his behavior is inexcusable.

Suppose she told him that he had nothing to do but look after his business. He would be quite justifiably outraged. Men among my clients, after hearing me explain this, ordinarily say "But it's not the same <u>thing</u>!" Followed by a paragraph about their work being important, putting the bread on the table, etc. This problem is not communication skills but ignorance, and that can be fixed.

DIALOGUE FOUR

M: "I had some extra time today, so I did the laundry for you."

F: [Silence]

M: "Hey, don't I even get a thank you?"

In her book, *In the Men's House*, Barkalow quotes another Army captain (male) as saying that "simply sharing the housework from time to time isn't the problem. I do that. Rather, it's assuming <u>equal responsibility</u> for the housework." Notice how he puts that . . . he says he doesn't mind sharing the housework "from time to time." Like the man in the dialogue, he presupposes that housework is Women's Work and that women should be grateful when men "from time to time" do some of it; but the women must continue to see that it gets done, no matter who does it.

Suggestion for Him: If you are a man who believes this to be true, keep it to yourself. You could not possibly be unaware that your partner disagrees with you. All you have to do to achieve this is to get rid of the "for you" phrase. Just say "I had some extra time today, so I did the laundry." Chances are good that the response will be "Thanks; that's a help."

Suggestion for Her: Tiresome as it is, if changing his behavior in this regard is one of your goals, you will have to confront the issue directly. You'll have to Level, but mixing in some Computer Mode will damp the hostility down a bit. Like this:

M: "I had some extra time today, so I did the laundry for you."

F: "It's amazing how many men still believe that total responsibility for the housework belongs to the woman; I'm sorry to hear that you feel that way."

Now he can't just demand that you express your gratitude; he has to turn to the issue of responsibility for the housework.

If you hold down an outside job, you may want to approach this differently. Let the remarks in the dialogue pass without comment. And then, when you come home the next day, say to him (with the same intonation he used), "I had some extra time today, so I earned some money for you." This isn't done for revenge, and it isn't "stooping to his level." It's a way of making it easier for him to share your reality by using a metaphor to tie the two realities together. Warning: If you know your male partner feels insecure about the fact that you work, especially if you earn more money than he does, this would cause him to lose far too much face. In that case, do it more gently. Say this:

> "Suppose I were to come home and say to you that I had had some extra time, so I'd earned some money for you. Would you think that was courteous?"

DIALOGUE FIVE

F: "Please don't ever do that to me again!"

M: "What? What did I do?"

F: "Please don't kiss me like that in public. I was really embarrassed. . . . I didn't know where to look!"

M: "Wait a minute! I understand about no passionate kisses in public! I wouldn't like that either. But we weren't in public, honey. There was nobody here except my family."

This is an example where his definition of "a public space" and hers are different. They fully agree that displays of passion are inappropriate in public, which gives them a chunk of shared meaning to work from. They should explore the meaning difference, to negotiate either a shared definition of "in public," or a rule about limits on public displays of affection that they can both live with.

The same strategy should be used whenever it becomes obvious that arguments are being caused by differing definitions of key spacetime words and phrases.

CHAPTER 13

◆

How to Achieve Intimacy

"Isn't this nice, John?" Paula said.

"Isn't what nice?"

She leaned over and rubbed her cheek against his shoulder. "You know," she said. "Sitting here like this. Nobody around to bother us . . . no kids . . . no television . . . no neighbors . . . just us."

"It's sure quiet."

"Yes, it is. It's lovely."

Paula moved closer, and leaned against him. "Why are you so tense?" she asked him. "Don't you like being alone with me?"

"That's a silly question. Of course I do."

"Then why don't you put your arm around me? After twenty years, surely you know that's not dangerous."

John laughed, and gave her a gentle hug. "There," he said. "How's that?"

"Nice!" she said. "I like being here with you like this, with Larry gone for the evening, and nothing that we have to do for once except enjoy each other's company."

"You're absolutely right," John said, and hugged her close.

Thirty seconds went by, and then he said, "Well, what do you want to do?"

"I don't want to 'do' anything," Paula told him. "I just want to sit here with you and watch the fire. Maybe talk about things."

"I see," said John. "Okay."

Paula sat up straight and looked at him hard. "You don't want to, <u>do</u> you?" she said. "You'd rather watch television, or read, or something."

"I didn't say that, honey."

"No—but I can tell."

"<u>Look</u>, Paula," he said patiently, "you said you want to just sit here and do nothing, and I said okay! What do you expect me to do, set off rockets?"

"Oh, well," she said. "Never mind, John. It was a dumb idea anyway." She patted him on the knee, smiling. "I'll go make some onion dip; you see if you can find anything decent to watch."

"<u>Why</u> do you always do that?" he demanded.

"Make onion dip, you mean?"

"Why do you always go through that whole cuddle-cuddle-kissy-face routine? And then turn into my mother when I don't sweep you up in my arms and smother you with passionate caresses?"

"Nobody asked you for 'passionate caresses'!" she said indignantly.

"Well, nobody asked <u>you</u> for <u>onion</u> dip!" he retorted.

"John," Paula sighed as she headed for the kitchen, "some day we've got to stop meeting like this and get to know each other."

"Now, what is <u>that</u> crack supposed to mean?" he said, grinning at her.

"Find something we can <u>watch</u>!" she said from the kitchen door. "Not just one chase scene after another, please—something for the Thinking Adult."

And she disappeared into the kitchen.

◆

What's Going On Here?

Paula's Point of View

Paula is not a demanding woman, or a naively romantic one; she doesn't expect to be swept up in anybody's arms and smothered in caresses, passionate or any other kind. What she *would* like, however, is a little more closeness with John. It sometimes seems to her that they're almost strangers. She has no serious complaints about their sexual relationship; it's what happens when they're alone together *outside* the bedroom context that troubles her. But she has tried explaining this to John scores of times, without success. His response is always the same:

- If she'll provide the script, he'll be more than happy to follow it.
- If she'll tell him what to say, he'll say it.
- If she'll explain exactly what she wants, he'll do his best to provide it for her.

She has tried many variations on her basic complaint: "I want you to be my friend as well as my husband and lover." Always, he responds with the polite tolerance and transparent distaste he shows toward people who insist on talking to him about their surgeries.

Every once in a while, when the occasion offers itself, Paula checks in with John again—just in case. But nothing ever changes.

John's Point of View

John is an intelligent man who understands perfectly well—in an intellectual sense—what Paula wants of him. It's not something *he* wants, however, and it makes no *emotional* sense to him at all. If he wants friends, he has plenty of them, and so, it seems to him, does Paula. When he gets home after working all day and putting up with a world full of incompetents and flakes, he wants a *wife*, not a friend. However, he knows that putting up with the "Can't we be closer, darling?" routine is one of the things required of a considerate husband who is fortunate enough to have an otherwise satisfactory wife. He prides himself on meeting that standard, just as he prides himself on maintaining the obligatory nonsexist façade toward women in the workplace. Within reason, of course. When Paula carries this "Let's be close" routine too far, he lets her know that he's not going to go along with it.

John would be amazed to learn that Mary Clayton's husband would be delighted to be "friends" with Mary if he could only figure out how to go about it, and that his inability to do so causes Frank great concern. That would confirm John's opinion: that Frank is a wimp, and that his wimpiness is a major reason for Mary's bizarre ideas about what constitutes normal behavior between the sexes.

Scenario Thirteen is of course a cliché. Like the man reading the newspaper at the table while his wife sits eating in martyred silence, the wife who tries for intimacy while her husband struggles for air is a cultural staple. The responses AME-speaking men offer in such altercations vary. Some men are brutal—"Oh, for god's sake, <u>get off my back</u> with that stupid stuff!" Others are like John, tolerant within limits. Some are sarcastic; others are argumentative. Some deal with the conflict by making sure they're never alone with their wives except in a bed, where the expected variety of intimacy is one that *does* have a script and that cannot be confused with the intimacy between close friends. After all, if you have a script and you follow it, you can't get into trouble.

It's true that almost all little girls have a "best friend"; it's not true that adult women therefore expect their male partners to assume the Best Friend role. It's not true that men have no friends except a "drinking buddy" or some nondrinking equivalent, or that "male bonding" is the only nonsexual intimacy men are able to achieve. It's not true that deep and intense conversation between men and women is impossible because they speak different languages. All these things are true of some men and some women, and they make extremely convenient excuses. But they are not *generally* true. Not beyond high school.

The truth concealed behind these stereotyped ideas is that the American Mainstream English culture places no particular value on conversation, offers few useful models of conversation to its young people, and teaches people no strategies for building the kind of mutual trust that makes real conversation—intimate or otherwise—possible. When the only kind of conversation a man is comfortable with is conversation-as-sport or conversation-as-combat, and he realizes that the woman isn't asking him for either of those, he feels certain in advance that if he tries to comply he'll be in hot water. Unless there is a very solid foundation of trust, he won't risk it. *Especially* if the woman is someone he lives with!

Women are often deeply hurt when they learn that their male partner has spent hours in close conversation with a woman he met by chance—someone who, like him, was stranded in an airport waiting for a delayed flight, for example. Their reaction is, "How could he possibly talk to a woman he doesn't even know, and not be willing to talk to <u>me</u>?" This is a misunderstanding of the situation. Trying for conversation-as-intimacy with a woman he'll never see again is different, not because she's preferable to the woman he knows but because it's *safe*. Suppose it's a fiasco;

no one will ever know but her, and she's not going to be around to remind him of it. The same thing is true of men who talk to their mothers but not their wives. Their mothers changed their diapers, and have seen them at their most vulnerable many times. Plus, men don't have to live with their mothers. This is a matter of *face*, and both sexes are guilty of creating the conditions that make it so, in their roles as the parents and teachers of little boys and little girls.

Sugar and Spice; Snakes and Snails

As soon as they're old enough to walk, males start learning that they must not cry and that it's not "manly" to show any emotions other than greed and patriotism except in the most extraordinary situations. They are taught that when "real men" feel pain they keep it to themselves; they're taught that real men must pretend to feel no fear. They are given a specific list of situations in which it is acceptable for them to show emotion (at a military funeral, for example, where even a United States President is permitted to cry) with specific rules about the extent to which the emotions may be expressed. The AME culture makes it very clear to them that these are limits they must not go beyond. As Jack W. Sattel says in *Men, Inexpressiveness, and Power* (Newburg House 1983) "John Wayne may be dead, but the masculine style stressing silent strength and the masking of emotions is still very much alive." At the same time, men are taught that these rules are only for males; girls and women don't have to follow them. (Thorne et al. 1983)

When my female clients say of their male partners, "He acts as if he's <u>afraid</u> to really talk to me!" I tell them, "He's not acting; he <u>is</u> afraid. And with good reason." Men are afraid that if they become involved in intimate conversation with a woman they'll find themselves showing emotions that aren't on the list or in ways that are forbidden by the rules, or both. The last thing they want is to have that happen in front of a woman who might use it against them at some later time, and who, every time they see her, will be a reminder that she's *seen and heard* them being unmanly. How in the world, under these circumstances, can men be expected to let down the barriers to intimate communication that have been trained into them over an entire lifetime? It's not surprising that intimate communication between the genders goes so badly in AME-speaking society today. What's surprising is that it ever happens at all.

Often a man's attempts to avoid intimate conversation with a woman are a direct measure of his high regard for her. This is the male equivalent of another female cliché: "I won't let you do what you want to do, because you wouldn't respect me afterward." *Men are afraid that the women whose good opinions they value the most will not* respect *them after linguistic intimacy.* They fear this in the same way women fear loss of male respect after *sexual* intimacy, and for exactly the same reasons. Not because of their genes, but because of the way they've been brought up. The metaphor is a nearly flawless one, with the primary difference being that the possible disastrous *consequences* aren't a perfect match. Neither pregnancy nor AIDS can result from linguistic intimacy.

The only remedy for this problem, other than a radical change in the way we teach gender roles in this society (a subject beyond the scope of this book), is to build *trust*. Trust deep enough and strong enough so that a man will know that violating the manliness code in front of the woman he shares his life with is not going to make her despise him or give her a weapon to use against him ever after.

It's easy to say, "Oh, well, there's no point in trying to talk to each other—we don't even speak the same language!" Or "Naturally we have trouble communicating intimately—we have entirely different motivations and goals!" It's not so easy to build the kind of trust that makes those facile excuses unnecessary, but it's far from being *impossible*.

For a woman seeking intimacy to say to a man, "It's all right—you can trust me" won't help. On the contrary; it will probably result in *less* trust. Remember that men have a great deal of experience in conversation-as-sport, where the focus is on racking up points, and on winning and losing. In sports you do everything you can to get your opponent to trust you, for just one reason: *so that you can take advantage of that trust.* One of the most striking of the "Peanuts" comic strips is the ongoing one in which Lucy holds a football for Charlie Brown to kick and insists to him that he can trust her—of *course* she won't move the ball, she promises. But when he runs at the ball she always moves it, so that he falls down—*always*. This is what men fear when women claim that it's safe to engage in intimate conversation with them. They're afraid of looking like foolish Charlie Brown, perpetual sucker, who never learns.

It's a rare man indeed in whom these fears aren't reinforced by the memory of childhood incidents in which he *did* show emotion, and he *was* made fun of, often by someone he had thought he could trust. Most men have at least one adult memory of having been mocked by an adult woman for showing emotion. In a "Men's View" column in the October 1991 issue of *Self*, Owen Edwards complains that . . .

> just when we start to get comfortable with the whole idea of liberated lips, we run into an unexpected and possibly insurmountable obstacle. Women don't really *want* to hear about our feelings.

And he reports having overheard a woman in a San Francisco restaurant ask a friend whether she's noticed "what whiners men have gotten to be."

Finally, and probably most compellingly, there is the effect of the metaphor: CONVERSATIONAL INTIMACY IS LIKE SEXUAL INTIMACY. Every adult male remembers going through the following sequence:

• He urged some female to give in to his sexual demands.

• She protested that if she did he wouldn't respect her.

• He insisted that he *would*.

• And then, after she believed him and did as he asked, he *didn't* respect her.

Why should he assume that things will be any different with a woman who appears to him to lust after intimate talk? As Dianne Hales notes in her article, "Talk to Me!" (*Working Mother*, June 1990), "Talk is secondary only to sex as a way for two people to share their most intimate feelings." And men are familiar with the recent surveys showing that many women would reverse that ranking and put talk first.

Getting over all these walls is a labor entirely suitable for Hercules, Male Hero. But as long as AME mothers and fathers and teachers and clergy . . . and society at large . . . continue to train AME males in the standard fashion, most of the work of getting past the barriers will have to be done by women. Fair or not, that's the way it is. Men cannot be expected to do what they've spent a lifetime learning *not* to do. Not on their own, and not without a tremendous amount of help. They weren't taught to be Alan Alda. They weren't taught to be the male heroes in soap operas, who are always willing to engage in lengthy intimate conversation. (I am convinced that the powerful appeal the soaps have for many women is due not to the romance or the erotic scenes but to these portrayals of men and women *talking*.) Most AME males have been taught to be John Wayne; even those who think for a while that they might be Alan Alda usually discover that John Wayne has his foot firmly on Alan Alda's throat.

Men as Reluctant Maidens: Using the Metaphor

Women should begin by applying Miller's Law and recognizing the metaphor that is being used. They will understand men's resistance to intimacy far better if they interpret it in terms of its parallels in their own experience. These parallels are encoded in the metaphor of The Reluctant Maiden. Within that metaphor, no man respects a woman after *sexual* intimacy unless he is married to her, and even then she should continue to be a *little* reluctant. Women need only remember how Reluctant Maidens behave when sex is urged upon them. They will then be able to predict— and understand, and more skillfully cope with—the behavior of males who are urged to consent to linguistic intimacy.

Similarly, although women are free to cry (if not running for political office at the time) and free to talk about their emotions, every little girl learns a list of topics that "nice people don't talk about" and "decent women (including Reluctant Maidens) never discuss." This list is exactly the sort of list men have; it's just that the men's list has different items on it and is probably longer. A man asked to talk openly and easily and in detail about his feelings is like a woman asked to talk openly and easily and in detail about her urination. Women need to keep that in mind.

Women who want intimacy will have to behave toward men who make tentative steps in that direction just as males behave toward very nervous virgins they are attempting to achieve sexual intimacy with. The rules include at least the following:

✦ **RULE ONE:**   Be satisfied with just an intimate sentence or two at first; don't immediately pressure the man for *paragraphs*.

✦ **RULE TWO:**   Don't take off verbally in hot pursuit.

Men complain that when a woman asks an intimate question and gets an honest attempt at an answer it only makes her want more and more. Instead of appreciating it, she asks another question, and then another, and then another, like the greedy seducer who is never satisfied.

✦ **RULE THREE:**   Always treat a man's attempts at intimate talk seriously and courteously.

Women have to demonstrate to men that if they do volunteer intimate conversation they will be safe. They won't be laughed at, they won't be mocked, their efforts will be recognized as significant and worthwhile, and they won't be met with an interrogation.

✦ **RULE FOUR:** Never betray a man's intimate confidence by using the information against him.

A woman cannot allow herself to use information volunteered by a man in intimate conversation as a weapon against him. No matter how vicious the fight she and the man are engaged in at the time; no matter how badly he has hurt her; no matter how justified she may be in hurting him back. *Not if she wants to continue the relationship and make it one of intimacy outside the bedroom as well as in it.* She will only have the opportunity to use this play against him once; from then on, she will have no greater chance for nonsexual intimacy with him than she has with a marble statue. Adult males are a lot smarter than Charlie Brown, and in this one regard they are totally unforgiving.

✦ **RULE FIVE:** Be *gentle*.

Women are trying to get past the conditioning of decades—it's going to take time. Only after dozens of occasions of saying a few intimate words and suffering no negative consequences will men risk a few intimate sentences, even with other *men*. You don't have to take my (female) word for this; here's Jack Sattel again.

> Even among equal-status peers, men seldom make themselves vulnerable to each other, for to do so may be interpreted as a sign of weakness, an opportunity for the other to secure advantage.

Patience, please. If you frighten him, the process of achieving intimacy will take even longer and be even more difficult.

What Men Can Do

Like women, they can try to be aware of the metaphor and to use their knowledge of its rules to understand what's going on. They are very familiar with the motives and behavior of males seeking sexual intimacy.

They would be the first to agree with all of these statements about such males:

- They mean no harm.
- They don't *intend* to be greedy and inconsiderate and hasty.
- They don't mean to frighten the woman.
- They sincerely believe the woman who cooperates will enjoy the experience, and deeply regret it when she doesn't.
- They are trying to *build* the relationship rather than destroy it.

They should have no difficulty seeing the parallels and they should be willing to give women who are seeking linguistic intimacy credit for the *same good intentions*. Finally, they should be willing to cut women the same amount of slack when they're clumsy that they expect women to cut for them in the sexual domain.

I would also like to suggest (in the face of the entire Old West rampant) that men remember that women, too, are only human. Suppose that—in a context where passions are running high and both of you say things you later regret—a woman *does* confirm your worst expectations, by using against you some emotional tidbit you had previously trusted her with. Try to find enough strength of character to give her another chance. Don't use this one bad episode as justification for never again sharing linguistic intimacy with her—or any other woman. She shouldn't have done it; that's true. But you were *both* doing things you shouldn't have done and saying things you shouldn't have said. Try to be fair.

Thirteen Ways to Stifle
Intimate Conversation

The list below is based on one assembled by Thomas Gordon; I've revised it, added categories, and provided examples of each. Nothing is intrinsically wrong with these language patterns, but they contain boobytraps for the unwary. When they're used as in the examples below, their primary effect—whether their semantic content is positive or negative—is to bring conversation to an abrupt *halt*. All offer multiple opportunities for violations of this basic rule:

✦ UNLESS IT IS YOUR <u>GOAL</u> TO CUT OFF COMMUNICATION ABRUPTLY, DON'T SAY THINGS THAT MAKE PEOPLE THINK: "WHAT ON EARTH AM I GOING TO SAY <u>BACK</u>?"

In the examples to follow, unlike my usual practice, I haven't given extra information about intonation. As is true for any utterance of English, these examples could be made harmless by scrupulously careful intonation in a proper context. However, with almost all likely melodies they cut off conversation by making response difficult or impossible.

1. NAMES AND EPITHETS

- "You sexist pig!" "Airhead!" "Creep!" "You're a saint!" "You genius!" "You wonderful, generous person!"

2. EVALUATIONS

- "You lost your job because you weren't willing to turn in your work on time."
- "You're always so good to other people; you never think of yourself at all."

3. DIAGNOSES

- "I know why you won't go out with me. It's because I remind you of your mother."
- "You're only saying that because you're so tired; you don't really mean it."
- "You wouldn't say no if I had a bigger car and more money to spend."

4. DIRECT COMMANDS

- "Go take off that awful tie!"
- "Don't just throw the tinsel at the tree! Put it on there one strand at a time, carefully!"
- "Don't do that! Here, let me do it!"

5. PROPHESIES

- "If you marry that woman you'll regret it for the rest of your life."
- "You're going to hate yourself in the morning."

6. SERMONS

- "It's wicked for you to dress like that. The money you spend on your suits would clothe a large orphanage."
- "Because you spend more money than you earn, you are always going to be in debt. Decent people budget. You should lie awake

at night and thank Providence that you aren't living in an alley and eating out of a dumpster.''

7. INTERROGATIONS

- ''Why did you do that? What did you have in mind when you decided you were going to behave like that? Why didn't you talk to me about it first? What was going on in your head?''
- ''What did she say to you? How did she look? Did she look like she was angry or did she just look bored? What kind of expression did she have on her face?''

8. UNSOLICITED ADVICE

- ''Let me tell you what I'd do if I were you.''
- ''The first thing you have to do is find an apartment. I'll tell you where to look first.''

9. HIJACKINGS

- ''You think you had a bad day? Let me tell you what happened to me today.''
- ''You think you work hard, but you don't know the meaning of the word! I'll tell you about hard work.''
- ''Before you go on, that reminds me of a story I heard this morning.''

10. REDUNDANT INFORMATION

- ''You have long red hair.''
- ''You're very tall.''

11. REASSURING SQUELCHES

- ''You'll get over it; you'll see. A year from now you'll look back on this and laugh about it.''
- ''Just put it out of your mind and don't worry about it anymore. By the end of the week, you won't even remember that it happened.''

12. CUTESIPATION

- ''You're so cute when you're mad!''
- ''Well, of course I think your little stories are worth reading; they're charming.''
- ''That shirt almost makes you look tall.''

13. CONTRADICTIONS

- "You are not hungry. You just finished eating."
- "You're not tired. You couldn't be tired."

You can't eliminate these structures from your speech. There are going to be times when you need them, times when they are the proper and appropriate way to communicate. But you can be aware of the hazards they present and use them with special care. It's difficult enough to keep intimate conversation moving without adding these additional roadblocks.

It's important not to fall into the trap of thinking that as long as what you're saying is "a nice thing to say," everything will be all right. Many people who never allow an unkind word to cross their lips are baffled by the efforts others make to avoid conversation with them. It's hard to think of a response to "You're a pig! I can't stand the sight of you!" that will allow the conversation to continue. But the same is true of "You're so brilliant. I'd give my right arm for a mind like yours—it's a privilege just to be around you!" The speaker may mean that sincerely and deeply; that doesn't make it any better. The listener can't say "Thank you" without appearing conceited. A modest "No, I'm not," will only lead to "Yes, you are!" and another utterance like the first one. There's no way for the conversation to go on after something like that, and the most usual response is an uncomfortable silence while the listener searches for words.

Technique #12

Semantic Mapping for Couples

You will probably have come across at least one of the "free association" techniques that have become popular in recent years, such as Tony Buzan's "mind-mapping" or Gabriele Rico's "clustering." If you've read my *Staying Well with the Gentle Art of Verbal Self-Defense*, you'll be familiar with my "dream-mapping" technique. All of these procedures are "brainstorming" methods designed to help you break out of the cognitive straitjacket of your routine *thinking* habits, so that you can find new and creative ways to solve problems. Couples can adapt the dream-mapping technique as an alternative way to investigate the differences between their definitions of key words and phrases. If you've found that sitting down and trying to carry on a logical discussion as a couple doesn't seem to work for the two of you, this technique may be exactly what you need.

Each partner needs a large sheet of paper, a black pen, and pens in at least two different colors. Then follow the steps below, working independently of each other and without comparing notes as you go along. (For the sake of clarity, I'll assume that the set of pens is black, red, and green.)

Step One: In the center of the sheet of paper, with the black pen, write the word or phrase you both want to investigate, and draw a circle around it.

Step Two: Use the red pen to represent Level One for you. As quickly as you can, write down around the central word six or seven words or brief phrases that *it makes you think of*, leaving plenty of space to do more writing. Draw a red circle around each item. Finally, connect all your Level One circles to the black circle in the center with a red line.

Don't struggle as you do this step. Don't worry about being "logical" or "making sense." You want your most immediate reactions to the word, without any interference.

Step Three: Stop and look at your work. Do you see any connections between the circles? Does the third item you wrote down seem to you to have an obvious link to the fifth one? If so, connect them with a red line.

Step Four: Use the green pen to represent Level Two. Proceed exactly as you did in Step Two, for each of the items in red. Around each of the items, write down six or seven words it makes you think of, in green. Circle them and connect the green circles to the red ones with green lines. Work quickly; don't struggle. If you get stuck on one item, move to another one; you can come back at any time to the one you skipped.

Step Five: Take a final careful look at your semantic map. This time, don't worry about working quickly.

- Do you see connections between circles? If so, draw connecting lines.

- Can you now fill in spots that were empty because you couldn't think of an associated word or phrase earlier? Write them in, circle them, and link them, being careful to use the right color.

- Do the items you put down for Level Two make you think of new items for Level One? If so, add them.

By this time you will probably have a sheet covered with an amazingly complicated map of criss-crossing lines and crowded scribbling; this is why you need different colors for the different levels.

Step Six: Now it's time to compare your semantic map (of "violence" or "being in debt" or whatever other sequence you chose) with the one your partner prepared. If the two are identical, congratulations; if they are different, discuss the differences until each of you understands the other's definition. (Whether you *agree* with it or not isn't relevant; you just want to understand what it *is*.)

It's important to remember that there is NO RIGHT ANSWER that you're supposed to find. Words for which the definition is absolutely rigid—the word "five," for example—will be words whose meaning you already agree on. Your goal is to find each person's personal definition, the one that is valid *for that person*, so that you can compare the two and find out where the meaning differences lie. This is impossible if either partner looks at the other's semantic map and says something like "Well, that's stupid! You obviously just don't know what the word means!" or "I don't believe you! You're making it up!" If you can't keep from doing that, don't use this technique.

Advanced Semantic Mapping for Couples

After you've done one or two of these maps and you've got the hang of it, try working together—at the same time—on a single sheet of paper (a very large one, obviously). Be careful to use different colors, so that you'll be able to tell who wrote what.

Now, let's go back for . . .

Another Look at Scenario Thirteen

Paula and John have a marriage that, like all marriages, has flaws. But it's also a marriage that *works*. In this scenario, John is too domineering, and less cooperative than would be ideal. Paula gives in more often than she ought to and shows him too much tolerance. They use patterns that cut off conversation, and come perilously close to using VAPs. But compromises are made on both sides, and neither John nor Paula takes advantage of the many points in the interaction when starting a fight would be overpoweringly easy. It could have gone very differently. For example . . .

Paula: "You don't want to, <u>do</u> you? You'd rather watch television, or read, or something."

John: "I didn't say that, honey."

Paula: "No—but I can tell."

John: "Look, Paula," he said patiently, "you said you want to just sit here and do nothing, and I said okay! What do you expect me to do, set off rockets?"

Paula: "Why do you have to be so CRUEL, John? Does it give you some kind of warped pleasure to make me feel awful?"

John: "I don't understand."

Paula: "You do understand! I heard what you said! You said that spending an evening talking to me is just 'sitting here doing nothing!' That's a TERRIBLE thing to say!"

John: "Paula, I was just stating the simple truth. I work hard. I resent being asked to waste the very limited leisure time I do have. I could have gone to the club tonight, you know, but I didn't. I stayed here with YOU."

Paula: "Well, how generous of you, Your Majesty! I do hope I seem appropriately GRATEful!"

John: "No, Paula, you don't seem grateful. But then you never do. It makes no difference how much I do for you, it's never enough. You can ALways find something ELSE to complain about!"

Paula: [Silence]

John: "Oh, terrific—now I suppose you're going to CRY!"

Almost every line in the scenario's dialogue presents a tempting opportunity to switch to a fight like this one. It's a compliment to John and Paula's communication skills—and to their tolerance—that it didn't happen.

Dialogues for Analysis

DIALOGUE ONE

F: "I know this is a stupid question, but can the microwaves hurt anything after you take the food out of the oven?"

M: "You're right; it is a stupid question. What do you mean, can the microwaves 'hurt' anything?"

F: "Well . . . you're not supposed to use a microwave oven if it's leaking radiation, right? But the food goes on cooking after you take it out. So I wondered—"

M: [Roaring with laughter] "Oh lord, I can't believe it! Only from the lips of a woman!"

He's wrong. It's not just women who are ignorant of basic science and technology in this country, unfortunately. But even if he were right, his speech demonstrates his vast ignorance of the science and technology of *language*.

Suggestion for Her: Never use a Hedge—as in "I know this is a stupid question, but . . ." or "I know this is going to make you mad, but . . ."—even when it states the facts accurately. Hedges are irritating; they are a way for the speaker to preempt the most likely expression of that irritation; they are an invitation to verbal abuse. Just ask the question. And when you really need an answer—as in this case, when you don't want to accidentally endanger yourself or anyone else—don't let his ridicule prevent you from getting it. Wait until he's quiet enough to hear you, and then ask him again.

Suggestion for Him: Let's apply Miller's Law and assume that you live in a reality where all adult males—and only adult males—understand how a microwave oven works. In that reality, men would have a store of information that women didn't have, and about which they were likely to ask questions. No man likes it when he shares information about his intimate feelings with a woman and she then laughs at him; when that happens, men decide such sharing is dangerous. Women who are ridiculed after asking what they feel are "stupid" questions react in the same way and for the same reasons: They have left themselves vulnerable, and if they are laughed at they will decide not to risk that again.

Suppose you suddenly had to make decisions about an area of life in which women are better informed—childbirth, for example. Your questions would be equally laughable. Be glad this woman cares more about using the microwave oven safely than she does about avoiding your ridicule, and answer her question. Courteously.

DIALOGUE TWO

F: "Aren't you going to stay here with me?"

M: "I don't know; I thought I might move around a little and find out what everybody's been doing."

F: "Why don't you stay here with me?"

M: "I'll be back in a few minutes."

F: "Don't you want to talk to <u>me</u>?"

M: [He walks away, pretending he didn't hear her final question.]

She is making the same mistake over and over again. Like Paula Gellis in Scenario Thirteen, she's using *negative questions*. (Paula's were "Don't you like being alone with me?" and "Then why don't you put your arm around me?") Negative questions *support* the negative, are frequently perceived by the listener as confrontational, and are an especially poor choice for attempts at persuasion. They should always be avoided unless they're absolutely necessary. I suggest this rewrite.

F: "Are you going to stay here with me?"

M: "I don't know; I thought I might move around a little and find out what everybody's been doing."

F: "I'd rather you stayed here with me."

M: "Why? I mean, I don't mind staying, but why are you insisting?"

F: "I don't know anybody in the room, and I feel conspicuous standing here by myself."

M: "I know that feeling. Tell you what . . . you come with me, and I'll introduce you to some of these people."

(There is also a "Why don't you . . ." construction that's not a negative question but an indirect command, as in "Why don't you close the window?" The context will make clear which speech act is intended.)

DIALOGUE THREE

M: "You're seeing an awful lot of Theresa, it seems to me. What's the attraction?"

F: "I like her very much. She's fun to be around, and she's interesting to talk to. Is there some reason why I shouldn't see her?"

M: "Yeah. She's a feminist."

F: "So?"

M: "So you know what I think of feminists."

F: "Well, you're going to have to <u>change</u>! Feminism is one of the most important cultural movements of this century, and it's not going to go away—you'd better crawl up out of the primordial slime and try to <u>learn</u> something from it.''

M: ''Let <u>me</u> tell <u>you</u> what feminism is! Feminism is a bunch of bra-burning hysterical women that don't have anything useful to do, so they decide it would be fun to destroy everything good and decent in this society!''

F: ''Well, at <u>least</u> they don't run around in the woods naked, howling and pounding on drums!''

M: ''I feel the same way about the so-called men's movement that <u>you</u> do! I'm talking about <u>real</u> men!''

F: ''Sure—real men! Real men like the ones that gave us World War I and World War II and <u>Vietnam</u>!''

It's possible that, given many hours of intense conversation with few interruptions, one of these two people might convert the other. It's possible; we've all seen it happen in the movies. But very few couples have the time for that sort of negotiation, and even when the time is available, the process demands a rare degree of commitment and energy. It's far more common for a couple like this one to be faced with the following three facts:

- They are never going to agree about feminism (or abortion, or the existence of a deity, or gun control, or cheating on taxes).
- They have no desire to spend all their time arguing.
- They want to continue their relationship.

In that case, they must agree to disagree. And they must either set up formal constraints or learn not to allow themselves to be drawn into fights like the one in the dialogue. Here are some possible ways to do that.

M: ''You're seeing an awful lot of Theresa, it seems to me. What's the attraction?''

F: ''I like her very much. She's fun to be around, and she's interesting to talk to. Is there some reason why I shouldn't see her?''

M: ''Yeah. She's a feminist.''

F: ''You're right. But that's only a reason why <u>you</u> shouldn't see her, honey. I enjoy her company.''

M: "Okay; it's your decision."

M: "You're seeing an awful lot of Theresa, it seems to me. What's the attraction?"

F: "I like her very much. She's fun to be around, and she's interesting to talk to. Is there some reason why I shouldn't see her?"

M: "Yeah. She's a feminist."

F: "We have a rule, you and I; we don't talk about feminism."

M: "You're right. My apologies."

M: "You're seeing an awful lot of Theresa, it seems to me. What's the attraction?"

F: "I like her very much. She's fun to be around, and she's interesting to talk to. Is there some reason why I shouldn't see her?"

M: "Yeah. She's a feminist."

F: "Some people like feminists; some people don't."

M: "Right."

F: "Did Ted Cartwright call you this afternoon?"

M: "You're seeing an awful lot of Theresa, it seems to me. What's the attraction?"

F: "I like her very much. She's fun to be around, and she's interesting to talk to. Is there some reason why I shouldn't see her?"

M: "No. I just wondered."

DIALOGUE FOUR

M1: "Honey, you're unhappy . . . what's wrong?"

F: "I'm not unhappy; I'm fine."

M1: "Look, I <u>know</u> you! And I'm not going to just sit here with you and pretend I don't know you're <u>miserable</u>."

M2: "Maybe she doesn't feel good. There's a lot of flu going around."

M1: "I hadn't thought of that. Honey, have you got a fever?"

F: "I do not have a <u>fev</u>er. I am <u>fine</u>."

M2: "Maybe she just doesn't want to talk about it."

M1: "We don't have that kind of relationship, I'm glad to say. She tells me <u>everything</u>; I have no secrets from <u>her</u>. And she's going to tell me what's bothering her right now, I promise you."

There are in this world people of both genders who *enjoy* making an obvious demonstration of unhappiness and then being endlessly and fruitlessly wheedled to explain its cause. If this woman is one of those people, the man presumably knows it; he shouldn't encourage her. Once she's answered his first question with "I'm not unhappy; I'm fine" he should change the subject and talk about something else.

It's more likely, however, that the reason she behaves as she does is because whatever is wrong is something she doesn't feel comfortable discussing in front of the second man present. In which case, once she's said she's fine, he should *still* change the subject and talk about something else.

In both cases, these men should stop talking about her as if she weren't there, or as if she were incapable of talking for herself. It's insulting, and it's inexcusable.

DIALOGUE FIVE

M: "All <u>right</u>. <u>Okay</u>. You're right, I <u>do</u> know why I hate to go to zoos."

F: "I knew it!"

M: "When I was four years old my folks took me to a zoo in Tulsa, and a lion roared at me and scared me so bad I wet my pants."

F: [Laughing] "When you were <u>four years old</u>? Boy, you'd been out of diapers a <u>long</u> time to pull a stunt like <u>that</u>! That's really <u>funny</u>!"

M: "Yeah. Sure."

F: "You know, that's a really dumb reason to stay away from zoos . . . you're all grown <u>up</u> now, don't you realize that?"

This could hardly be worse; he will never, never again trust her with anything that might provide her an opportunity to repeat this behavior.

What she should have said, after he gave in and confided in her, is something like this: "That must really have been embarrassing. You were old enough to feel awful about it."

Any man so humiliated has every right to be outraged, and would be performing a public service by explaining to the woman the error of her linguistic ways. The same holds true for any woman whose confidence is ridiculed by a man.

DIALOGUE SIX

F: "Yes, I know why I'm scared of dentists, but you wouldn't find it interesting."

M: "Sure I would. Tell me."

F: "I really don't like to talk about it."

M: "Come on! Are we friends, or _what_? If you can't talk to me, who _can_ you talk to? Don't you trust me?"

F: "Well, the first dentist my folks ever took me to was a real brute. He'd just start drilling and keep on until the cavity was gone, no matter how long it took and no matter how hot the drill got. The pain was terrible . . . and he never used any kind of anesthetic."

M: "Hey, you think _that's bad_? Listen, the dentist I went to when _I_ was a little kid pulled one of my molars—a back molar, can you believe that?—with no anesthetic! Just stuck his fist in there with some kind of big clunking instrument in it and pulled till he tore it out of my head! Let me tell you, that _hurt_."

F: "I'm sure it did. It sounds terrible."

M: "And then, as if that wasn't bad enough, I got spanked for yelling. My mother said she'd never been so humiliated in her life. And when we got home. . . ."

He pressures her to confide in him, and she does. And he doesn't laugh at her, which is good. But he proceeds to violate the language traffic rules, which is a mistake. The topic she has introduced—reluctantly, and as a demonstration of trust—is _her_ bad dental experience. For him to immediately switch to a comparable experience of his own, without so much as a comment on hers, is both a failure to support her topic and an abrupt change of subject. The fact that this happens in a context so charged with emotion makes it even worse—it's like cutting ahead of someone at an intersection who is trying to get an injured person to an emergency room.

Fixing this would be quick and simple. After she tells him her childhood trauma, the dialogue should continue like this:

M: "No wonder you don't like dentists! That's horrible."

F: "It was. I <u>know</u>, intellectually, that no dentist would behave that way today, but I just can't seem to get over the phobia."

M: "I understand. I have the same problem. The dentist I went to when I was a little kid. . . ."

DIALOGUE SEVEN

M: ". . . and so, ever since, whenever anybody starts talking about religion, I get all tied up in knots inside."

F: "Hmmmm. You feel as though every clergyperson is going to treat you the way that priest treated you."

M: "I guess I do. It's not rational, I know, but that's what happens."

F: "You think it's not rational for you to be unable to shake off the trauma of that childhood experience."

M: "Right."

F: "You feel that you ought to be able to set aside your emotions and—"

M: "Hey! If I wanted <u>therapy</u>, I'd hire a professional!"

Here we have a woman who responds to the man's confidence not with ridicule or by trying to top his story but by amateur psychoanalysis that he hasn't requested. That's not appropriate, and it will always be resented. The presuppositions behind doing therapy include: "You're sick; you need treatment; I am qualified to provide treatment, and I have the right to do so in your case." Unless those presuppositions are true, doing therapy at someone is an excellent way to make future intimacy impossible.

DIALOGUE EIGHT

F: "You weren't <u>born</u> so nervous and moody and hyper . . . there has to have been something about the way you were brought up, or the way you were treated, that's responsible for it. And I need to know what it <u>was</u>, darling. Otherwise, I'll never be able to figure out why you're upset or how to avoid it."

M: "You really want to talk about that kind of stuff?"

F: "I really do. It's important, if we're going to survive as a couple."

M: "Okay. The reason I'm so moody, honey, is a woman named Marilyn. She was gorgeous; you've never seen such a perfect body. She had the face of an angel. Her eyes were the most incredible color, a kind of deep blue, and her skin? Her skin, when you touched it, felt like satin. When she walked, every man within looking distance got high blood pressure. And when we . . ."

As you see, there's no end to the number of ways that intimate conversation can cause trouble. She has explained, Leveling, that she needs more information about the possible reasons why he is nervous and moody and so on, and he is doing his best, also Leveling, to give her what she asked for. If he was always an easygoing sort of man until he became involved with Marilyn, that's useful information for his partner. But she has no need to know every last detail about Marilyn's physical appearance or (as appears to be next) about her sexual behavior. Since the woman started this sequence, she should stop it, before it gets out of hand. Like this.

M: "Okay. The reason I'm so moody, honey, is a woman named Marilyn. She was gorgeous—"

F: "I'm glad she was gorgeous. That was nice for you. But it's not what I need to know, and I'm sure her beauty isn't responsible for your moods. Tell me <u>why</u> Marilyn is the reason you're moody. Tell me what she <u>did</u>."

DIALOGUE NINE

F: "<u>Tell</u> me!"

M: "I'm not going to, and that's all there is to it."

F: "I'm your wife; I have a right to know."

M: "You do not. You have a right to know lots of things, but you have <u>no</u> right to know the story of my life, minute by minute, from birth."

F: "If you <u>really</u> loved me, you wouldn't keep <u>secrets</u> from me!"

M: "Why not? Will you explain that to me, please?"

F: "Because people who really LOVE each other don't <u>want</u> any secrets between them, <u>that's</u> why!"

M: "Honey, that idea belongs in your scrapbook, with your senior prom picture."

He is absolutely right. By the time human beings reach adulthood, they've usually done lots of things they'd rather other people didn't know about. I'm not talking about axe murders, just the ordinary thoughtless and foolish behavior typical of ordinary youngsters. If those experiences come up in conversation without pressure, as is likely to happen over the years of a long-term relationship, that's fine. It should happen that way or not at all. Many women in the AME-speaking culture have gone through a period in their lives when the way you proved your loyalty to close friends was by exchanging "secrets" with them. But this particular test of loyalty is something that should be looked back on with affectionate amusement, not carried into adult life.

DIALOGUE TEN

M: "I'm sorry. I just don't care to talk about that subject, that's all. It doesn't serve any purpose, it makes me feel terrible, and I'm not going to do it."

F: [Bursts into tears]

M: "Oh, for the love of . . . Will you <u>please</u> not cry?"

F: [Sobs, shaking her head]

M: "Go ahead, <u>cry</u>! Women ALWAYS do that! The minute they think they might lose an argument, OUT COME THE WAterworks!"

F: [Sobs harder]

Crying is a difficult subject, surrounded by myths and misconceptions. AME-speaking little boys, barely able to toddle, are sternly told not to cry, while little girls who cry are comforted and cuddled. The problem with crying isn't that it's immoral or irrational. The problem with crying is, as shown in the dialogue, that a person who is crying can't talk (and often can't observe the body language of those who *are* talking). *Being unable to talk means being unable to defend yourself or negotiate— it means being* helpless.

Men, whose upbringing includes training in controlling their tears because the roles they fill as adults don't permit helplessness, pay a physical price for that skill, but in every other way it's something they should be grateful for. And they need to realize that far from prizing their tears as a weapon for use in verbal confrontations, women would like to have that skill, too—to be able to cry only when (and only as long as) it's appropriate to do so and doesn't interfere with communication.

CHAPTER 14

◆

Conclusion: Speaking the Same Language

─────────── **Scenario Fourteen** ───────────

"What do you suppose they're talking about out there?"

"The women?"

"Yeah." He jerked his head sharply, once, toward the sliding glass door to the patio, where the women were sitting outside in the last evening light. Their voices could be heard, but too softly to understand the words. "What do they find to talk <u>about</u> all the time, for crying out loud?"

"Who knows?" said one of the other men. "We're probably better off not knowing."

"Yeah! You want ulcers? You want chest pain? You want to have a nervous breakdown? You go out there and take notes, my friend!"

"They never <u>stop</u> talking, but damned if anything they say ever makes much sense . . .''

"It makes sense to <u>them</u>, maybe."

"Maybe. Who knows?"

"Women!" said the man who'd spoken first, shaking his head from side to side. "They're wonderful. I love them all. I wouldn't want to be without them. But you can't <u>talk</u> to them! It's like trying to talk to some alien being or something! Let me tell you what happened to me yesterday when I made the mistake of trying to tell my wife why we don't need two cars any more . . .''

Out on the patio, the women could hear the men's voices from the living room inside, where they were gathered around the television set watching the football game.

"I wonder what they're talking about in there."

"The men?"

"Mmhmm. They sound like a hive of bees . . . how can they keep track of the game if they never stop talking?"

One of the women chuckled softly. "Bob doesn't even like football," she said. "He hates it. If he couldn't keep his mouth moving while he is—quote—watching the game—unquote, he'd go out of his mind with boredom."

"Do you suppose they all feel like that? I mean, do they just sit around the television set with the football game on so they'll have an excuse to sit and talk?"

"I don't think so . . . but then you never know. You can't ask them. If you did ask them, they'd only start giving a lecture on the wonders of blitzing, or some such nonsense."

"Gary would take my head off if I suggested that he only pretends to like football so he can shmooze with the rest of the guys . . . wow, he'd be mad if I said that! I think."

"How could you know? It's impossible to talk to men!"

"Do you understand why that is?" asked the woman who had spoken first, and the rest burst into laughter.

"Are you kidding? Do I understand the mystic secrets of the universe? Come on!"

"Well, try this one for me, anyway; I could use some input. Let me tell you what happened yesterday when I tried to explain to that man why we've still got to have two cars. . . ."

◆

What's Going On Here?

The Men's Point of View

As these men perceive things, the women talk constantly, and it takes them five times as long to get through any conversation as it would take a similar group of men. They perceive the women's speech as less logical, less informed (except on "women's" subjects that don't interest men anyway), and more emotional, than their own. They assume that when they hear a buzz of talk from a group of women the subject is gossip, what to wear, or what to cook; when they overhear women "trying to talk politics or business" they are very amused. They find the women's behavior in mixed conversation irritating—the women talk all the time, won't listen to other people, interrupt, talk about things nobody in his right mind would be interested in, act as if they'd never heard a four-letter word in their lives, and are forever getting their feelings hurt. Better to separate into groups and let men talk to men while women talk to women, unless you've got two or three couples who are close friends; and even then, the women keep wanting to monopolize the conversation.

These men genuinely like women, and enjoy the company of many of the women they know—but they are convinced that attempts at real conversation with women can only lead to trouble.

The Women's Point of View

As these women perceive things, the men talk constantly, and as long as they're talking to one another they seem to enjoy themselves—provided they have "something to do," like bowling or playing golf or watching a football game. Otherwise, they feel they have to start talking about a subject they consider "serious," which always means competing with one another for the floor and for points in a way that strikes the women as unpleasant and unsettling. And they appear to be entirely unable to talk to women, or to give women a fair opportunity to talk, when the company is mixed. The men interrupt, they hog the conversational space, they don't listen to others who have the turn, they use language that belongs only in the locker room, they get all worked up over nothing at all, and first thing you know they're yelling at each other. It's better, the women feel, to divide up by gender and let each group go off and have a conversation in *peace*.

These women genuinely like men and enjoy the company of many of the men they know; they would like very much to be able to carry on intimate conversations with the men they live with. But it seems to them that men speak some different, alien language, and they have very little hope of getting past that communication barrier any time soon.

The Author's Point of View

It is my conviction that men and women do *not* speak different languages, or even different dialects. I am convinced that the choice of conversational styles and strategies differs not according to gender but according to the personality and history of the individual, and according to the real-world context.

The "different language" idea, in any of its variations, is an almost irresistibly convenient excuse. When a couple (or a man/woman pair who spend significant amounts of time together in the workplace or elsewhere) have communication breakdowns, this excuse lets them avoid any responsibility for the problem. They don't have to consider the possibility that the reason they're having trouble communicating is not that they're different genders, but that—

- They don't listen to one another.
- They aren't really *trying* to communicate.
- They're stressed and tired.
- They have bad language habits they learned as kids.
- They dislike each other.
- They don't believe they should have to be courteous in an intimate relationship.
- They're in too much of a hurry.

—or any of a multitude of other common and probable reasons. All these reasons share one inconvenient property: They are things that—if you're willing to make the effort—you could do something *about*.

It's far easier to say that it's useless to try to do better, because male and female communication is *inherently* different and nothing can be done. Men are particularly pleased when claims of difference come from women who are recognized scholars, enabling them to say, "Hey, it's not my fault we can't communicate! There's nothing either one of us can do about it. We don't even speak the same language! And it's not men saying that, by the way, it's women. Women with Ph.d's!" In this context, women's alleged inability to speak and write and understand the language of men becomes yet one more reason why women "have no place in business," "aren't suited to executive roles," and the like; it helps hold up the infamous Glass Ceiling.

I believe that the language patterns called "feminine" are used by both genders in situations of subordination; those called "masculine" are used by both genders in situations of dominance. Both genders know both patterns and can use them appropriately—women tend to get more practice in the subordinate ones and men more practice in the dominant ones because of the way power is structured in our society. And the clever trick of saying that a man using subordinate patterns is "talking like a woman," or that a woman using dominant ones is "talking like a man," is simply that—a clever trick. It has no basis in reality.

Most of the real cross-gender communication breakdowns are the result of differently defined key words—reality gap words—growing out of differing metaphors that filter perception and constrain behavior. When this is understood, the mysteries disappear and the breakdowns can be either prevented or repaired—especially since only a small number of unifying metaphors function in this way in a single culture at any one time.

There is no valid reason why men and women cannot communicate with the opposite sex efficiently and effectively, using their basic intelligence and common sense plus the techniques and information presented in this book. It's more work than saying "Oh, we don't even speak the same language—of <u>course</u> we can't communicate with each other!" But the payoff for setting that comfortable excuse aside and doing something constructive to improve cross-gender communication is well worth the effort. It can be done, and it would mean a revolution for the better in this world.

What to Do About It

Most communication breakdowns between men and women happen when they try to talk to each other across *reality gaps*: situations in which their differing perceptions of reality cause their language to become inadequate, temporarily. What's needed are ways to build reality bridges across those gaps.

Building Reality Bridges—Review

A reality bridge is always made up of what the two groups on either side of the gap have *in common*. When one group is AME women and the other is AME men, that includes at least the following:

1. They speak the same language. They have the same grammar rules for making statements, asking questions, making promises and threats, giving commands—for carrying out all the speech acts. They make items plural or negative or possessive according to the same rules. They assemble words into sentences using the same word order constraints. Their vocabularies come out of the same mental and physical dictionaries.

2. They have a shared cultural heritage. They celebrate the same holidays, get choked up over the same symbols, have many of the same values, are educated in the same schools and churches and by the same mass media. They come out of Mainstream America.

3. They have a shared self-interest in learning to get along together better—so that life can run more smoothly, so that we can stop the epidemic of violence that is destroying both the lives of Americans and the American economy, and so that each one of them personally will not have to face the terrible health penalties that come from chronic hostility and/or loneliness.

4. Many of them *love* each other—as couples, as parent and child, as relatives, as best friends. Many others, although love is too strong a word, are very fond of individuals of the opposite sex with whom they are associated in their personal and professional lives.

With all of this in common to serve as the planks and cables and bolts of the reality bridge, AME-speaking men and women are well prepared for the task. *The Gentle Art* system then provides them with the tools they need for combining those materials and making the bridge strong and safe. Women and men, men and women, can do all of the things listed below. They can:

1. Substitute valid definitions of *language*, *dialect*, *communication*, etc., for the inaccurate traditional ones.

2. Apply Miller's Law when they hear language that strikes them as illogical, or outrageous, or otherwise difficult to understand. They can assume at least temporarily that the language is true, and ask themselves what it could be true *of*? In what sort of reality would it be a true thing to say? What *else* would be true?

3. Apply the technique of semantic analysis when someone they consider rational suddenly seems to be behaving in an irrational way. They can look for the key words that are triggering that perception; they can use semantic features and reality statements to isolate the differing definitions of those words that are barriers to communication. And they can use their shared language to negotiate toward a definition—or an agreement about the *differing* definitions—that both sides can live with.

4. Use semantic mapping to provide an alternative pathway when the semantic analysis techniques don't seem to move them toward negotiation.

5. Apply the techniques of simultaneous modeling and careful observation to improve their body language skills and minimize the problems that are created by inadequate ones, paying particular attention to the intonation of the voice.

6. Pay attention to the Satir Modes being used and follow the rules for responding to them, to minimize the problems that result from feeding negative communication loops.

7. Pay attention to the Sensory Modes being used and follow the rules for responding to them, to increase trust and rapport and to reinforce the idea that both parties are "speaking the same language."

8. Use the technique of the three-part message to state complaints when complaints are genuinely necessary.

9. Use the presuppositions in time words, and the "illusion of choice," instead of direct commands.

10. Apply the technique of semantic modulation when differing metaphors are filtering perceptions in significant ways. They can use their shared language—and Miller's Law—to identify and investigate the model of reality that the other person is using, as well as their own personal model, and to repair the communication breakdowns that result from the differences between the models. In many cases they can use these tools to develop a *shared* metaphor.

11. Follow the language traffic rules.

12. Recognize the English Verbal Attack Patterns and follow the rules for responding to them.

13. Be sensitive to the problem of sexual harassment and the genders' very different perceptions about the problem. They can use their shared language to find the boundaries of behavior acceptable to both genders and negotiate ways to observe them without resentment and strain.

14. Use their shared language to negotiate ways around the problems caused by the male tendency to run on monochronic time and the female tendency to run on polychronic time.

15. Give up the Tender Telepathy Myth.

16. Give up the idea that communication breakdown between genders is something you just have to live with and about which nothing can be done.

17. Take into consideration the very different perceptions men and women have regarding conversational intimacy—with men facing the problems women face regarding *sexual* intimacy—and use their shared language to negotiate behaviors that both can live with comfortably.

18. Try for the five Ts: Truthfulness, tolerance, tenderness, togetherness, and tinsel. (Tinsel is the *fun* part of communicating with each other . . . it matters, too.)

You can do this. It takes motivation, it takes practice, and it takes patience—but you can do it. The stakes are high enough to make it worth the effort many times over.

APPENDIX

$$\blacklozenge$$

The Gentle Art of Verbal Self-Defense: An Overview

Just as there is a grammar of English for such things as word endings and the order of words in sentences, there's a grammar of English for verbal violence and verbal self-defense. All native speakers of English know this grammar flawlessly, although many factors—stress, nervousness, illness, lack of time, and the like—interfere with their demonstration of that flawless knowledge. The problem is that the information is not available at a level of conscious awareness, and people therefore cannot conveniently make use of it. The *Gentle Art* system is designed to help correct this problem and to make it clear that every human being is an expert in the use of his or her language.

When you use this system for verbal self-defense, you won't be restricted to sarcastic comebacks and counterattacks. Instead, you will be able to create for yourself a language environment in which such confrontations will be very *rare*. And when they do occur you will be able to deal with them quickly and competently, with no sacrifice of your own self-respect, and with no loss of face on either side of the interaction.

This is a brief overview of the basic concepts of the system, together with three examples of techniques for putting it to use. (For more detailed information about these and other techniques, please refer to the books, tapes, and videos in the *Gentle Art of Verbal Self-Defense* series.)

Reference Items

The Four Basic Principles

+ **ONE:**   KNOW THAT YOU ARE UNDER ATTACK.

+ **TWO:**   KNOW WHAT KIND OF ATTACK YOU ARE FACING.

✦ **THREE:** KNOW HOW TO MAKE YOUR DEFENSE FIT THE ATTACK.

✦ **FOUR:** KNOW HOW TO FOLLOW THROUGH.

The first principle is important—because many verbal victims are not aware that they are victims. Typically, they feel miserable but they don't know why, and they tend to blame not those who abuse them but themselves. For English, the most important clue for knowing that a verbal attack is taking place is not the words being said but the intonation of the voice that's saying them—the "tune" the words are set to.

The second and third principles work together to help you tailor your responses. When you learn to recognize language behavior modes (like the Sensory and Satir Modes described below) and to construct responses based on rules for their use, you are applying these two principles.

The fourth principle is often the hardest. There are two barriers to its use:

1. The idea that if you don't participate in the power game of verbal abuse you're letting the abuser "get away with it"

2. The problem of feeling guilty about defending yourself (especially common among women)

Both of these barriers are based on misconceptions. When you play the role of victim in verbal confrontations, you're training your attacker to be a more skilled verbal abuser—you're providing the attacker with practice and encouragement. That's not kind or nurturing. And when you allow someone to involve you in verbal violence, *that*—not the words said—is letting the person get away with it. (We'll come back to this point later, in the section on Verbal Attack Patterns.)

Consider the principle that I call Miller's Law:

In order to understand what another person is saying, you must assume that it is true and try to imagine what it could be true of. (George Miller, 1980)

Notice that you don't have to *accept* that it's true—just *assume*, for purposes of discussion, that it is. And ask yourself what it could be true *of*. Often what we do is use a kind of "Miller's-Law-in-Reverse," where we assume that what's being said is *false* and then we try to imagine what could be wrong with *the person speaking* to make them say something so outrageous. This guarantees communication breakdown; apply Miller's Law instead.

✦ **Syntonics.**   Syntonics, in the *Gentle Art* system, is the science of *language harmony*.

The name is taken from the term "syntonic," used in radio telegraphy to describe two radio sets sufficiently well tuned to one another to allow the efficient and effective transmission of information. When people attempt to communicate with each other, they need to try for a similar syntonic state. When the speaker is using Channel 6 and the listener is using Channel 11, communication is sure to fail. The *Gentle Art* techniques provide you with methods for making sure that speaker and listener are on the same channel and are syntonic.

✦ **Presupposition.**   A presupposition is anything that a native speaker of a language knows is part of the meaning of a sequence of that language even when it does not appear on the surface of the sequence.

For example: Every native speaker of English knows that the meaning of the sentence "EVen JOHN could pass THAT course!" includes two more propositions saying that the class is somehow second-rate and so is John. The sentence means: "Even John (who, as everybody knows, is no great shakes as a student) could pass that course (which, as everybody knows, is really trivial)." But the negative comments about John and the course are not there in the surface structure of the sentence: *They are presupposed.* Most verbal attacks, with the exception of the very crudest ones, are at least partly hidden away in presuppositions.

First Technique—Using the Sensory Modes

Human beings can't survive without information. We need data from the outside environment and from our bodies; we need data from other human beings and living creatures. Without a system for *managing* all this data, it would be impossible to deal with. Information that's coming in has to be processed. It must be selected, and (if possible) understood; then it must be either discarded, or indexed for storage in memory. Information going out has to be processed also, so that it can be expressed for other people to understand. Our primary tool for this processing is the set of sensory *systems*—sight and hearing and touch, taste and smell, etc.

Each of us has a preferred sensory system that we find easiest to use, and that helps us the most in understanding and remembering. And when we express ourselves we often demonstrate that preference by using one of the language behavior modes called Sensory Modes. Like this—

SIGHT: "I really like the way this looks."

HEARING: "This just sounds great to me."

TOUCH: "I really feel good about this."

SMELL: "This whole plan smells fishy to me."

TASTE: "This leaves an awful taste in my mouth."

People who hear you matching their preferred Sensory Modes are more likely to trust you and to listen to what you say. They think of you as someone who speaks their language and shares their perceptions. This is the easiest of all the *Gentle Art* techniques, and one that you can put to use immediately.

Under normal circumstances, people can switch from one Sensory Mode to another without any difficulty. But when they're under stress they tend to get locked in to their preferred Mode. The more upset they are, the more trouble they will have understanding communication in other Sensory Modes, and the more trouble they will have using other Sensory Modes to express themselves. In such situations, you will improve communication dramatically if you *match* the Sensory Mode the other person is using.

You'll have no trouble identifying the Sensory Mode coming at you. Any fluent speaker of English does that *automatically*. You can then tailor your own response for maximum efficiency and effectiveness by following two simple rules:

✦ **RULE ONE:** MATCH THE SENSORY MODE COMING AT YOU.

✦ **RULE TWO:** IF YOU CAN'T FOLLOW RULE ONE, USE NO SENSORY MODE LANGUAGE AT ALL.

For example: asked "How does the new paint job look?", use Rule One and say "The way I see it, it's beautifully done"; or use Rule Two and say "I think it's beautifully done." Rule Two doesn't give you the same advantages as Rule One, but it's a *neutral* alternative.

Second Technique—Using the Satir Modes

Dr. Virginia Satir was a world-famous family therapist. As she worked with clients, she noticed that the language behavior of people under stress tends to fall into one of the following five categories, which we call the *Satir Modes*.

Blaming:
>"WHY don't you ever think about anybody ELSE's feelings? DON'T you have ANY consideration for other people at ALL?"

Placating:
>"Oh, YOU know how I am! Shoot—whatever YOU want to do is okay with ME!"

Computing:
>"There is undoubtedly a good reason for this delay. No sensible person would be upset."

Distracting:
>"WHAT IS THE MATTER with you, ANYway? Not that I care! YOU know me—I can put up with ANYthing! However, common sense would indicate that the original agreement should be followed. And I am really FED UP with this garbage!!"

Leveling:
>"I like you. But I don't like your methods."

Each of the Satir Modes has a characteristic style of body language. Blamers shake their fists or their index fingers; they scowl and frown and loom over people. Placaters cling and fidget and lean on others. Computers are stiff and rigid, moving as little as possible. Distracters cycle through the other Modes with their bodies just as they do with their words. The body language of Levelers is distinguished by the absence of these other patterns, and by the fact that it's not in conflict with their words.

The first four Satir Modes are examples of the lack of a *personal* syntonic state. People use Blamer Mode because they are insecure and afraid that nobody will respect or obey them. People use Placater Mode—

saying that they don't care—because they care so very much. They use Computer Mode—saying "I have no emotions"—because they are aware of an emotion they actually feel and are unwilling to let it show. Distracter Mode cycles through all of these states of mismatch and expresses panic. Only with Leveler Mode (or with Computer Mode used deliberately for strategic reasons) do you have a syntonic state. To the extent that they are capable of accurately judging their own feelings, people using Leveler Mode use words and body language that match those feelings.

As with the Sensory Modes, people can ordinarily switch from one Satir Mode to the other, but they tend to become locked in to preferred Satir Modes in situations of tension and stress. The rules for using the Satir Modes are based on the same metaprinciple as those for using Sensory Modes: ANYTHING YOU FEED WILL GROW. All language interactions are *feedback loops*. When you match a language pattern coming at you, you feed it and it escalates. The difference between the two techniques is that it's always a good thing to match another person's Sensory Mode—because increasing the level of trust and rapport is always a good thing—but you should only match a Satir Mode if you *want* the behavior it produces to grow. Here are the results you can expect from feeding the Satir Modes:

- BLAMING AT A BLAMER causes fights and scenes.
- PLACATING AT A PLACATER causes undignified delay.
- COMPUTING AT A COMPUTER causes dignified delay.
- DISTRACTING AT A DISTRACTER is panic feeding panic.
- LEVELING AT A LEVELER means an exchange of the simple truth, going both ways.

In any language interaction, once you've recognized the Satir Mode coming at you, you have to choose your response. You make your choice based on the situation, on what you know about the other person, and on your own communication goals. Here are the two rules you need:

✦ **RULE ONE:** IF YOU DON'T KNOW WHAT TO DO, USE COMPUTER MODE.

✦ **RULE TWO:** IF IT WOULD BE DESIRABLE FOR THE SATIR MODE COMING AT YOU TO ESCALATE, MATCH THAT MODE.

Third Technique: Recognizing and Responding to the Verbal Attack Patterns of English

Many people don't realize that they are verbal victims because the verbal abuse they're subjected to isn't *openly* abusive. Most verbal abusers don't just spit out curses and insults. (That sort of behavior is usually part of a pattern of *physical* abuse.) Instead, they rely heavily on the set of verbal attack patterns (VAPs) that are part of the grammar of English verbal violence. These patterns are just as dangerous as shouted obscenities, but much more subtle.

The attack patterns discussed below have two parts. There is the BAIT, which the attacker expects you to respond to. It's easy to recognize, because it's the part that *hurts*. And then there is the attack that matters, which is usually hidden away in the form of one or more presuppositions. Here's an example:

"If you REALLY loved me, YOU wouldn't waste MONEY the way you do!"

The bait is the part about wasting money; it's what your attacker expects you to respond to. You're expected to take the bait and say, "What do you MEAN, I waste money! I DO NOT!" And then you're off to a flaming row, which is a poor way to handle the situation. The important part of the attack is not the bait, but the presupposition at the beginning—"YOU DON'T REALLY LOVE ME." Instead of taking the bait, respond directly to that presupposed attack. Say:

"When did you start thinking that I don't really love you?"

—or—

"Of <u>course</u> I love you!"

This is not what the attacker expects, and it will short-circuit the confrontation.

Here are some other examples of English VAPs.

"If you REALLY wanted me to get good grades, YOU'D buy me a comPUTer like all the OTHER kids have got!"

"A person who REALLY cared about his health wouldn't WANT to smoke!"

"DON'T you even CARE if the neighbors are all LAUGHING AT US?"

"EVen a woman YOUR age should be able to cook LUNCH!"

"EVerybody underSTANDS why you're so TOUCHY, dear!"

"WHY don't you ever LISTEN to me when I talk to you?"

"YOU'RE not the ONly person with PROBlems, you know!"

"You could at LEAST get to WORK on time!"

"EVEN if you DO forget my birthday, I'LL still love you!"

It's important to realize that what makes these examples attacks is not the words they contain. For English, more than half of the information is not in the words but in the body language, including the intonation of the voice. To recognize a verbal attack, you have to pay attention to the intonation—the melody of the voice—that goes *with* the words. Any time you hear a lot of extra stresses and emphasis on words or parts of words, you should be on the alert. THERE IS NO MORE IMPORTANT CUE TO RECOGNIZING VERBAL ATTACKS THAN ABNORMAL STRESS PATTERNS. The sentence, "Why do you eat so much junk food?" may be very rude and unkind, but it's not a verbal attack. The attack that goes with those words sounds like this: "WHY do you eat SO MUCH JUNK food?"

In dealing with verbal attack patterns, you have three rules to follow:

✦ **RULE ONE:** IGNORE THE BAIT.

✦ **RULE TWO:** RESPOND DIRECTLY TO A PRESUPPOSITION.

✦ **RULE THREE:** NO MATTER WHAT ELSE YOU DO, SAY SOMETHING THAT TRANSMITS THIS MESSAGE: "YOU'RE WASTING YOUR TIME TRYING THAT WITH ME. I WON'T PLAY THAT GAME."

Nobody can carry on a verbal attack alone. It takes two people—one to be the attacker, and one to be the victim. People who use verbal abuse do so because they want the fight or the scene—they want your *attention*—and they enjoy the havoc they create. When you take the bait in their attacks and go along with their plans, you're not showing them how strong and assertive you are, you are giving them *exactly what they want*. The more you do that, the worse the situation will get. EVERY TIME YOU TAKE THE BAIT IN A VERBAL ATTACK, YOU ARE PARTICIPATING IN A SELF-REINFORCING FEEDBACK LOOP.

Instead of doing that, use this third technique and break out of the loop. That's not "letting them get away with it." Letting them sucker you into an ugly row, giving them your attention on demand, playing verbal victim for them: *That* is letting them get away with it.

It's not true that victims of verbal abuse are helpless to protect themselves or that their only defense is to be even more abusive than the attacker. It's not true that verbal abusers can't change their language behavior, or that doing so will mean sacrificing their self-respect. The *Gentle Art* system is a practical method for tackling the problems of everyone involved in verbal abuse—attackers, victims, and innocent by-standers—with no loss of face or sacrifice of principle. Pollution in the language environment is just as dangerous to health and well-being as pollution in the physical environment; the *Gentle Art* system is a solution that *everyone* can put to immediate and effective use.

Suzette Haden Elgin, Ph.D.

For more techniques in the *Gentle Art* system (and detailed discussions of those introduced above), see any of the materials in the series. For additional information, write directly to Dr. Elgin at the Ozark Center for Language Studies, P.O. Box 1137, Huntsville, AR 72740.

References and
Bibliography

Articles

A.F.G. "Notes: Judges' Nonverbal Behavior in Jury Trials: A Threat to Judicial Impartiality." *Virginia Law Review* 61 (1975): 1266–98.

Addington, D. W. "The Relationship of Selected Vocal Characteristics to Personality Perception." *Speech Monographs* 35 (1968): 492–503.

Allis, S. "What Do Men Really Want?" *Time*, Fall 1990, pp. 80–82.

Arnott, N. "Trouble Spots." *Executive Female*, May/June 1988, pp. 45–48.

Beattie, G. W. "The Regulation of Speaker-Turns in Face-to-Face Conversation: Some Implications for Conversation in Sound-Only Communication Channels." *Semiotica* 34 (1981): 55–70.

———. "Interruption in Conversational Interaction, and Its Relation to the Sex and Status of the Interactants." *Linguistics* 19 (1981): 15–35.

Bell, C. "Family Violence." *JAMA*, 19 September 1986, pp. 1501–2.

Blakeslee, S. "Cynicism and Mistrust Tied to Early Death." *New York Times*, 17 January 1989.

Blanck, P. D. "Off the Record: Nonverbal Communication in the Courtroom." *Stanford Lawyer*, Spring 1987, pp. 18–23, 39.

———. "What Empirical Research Tells Us: Studying Judges' and Juries' Behavior." *The American University Law Review* 40 (1991): 775–804.

——— et al. "The Appearance of Justice: Judges' Verbal and Nonverbal Behavior in Criminal Jury Trials." *Stanford Law Review*, November 1985, pp. 89–163.

Blau, M. "Can We Talk?" *American Health*, December 1990, pp. 37–45.

Bozzi, V. "Crosstalk: Byline Bias." *Psychology Today*, November 1985, page 15.

Breslin, C. and M. Morris. "Please Leave Me Alone." *Working Woman*, December 1988, pp. 74–82.

Brock, D. "The Real Anita Hill." *The American Spectator*, March 1992, pp. 18–29.

Carlson, M. "It's Our Turn." *Time*, Fall 1990, pp. 16–18.

Cassileth, B. F. et al. "Psychosocial Correlates of Survival in Advanced Malignant Disease." *New England Journal of Medicine*, 13 June 1985, pp. 1551–55.

Cohn, C. "Slick'ems, Glick'ems, Christmas Trees, and Cookie Cutters: Nuclear Language and how we learned to pat the bomb." *Bulletin of the Atomic Scientists*, June 1987, pp. 17–24.

Colpitts, Michael. "Inside the Robot Kingdom." *BCS TECH*, November 1991, pp. 1–3.

Condon, W. S. "The Relation of Interactional Synchrony to Cognitive and Emotional Processes." In M.R. Key Ed. *The Relationship of Verbal and Nonverbal Communication* (The Hague: Mouton, 1980), pp. 49–65.

Cosmides, L. "Invariance in the Acoustic Expression of Emotion During Speech." *Journal of Experimental Psychology*, December 1983, pp. 864–81.

Crosby, F. and L. Nyquist. "The Female Register: An Empirical Study of Lakoff's Hypotheses." *Language In Society* 6 (1977): 313–22.

Crum, R. "Why Johnny Kills." *New York University Magazine*, January 1989, pp. 34–40.

DeFrancisco, V. L. "The Sounds of Silence: How Men Silence Women in Marital Relations." *Discourse & Society*, October 1991, pp. 489–502.

Dowd, M. "Power: Are Women Afraid of It—or Beyond It?" *Working Woman*, November 1991, pp. 98–99.

Dubois, B. L. and I. Crouch. "The Question of Tag Questions in Women's Speech: They Don't Really Use More of Them, Do They?" *Language In Society* 4(1975): 289–94.

Edelsky, C. "Who's Got the Floor?" *Language In Society* 10 (1981): 383–421.

Ehrenreich, B. "The Politics of Talking in Couples." *MS.*, May 1981, pp. 46, 48.

————. "Sorry, Sisters, This Is Not the Revolution." *Time*, Fall 1990, page 15.

Ervin-Tripp, S. et al. "Language and Power in the Family." In C. Kramarae et al., eds., *Language And Power* (Beverly Hills: Sage Publications, 1984), pp. 116–35.

Fellman, B. "Talk: The Not-So-Silent Killer." *Science 85*, December 1985, pp. 70–71.

Frankel, R. M. "The Laying On of Hands: Aspects of the Organization of Gaze, Touch and Talk in a Medical Encounter." (In S. Fisher and A. D. Todd, *The Social Organization of Doctor-Patient Communication* (Washington, D.C.: Center for Applied Linguistics, 1983), pp. 19–54.

Freeman, B. "Breaking the Code." *Savvy*, June 1988, pp. 55–6 and 94.

Friedman, M. MD. "Type A Behavior and Mortality from Coronary Heart Disease." *New England Journal of Medicine*, 14 July 1988, page 114. (And letters under the same title, through page 117.)

Gary, F. et al. "Little Brother Is Changing You." *Psychology Today*, March 1974, pp. 42–46.

Gleason, J. B. "Sex Differences in Parent-Child Interaction." In S.U. Philips et al., eds., *Language, Gender and Sex in Comparative Perspective* (London: Cambridge University Press, 1989), pp. 189–199.

Goleman, D. "Can You Tell When Someone Is Lying to You?" *Psychology Today*, August 1982, pp. 14–23.

Hales, D. 1990. "Talk to Me!" *Working Mother*, June 1990, pp. 28–30.

Hall, E. "Giving Away Psychology in the 80's: George Miller Interviewed by Elizabeth Hall." *Psychology Today*, January 1980, pp. 38–50, 97–98.

Hall, S. S. "A Molecular Code Links Emotions, Mind and Health." *Smithsonian Magazine*, June 1989, pp. 62–71.

Hankiss, A. "Games Con Men Play: The Semiosis of Deceptive Interaction." *Journal of Communication* 3 (1980): 104–112.

Heller, L. "The Last Angry Men? What Men *Really* Feel About Working With Women." *Executive Female*, September-October 1988, pp. 33–38.

Henley, N. M. and C. Kramarae. "Gender, Power and Miscommunication." In N. Coupland et al., eds., *"Miscommunication" and Problematic Talk* (Newbury Park CA: Sage Publications, 1991), pp. 18–43.

Higgins, L. C. "Hostility Theory Rekindles Debate over Type A Behavior." *Medical World News*, 27 February 1989, page 21.

Jacobs, S. and S. Jackson. "Speech Act Structure in Conversation: Rational Aspects of Pragmatic Coherence." In Craig, R. T. and K. Tracy, *Conversational Coherence: Form, Structure, and Strategy* (Beverly Hills CA: Sage, 1983).

Jones, E. E. "Interpreting Interpersonal Behavior: The Effects of Expectancies." *Science*, 3 October 1986, pp. 41–6.

Kaplan, D. A. et al. "Anatomy of a Debacle." *Newsweek*, 21 October 1991, pp. 32–36.

Kartunnen, L. "Implicative Verbs." *Language* 47 (1971): 350–58.

Katz, J. J. and D. T. Langendoen. "Pragmatics and Presupposition." *Language* 52 (1976): 1–17.

Kenner, H. "Plato in Vermont." *Harper's*, October 1981, pp. 84–85.

Kiparsky, C. and P. Kiparsky. "Fact." In M. Bierwisch and K. E. Heidolph, eds., *Progress In Linguistics* (The Hague: Mouton 1970), pp. 142–73.

Knotts, L. "Job-hunting Advice for Women: Talk Like a Man." *The Baltimore Evening Sun*, 28 May 1991.

Kobasa, S. O. "Test for Hardiness: How Much Stress Can You Survive?" *American Health*, September 1984, page 64.

Kramer, C. et al. "Perspectives on Language and Communication." *Signs* 3 (1978): 638–51.

Lakoff, G. "Hedges: A Study in Meaning Criteria and the Logic of Fuzzy Concepts." In P. Peranteau et al., eds. *CLS8*, 1978, pp. 183–228.

———. "Metaphor & War." *Express*, February 22, 1991, pp. 1–2, 13–18.

Lane, R. M. "A Man's World: An Update on Sexual Harassment." *Village Voice*, 16–22 December 1981.

Lynch, J. J., Ph.D. "Listen and Live." *American Health*, April 1985, pp. 39–43.

———. "Interpersonal Aspects of Blood Pressure Control." *Journal of Nervous and Mental Diseases* 170 (1982): 143–53.

Meade, W. W. "How to Be a Supporting Player When You Know You Were Born a Star." *Working Woman*, December 1988, pp. 103–4.

McCabe, M. "What Happened at Stanford?" *MD*, October 1991, pp. 35–38.

McConnell-Ginet, S. "Intonation in a Man's World." In B. Thorne et al., eds., *Language, Gender and Society* (Rowley MA: Newbury House, 1983), pp. 69–88.

Milstead, J. "Verbal Battering." *BBW*, August 1985, pp. 34–5, 61, 68.

Miron, M. S. and T. A. Pasquale. "Psycholinguistic Analysis of Coercive Communications." *Journal of Psycholinguistic Research* 7 (1978): 95–120.

Pfeiffer, J. "Girl Talk, Boy Talk." *Science 85*, February 1985, pp. 58–63.

Philips, S. U. "Sex Differences and Language." *Annual Review of Anthropology* 9 (1980): 523–44.

Pollitt, K. "Georgie Porgie Is a Bully." *Time*, Fall 1990, page 24.

Rudolph, B. "Why Can't a Woman Manage More Like . . . a Woman?" *Time*, Fall 1990, page 53.

Sacks, H. et al. "A Simplest Systematics for the Organization of Turn-Taking for Conversation." *Language* 50 (1974), pp. 696–735.

Sandroff, R. "Sexual Harassment in the Fortune 500." *Working Woman*, December 1988, pp. 69–73.

Sattel, J. W. "Men, Inexpressiveness, and Power." In B. Thorne et al., eds., *Language, Gender and Society* (Rowley MA: Newbury House, 1983).

Shea, M.J. MD. "Mental Stress and the Heart." *CVR&R*, April 1988, pp. 51–58.

Smith, M. E. "Sexual Harassment: Now You See It, Now You Don't." *Sojourner*, December 1991.

Stone, D. A. "Race, Gender, and the Supreme Court." *The American Prospect*, Winter 1992, pp. 63–72.

Stone, E. "Sons and Mothers: How Do Boys Respond to Enlightened Child-Raising? KAPOW!" *Savvy*, September 1988, pp. 114–116.

Toufexis, A. "Coming from a Different Place." *Time*, Fall 1990, pp. 64–66.

———. "They Just Don't Understand." *Time*, 1 June 1992, pp. 76–78.

Troemel-Ploetz, S. "Review Essay: Selling the Apolitical." (Review of Tannen 1990.) *Discourse & Society*, October 1991, pp. 489–502.

Weiner, E. J. "A Knowledge Representation Approach to Understanding Metaphors." *Computational Linguistics* 10 (1984): 1–14.

West, C. and A. Garcia. "Conversational Shift Work: A Study of Topical Transitions Between Women and Men." *Social Problems* 35 (1988): 551–75.

Whaley, B. "Toward a General Theory of Deception." *Journal of Strategic Studies*, March 1982, pp. 179–92.

Williams, R. MD. "Curing Type A: The Trusting Heart." *Psychology Today*, January/February 1989, pp. 36–42.

Zajonc, R. B. "Emotion and Facial Efference: A Theory Reclaimed." *Science*, April 5, 1985, pp. 15–20.

Items with No Byline

————. "How the Men in Your Office *Really* See You." *Working Woman*, November 1991, pp. 101–3.

————. "The Male Stress Syndrome." *Pest Control Technology*, June 1987, page 44.

————. "The Marketing Idea Exchange: Communicating Well with Women Helps Your Practice." *AAFP Reporter*, January 1987, pp. 13–14.

Books

Ader, R., ed. *Psychoneuroimmunology*. New York: Academic Press, 1981.

Argyle, M. *Bodily Communication*. London: Methuen, 1975.

Astrakhan, A. *How Men Feel: Their Response to Women's Demands for Equality and Power*. New York: Anchor/Doubleday, 1986.

Austin, J. L. *How to Do Things with Words*. London: Oxford University Press, 1972.

Barkalow, C., with A. Raab. *In the Men's House*. New York: Poseidon, 1986.

Beattie, G. *Talk: An Analysis of Speech and Non-Verbal Behaviour in Conversation*. Milton Keynes, England: Open University Press, 1983.

Belenky, M. F. et al. *Women's Ways of Knowing*. New York: Basic Books, 1986.

Bierwisch, M. and K. E. Heidolph, eds. *Progress in Linguistics*. The Hague: Mouton, 1970.

Blumenthal, M. D., et al. *Justifying Violence: Attitudes of American Men*. Ann Arbor: University of Michigan, 1972.

————. *More About Justifying Violence: Methodological Studies of Attitudes and Behavior*. Ann Arbor: University of Michigan, 1975.

Bolinger, D. *Intonation*. Harmondsworth: Penguin Books, 1972.

Bolton, R. *People Skills: How to Assert Yourself, Listen to Others and Resolve Conflicts*. Englewood Cliffs: Prentice Hall, 1979.

Butturff, D. and E. L. Epstein, eds. *Women, Language and Style*. Akron: L & S Books, 1978.

Buzan, T. *Use Both Sides of Your Brain*. New York: E. P. Dutton, 1983.

Chesney, M. and R. H. Rosenman, eds. *Anger and Hostility in Cardiovascular and Behavioral Disorders*. Washington DC: Hemisphere Corporation, 1985.

Clynes, M., ed. *Music, Mind, and Brain: The Neurophysiology of Music*. New York: Plenum Press, 1982.

Cole, P. and J. L. Morgan, eds. *Syntax and Semantics, Volume 3: Speech Acts*. New York: Academic Press, 1975.

Coupland, N. et al., eds. *Problem Talk and Problem Contexts*. Beverly Hills: Sage Publications, 1991.

Craig, R. T. and K. Tracy. *Conversational Coherence: Form, Structure, and Strategy*. Beverly Hills: Sage Publications, 1983.

Dubois, B. L. and I. Crouch, eds. *The Sociology of the Languages of American Women*. San Antonio: Trinity University Press, 1976.

Ehrenreich, B. *The Worst Years of Our Lives*. New York: Pantheon, 1990.

Ekman, P. *Telling Lies: Clues to Deceit in the Marketplace, Politics, and Marriage*. New York: W. W. Norton, 1985.

Elgin, S. H. *The Gentle Art of Verbal Self-Defense*. New York: Reston Press, 1985.

———. *The Gentle Art of Verbal Self-Defense Workbook*. New York: Marboro Books, 1987.

———. *More on the Gentle Art of Verbal Self-Defense*. Englewood Cliffs: Prentice Hall, 1983.

———. *The Last Word on the Gentle Art of Verbal Self-Defense*. Englewood Cliffs: Prentice Hall, 1987.

———. *Success with the Gentle Art of Verbal Self-Defense*. Englewood Cliffs: Prentice Hall, 1989.

———. *Staying Well with the Gentle Art of Verbal Self-Defense*. Englewood Cliffs: Prentice Hall, 1991.

———. *The Gentle Art of Written Self-Defense Letter Book*. Englewood Cliffs: Prentice Hall, 1993.

——— and R. Haden. *Raising Civilized Kids in a Savage World*. Huntsville AR: OCLS Press, 1989.

Everstine, D. S. and L. Everstine. *People in Crisis: Strategic Therapeutic Interventions*. New York: Brunner/Mazel, 1983.

Festinger, L. *A Theory of Cognitive Dissonance*. Evanston: Row, Peterson, 1957.

Fisher, S. *In the Patient's Best Interest: Women and the Politics of Medical Decisions*. New Brunswick: Rutgers University Press, 1986.

——— and A. D. Todd. *The Social Organization of Doctor-Patient Communication*. Washington, DC: Center for Applied Linguistics, 1983.

Forward, S. and J. Torres. *Men Who Hate Women and the Women Who Love Them*. New York: Bantam, 1986.

Good, N. *How to Love a Difficult Man*. New York: St. Martin's, 1987.

Gordon, T. *Parent Effectiveness Training*. New York: Peter H. Wyden, 1970.

————. *Leader Effectiveness Training*. New York: Peter H. Wyden, 1972.

Gray, J. *Men Are from Mars: Women Are from Venus: A Practical Guide for Improving Communication and Getting What You Want in Your Relationships*. New York: HarperCollins, 1992.

Hagan, K. L. *Women Respond to the Men's Movement*. New York: HarperCollins, 1992.

Haley, J. *Uncommon Therapy: The Psychiatric Techniques of Milton H. Erickson, M. D.* New York: Anchor Books, 1977.

Hall, E. T. *The Dance of Life: The Other Dimension of Time*. New York: Anchor/Doubleday, 1983.

Harragan, B. L. *Games Mother Never Taught You: Corporate Gamesmanship for Women*. New York: Warner, 1977.

Henley, N. *Body Politics: Power, Sex, and Nonverbal Communication*. Englewood Cliffs: Prentice Hall, 1977.

Hill, A. O. *Mother Tongue, Father Time: A Decade of Linguistic Revolt*. Bloomington: Indiana University Press, 1986.

Jespersen, O. *Language: Its Nature, Development and Origin*. New York: W. W. Norton, 1921.

————. *Growth and Structure of the English Language*, 9th edition. Oxford: Basil Blackwell, 1962 (originally published 1905).

Justice, B. *Who Gets Sick?: Thinking and Health*. Houston: Peak Press, 1987.

Key, M. R. *Male/Female Language*. Metuchen NJ: Scarecrow Press, 1975.

————, ed. *The Relationship of Verbal and Nonverbal Communication*. The Hague: Mouton, 1980.

Kramarae, C. *Women and Men Speaking: Frameworks for Analysis*. Rowley MA: Newbury House, 1981.

————, ed. *The Voices and Words of Women and Men*. Oxford: Pergamon Press, 1980.

Lakoff, G. and M. Johnson. *Metaphors We Live By*. Chicago: University of Chicago Press, 1980.

Lakoff, R. *Language and Woman's Place*. New York: Harper and Row, 1975.

————. *Talking Power: The Politics of Language in Our Lives*. New York: Basic Books, 1990.

Lazarus, R. S. and S. Folkman. *Stress, Appraisal, and Coping*. New York: Syringer, 1984.

Lerner, H. G. *The Dance of Anger: A Woman's Guide to Changing the Patterns of Intimate Relationships*. New York: Harper and Row, 1985.

Levy, S. M. *Behavior and Cancer*. San Francisco: Jossey-Bass, 1985.

Lewis, D. *The Secret Language of Success: Using Body Language to Get What You Want*. New York: Carroll & Graf, 1989.

Locke, S. MD and D. Colligan. *The Healer Within: The New Medicine of Mind and Body*. New York: New American Library/Mentor, 1987.

Lynch, J. J. *The Broken Heart: The Medical Consequences of Loneliness*. New York: Basic Books, 1977.

————. *The Language of the Heart: The Body's Response to Human Dialogue*. New York: Basic Books, 1985.

McConnell-Ginet, S. et al., eds. *Women and Language in Literature and Society*. New York: Praeger, 1980.

Montagu, M. F. A. *Touching: The Human Significance of the Skin*. New York: Harper and Row, 1971.

O'Barr, W. M. *Linguistic Evidence: Language, Power, and Strategy in the Courtroom*. New York: Academic Press, 1982.

Ornstein, R. and D. Sobel. *The Healing Brain: Breakthrough Discoveries About How the Brain Keeps Us Healthy*. New York: Simon & Schuster, 1987.

Penelope, J. *Speaking Freely: Unlearning the Lies of the Father Tongue*. New York: Pergamon Press, 1987.

Rico, G. L. *Writing the Natural Way*. Los Angeles: J. P. Tarcher, 1983.

Rothwell, J. D. *Telling It Like It Isn't*. Englewood Cliffs: Prentice Hall, 1982.

Ryan, E. B. and H. Giles, eds. *Attitudes Toward Language Variation: Social and Applied Contexts*. London: Edward Arnold, 1982.

Samovar, L. A. and R. E. Porter. *Intercultural Communication: A Reader. 4th edition*. Belmont CA: Wadsworth, 1985.

Satir, V. *Conjoint Family Therapy*. Palo Alto: Science and Behavior Books, 1964.

————. *Peoplemaking*. Palo Alto: Science and Behavior Books, 1972.

Sattel, Jack W. *Men, Inexpressiveness, and Power*. Rowley MA: Newbury House, 1983.

Scherer, K. and P. Edman. *Handbook of Methods in Nonverbal Behavior Research*. New York: Cambridge University Press, 1982.

Searle, J. *Speech Acts*. Cambridge: Cambridge University Press, 1969.

Spender, D. *Man-Made Language*. London: Routledge and Kegan Paul, 1980.

————, ed. *Men's Studies Modified*. Oxford: Pergamon Press, 1981.

Tannen, D. *That's Not What I Meant!: How Conversational Style Makes or Breaks Relationships*. New York: William Morrow, 1986.

————. *You Just Don't Understand: Women and Men in Conversation*. New York: William Morrow, 1990.

Thorne, B. and N. Henley, eds. *Language and Sex, Difference and Dominance*. Rowley MA: Newbury House, 1975.

Thorne, B. et al., eds. *Language, Gender and Society*. Rowley MA: Newbury House, 1983.

Todd, A. D. *Intimate Adversaries: Cultural Conflict Between Doctors and Patients*. Philadelphia: University of Philadelphia Press, 1989.

Treichler, P.A. et al., eds. *For Alma Mater: Theory and Practice in Feminist Scholarship*. Urbana and Chicago: University of Illinois Press, 1985.

Van Dijk, T. A., ed. *Handbook of Discourse Analysis*. London: Academic Press, 1985.

West, C. *Routine Complications: Troubles With Talk Between Doctors and Patients*. Bloomington: Indiana University Press, 1984.

Wolff, N. *The Beauty Myth: How Images of Beauty Are Used Against Women*. New York: William Morrow, 1991.

Index